MW01166575

Secrets of RSS

Demystifying the Sangh

Secrets of RSS

Demystifying the Sangh

Ratan Sharda

Manas Publications
(We Convert Fighters into Writers)
New Delhi-110 002 (INDIA)

MANAS PUBLICATIONS
(Publishers, Library Suppliers, Importers & Exporters)
4402/5-A, Ansari Road
(Opp. HDFC Bank)
Darya Ganj, New Delhi-110 002 (INDIA)
Off. ✆ 23260783, 23265523, Res. ✆ 23842660
Fax: 011-23272766
E-mail: manaspublications@vsnl.com
manaspublications@yahoo.com

ISBN 978-81-7049-319-8

Rs. 595

Typeset at
Manas Publications

Printed in India at
RK Print Services, Delhi
and published by Mrs Suman Lata for
Manas Publications, 4402/5-A, Ansari Road
(Opp. HDFC Bank),
Darya Ganj, New Delhi-110 002 (INDIA)

Contents

Acknowledgements

I thank all my colleagues in the RSS - each of them was a source of inspiration for me through my life, and whose silent work motivated me to write this book.

I have given real-life examples of many of my seniors and colleagues, without taking their consent. Many of them being publicity shy would surely grumble at their names being mentioned! But, I believe a story touches the heart when it presents somebody in real flesh and blood, hence this liberty.

My friend Sandeep Singh deserves to be mentioned for pushing me into writing this book as he seriously believed that there is a great gap between the public perception of the RSS and reality.

I thank senior prachaaraks and leaders of Rashtriya Swayamsevak Sangh who encouraged me when I discussed the idea of writing this introductory book on the RSS with them. The inspiration for presenting ideas in a simplistic way comes from the senior the RSS prachaarak Shri Ranga Hari ji. I have quoted him extensively in the book. My heartfelt gratitude to this great noble soul who represents the best in the prachaarak tradition of the RSS.

I would be remiss if I didn't express my debt to Shri Bimal Kedia who has actually encouraged me to get involved in writing and helping people write in the past few years. He has also been an inspiration as a live embodiment of a selfless RSS worker to the core.

My acknowledgements are due to the great scholars and Indologists who gave me a firm foundation for expounding the philosophy of the RSS in a way that is slightly at variance with the conventional as is presented by the RSS ideologues and theorists. I am specially inspired by the Koenrad Elst, Sitaram Goel, David Frawley and Prof. Rakesh Sinha for their meticulous way of presenting their ideas.

Great Gandhian Dharampal has thrown new light on what was supposed to be a mythical story of prosperous India of yore and I must thank him for this hard labour he put in and to Claude Alvares who has brought his viewpoints out so well. I may also mention Dr. Sadhana Modh whom I have quoted to give a management perspective about the organizational philosophy of the RSS. I have quoted many other authors and scholars also, whose contribution I have acknowledged in my References at the end of the book and I thank all of them.

I express my gratitude to my uncle (Chacha ji) Shri Jagdish Chandra Sharda 'Shastri' who encouraged me to follow the path of selfless service to the society through his own lifetime dedication to the cause of social service.

– Author

Editorial Notes

Roman spellings of Indian words: I have avoided diacritical marks for Sanskrit and other Indian words throughout the book to make reading easier. But, to overcome the problem of pronunciation, I have used phonetic spellings being used by internet service providers in providing transliteration of Indian languages. e.g. Asha could be written as Aashaa, to help those uninitiated in Indian languages pronounce the words properly. But, commonly understood words like Bharat will not appear as Bhaarat as people generally read it correctly.

Terminology: I have not used typical words used in the RSS but given them in brackets in most places so that the reader may not have to sit down with a dictionary from page one, and also to make things more familiar sounding. Thus, I have used words like volunteer, activist, swayamsevak interchangeably though purists from the Sangh school, as also linguists may not like it. Worker is not as dignified a word as kaaryakartaa, nor does it provide due weight to this word that people in the RSS give. It does not convey the commitment, seniority and experience of a volunteer (swayamsevak) who becomes 'kaaryakartaa'. I have taken this liberty to make reading easier. Similarly, I have not differentiated between India and Bharat, though a Sangh member or sympathizer generally prefers to use only Bharat. These two words have come to carry different connotations for the opinion makers but for common man they are same.

Annexure: There is a great deal of history that needs to be shared with the reader to give a proper perspective about the RSS. This centres around 1942 to 1948 i.e. from Quit India movement to the first ban on the RSS and its revocation. Critics have flung lot of mud casually at the RSS with reference to this period feeling secure that common people would not tend do tedious research to find the facts. I felt that these details might come in way of the narrative that is meant to give an overview of the RSS, its ideology, its structure and its reach in various social fields across India and bog it down. So, those chapters from recent history have been included in Annexure, making it larger than I had hoped for. However, any serious student of the RSS and current history would like to know these facts, so I decided to live with this larger than expected Annexure.

Preface

It amazes time and again when people confess that they don't know much about the RSS in spite of it being around for nearly 85 years and being quite open about itself. While critics blame it on the secretive way the RSS (Rashtriya Swayamsevak Sangh - or National Volunteers Corps) works, the RSS volunteers believe that critics don't really wish to understand the RSS and they only use this theory of secretiveness to cover their intellectual lethargy and, sometimes, bias. Apart from this, there are large number of people who simply don't understand its working as it is quite different from other organizations, nor its philosophy as that too goes against the established norms of ideological discussions of India, heavily influenced as they are with western notion of culture, nationalism and social organizations.

I am amused at the debates that take place between the RSS and its adversaries. It is like two people arguing with each other in different languages. So, all you hear is lot of noise but not an informed debate. A recent comment by the venerable number one newspaper of the world, our own *Times of India,* that the RSS is a secretive organization while giving the news of elevation of Shri Mohanrao Bhagwat to the august post of Sarsanghchaalak or Chief of the RSS, prodded me to shred away the veil of so-called secrecy over working of the RSS. So the title of the book does not denote an effort by me to have a sensational tag line for the book, but only have a title that would not leave any excuse for the critics for being uninformed. If it be so, it would be only out of choice.

I have been a member of the RSS for many years and held various responsibilities in the organization over years, right from the first rung 'gat naayak' (or group leader) to responsibilities in Mumbai working committee. But, I have tried to write it as an observer, standing away from it for some years. Still, I may be accused of certain bias. I leave it to readers' judgment about my neutrality or bias. In writing this book, I am not bothered about the heavily biased ruling intellectual class and political parties and groups influenced by it. The power of this class is heavily overestimated as it dominates the media and guides the intellectual discourse in this country. However, its footprints on the ground are minimal. I wish to engage that large mass of Indians who genuinely wish to do something for the country and are disappointed with what they see around them. They are not sure how to help build a better India in the absence of any alternative organization or viewpoint as they are ignorant of the RSS and its ways of working and its vast body of work.

In this small book, I will try to open up the supposedly secret world of the RSS to the public. These are not the views of a purist as I was never a purist swayamsevak. I may not interpret the RSS' work as an RSS purist would like it to be as I have been out of day-to-day working for some time. I have used simple anecdotes or live examples to illustrate a point rather than argue about it solely on the basis of theory and philosophy. For the ideologues and critics, another day, another place perhaps!

Like many volunteers of my age, I had a fairly diverse exposure to other political movements and leaders of other political parties during the emergency. This period also coincided with my second round as a student of Arts after my earlier Science stream days. I was fortunate to be encouraged as well as criticized as a student leader by some of my left leaning professors during this period who gave me a different perspective of looking at issues. I recall Prof. Manjrekar fondly, who considered himself a Gandhian Marxist and who encouraged us a lot in our fight for democracy, but was equally critical of me for being a member of the RSS, till his last days. I had fascinating discussions with my Communist and Socialist friends inside and outside the jail during this period. It also was a time when I went through the magical world of dialectical materialism, supposed achievements of Russian revolution, Solzhenitsyn, Vladimir Dudintsev, Ayn Rand - the whole spectrum of economic and political thoughts. I also had close encounters with senior and junior RSS full-time volunteers (prachaaraks) which itself was an unforgettable learning experience.

The RSS is a huge organization. As a cadre based organization that works on consensus; its strong culture of taking along everybody democratically tends to slow down decision making; and any effort to bring about changes tends to get bogged down many a time. This makes a worker, who wishes to move fast with new ideas, feel frustrated. Since, he cannot do much about changing this style due to very nature of the organization, he either moves out and takes a different path or becomes indifferent. Similar experiences led me to, ultimately, distance myself from its regular day-to-day working.

My frustration arose, primarily, out of the refusal of the RSS to address the critical issue of biased media and its failure to reach out to vast audience with more 'with it' communication approach in tune with modern times. Its refusal to join adversaries in debate due to various reasons left me highly dissatisfied time and again. For the RSS, the biggest reason for not engaging in media polemics and propaganda has been its guiding principle of avoiding self-promotion at all costs and simply keep on working silently. Its founder Dr Keshav Baliram Hedgewar firmly believed that propaganda and self-promotion creates ego and this ego at personal and organizational level ultimately leads to corruption at both levels - not monetary corruption but more importantly, intellectual corruption that feeds on ego. Though, I sincerely appreciate this point having experienced this from close quarters, I believe that no movement can expand its base without the use of modern tools of communication today.

This attempt to unravel the secrets of the RSS is born out of this urge to explain the RSS working to lay people, especially the younger generation in an objective manner. I believe that my long experience with different generations of the RSS volunteers - both general members and senior workers of age groups ranging from 80s to 20s - and my frequent run-ins with my seniors due to my impatience with the RSS' style of working would tend to iron out any bias that an observer with limited exposure or contacts with such a vast organization may carry, thus influencing an objective analysis.

- Ratan Sharda

Prologue

"The RSS is a revolutionary organization. No other organization in the country comes anywhere near it. It alone has the capacity to transform society, end casteism and wipe the tears from the eyes of the poor... ...I have great expectations from this revolutionary organization that has taken up the challenge of creating a new India."

- Shri Jai Prakash Narayan, 1977

1

RSS and Fight for Democracy during Emergency

Let me begin from the middle. The emergency imposed by Mrs. Indira Gandhi on June 25 in 1975 was a watershed event in the annals of independent India. It was also a defining moment for the Rashtriya Swayamsevak Sangh or the RSS. It was an event which brought together all anti-Congress parties on a single platform, the incarceration of various political leaders in common jails and gave them a chance to know each other better. At the end of it all, the Janata Party was born which brought down the curtains on this digression from our democratic traditions. This era of emergency is a landmark event in the history of the RSS too. People of my generation look at this struggle for restoration for democratic values as our signal contribution to the society. The current generation doesn't have a collective memory beyond 1984 Sikh riots and 2002 Godhra train burning and subsequent riots. To them Emergency is a distant non-event. But, for the independent India, it was one of the most significant episodes in modern history. I thought, it would be a good idea to begin from this milestone in the life of the RSS.

For the people of our generation, who were in the prime of their youth, Shri Jai Prakash Narayan's (JP) movement for probity in public life had fired their imagination about 'sampoorna kranti' - total revolution - to throw out old decaying system and bring about a fundamental change throughout the political system. That it didn't end up that way is a sad commentary on our political leadership and a deep sense of disappointment for us who gave their all to restore democracy and fight for ideals personified by JP at that moment in history. This pain is exacerbated further when we note that people like Laloo Prasad Yadav and Ram Vilas Paswan who have mocked at the ideals of JP by following a blatantly casteist and communal agenda to fulfill their political ambition, are also the products of that struggle. The Hindu mythology of churning of the oceans (saagar manthan) tells us that every churning that throws up nectar will also throw up poison. How true!

Let me not jump the gun and give a little idea about what was this Emergency all about. After the heady days of 1971 decisive victory of India over Pakistan ending with liberation of Bangladesh, Indira Gandhi and her courtiers raised her to a very superhuman pedestal. They presumed that that they could do anything. This sense of arrogance of absolute power was like an aphrodisiac for this crowd of the Congress leaders who basked in the shadows of Smt. Gandhi. Those were the days when the Congress chief minister of Assam Shri P. C. Barooah declared that "India is Indira and Indira is India". All this led to various acts of omission and commission. This arrogance went overboard with persecution of opposition wherever possible. With power going to the heads of the ruling class, corruption became rampant.

First, Gujarat came into the grip of 'Navnrimaan Andolan' led primarily by students, that wished to displace highly corrupt regime of Chimanbhai Patel propped up by the Congress. It was essentially a non-political movement spearheaded by students. As it picked force, the RSS members, erstwhile Jan Sangh and other opposition groups also supported the agitation actively which ultimately led to the downfall of Patel and installation of the first non-Congress government headed by Babubhai Patel. The agitation inspired a parallel agitation in Bihar. JP was persuaded to come out of virtual retirement and led the agitation fuelled by the idealistic youth and students. A forum called Lok Sangharsh Samiti was formed and Nanaji Deshmukh, a veteran RSS prachaarak, was nominated as the general secretary of this forum which had members from the whole spectrum of political and student organizations and a few non-political social organizations too. This was also the time when JP came very close to the Jan Sangh and the RSS leaders seeing their great work on the ground. This intense ferment in the society shook up the Congress and Indira Gandhi badly. In the meanwhile, her election was declared void by the Justice Jagmohan Lal Sinha of Allahabad High Court which led to a political chaos.

The coterie around Smt. Gandhi played on her insecurity and convinced her about taking strong action to suppress this agitation and opposition. She declared a 'state of emergency' at midnight of 25th June, 1975, citing grave internal security threat to the nation. It was the first time that an Emergency was imposed citing internal security of India. A draconian act Maintenance of Internal Security Act (MISA) was revived to quell any dissidence, wherein a person could be detained without trial for at least two years. All the important opposition leaders were arrested overnight and the RSS was also banned for the second time in its chequered history. A few sundry organizations like Anand Marg and Jamat-e-Islami were also banned as tokenism to show that law was even handed and there was no bias.

Emergency pitch forked the RSS into this battle for restoration of democracy as the central player. Just to give reader an idea of the RSS's contribution to this fight, nearly 1,00,000 of the 1,30,000 satyaagrahis arrested during the emergency were from the RSS ranks. Of 30,000 people under dreaded MISA (Maintenance of Internal Security Act, something similar to anti-terror current MCOCCA of Maharashtra), 25000 were the RSS activists. We realized during this time that other political parties like Socialists of different hues had more leaders than cadres so it was very rare to see a socialist activist take part in the satyaagrahas. Thousands of activists spent nearly 18 months under MISA, or jailed under some IPC sections for staging satyagrah for six months or more; while some like me spent a month or so before being released due to a historic decision by Justice Lalit of Nagpur High Court who declared that Emergency didn't mean suspension of basic democratic rights.

It will be interesting to point out that Justice Lalit was virtually blacklisted and did not get his due promotions later. Those were the days of 'committed judiciary' as propounded by Indira Gandhi who was heavily influenced by a Communist coterie at that time led by late Kumarmangalam. Communist Party of India (CPI) had supported Smt. Gandhi's actions to 'suppress and defeat forces of fascism'! It would also be appropriate to note at this juncture that Communists had played dubious role during Quit India movement of 1942 as well as during Chinese attack of 1962. The pro-Chinese section of Communists at that time justified the Chinese attack and indirectly supported it by engineering a transport strike in West Bengal. Honourable comrades like Jyoti Basu were put behind the bars for a short duration during this time. This section later split up the CPI and formed CPM.

It is a telling commentary on the bias of the so called scholars and of modern Indian history chroniclers like Ramchandra Guha that they simply gloss over these facts of history or write disparagingly about the RSS' contribution rather than highlight the exemplary way they bore the brunt of atrocities in and outside jails even as their careers, family lives and businesses were damaged or ruined.

The RSS and its associate organizations' leadership in consultation with other political parties, who were part of the democratic struggle, instructed volunteers of all the associate organizations to organize satyagrah all over the country to create awareness amongst people about atrocities committed in the name of saving India. This agitation was propped up by the RSS across the length and breadth of the country. Satyagrahis would pop up in most unlikely of places with high security cordons in public functions. Many of these acts of defiance got covered in international media too.

In a small place like my college, Parle College (today's Sathaye College) in Mumbai, where I was the General Secretary of its students union and we had a very lively young band of the RSS volunteers, we were able to sustain satyagrah for months and courted arrests on weekly basis, creating big headache for the police. Our principal, Mr. Potdar was so pained with regular disturbance and even a college bandh after my arrest that he threw me out of college like many students of my times and I ended up in St. Xavier's College under the benign guidance of late Professor Oza, a well known Marxist economist. For this same crime a fellow volunteer Girish Bodas, a student of IIT Mumbai, was put behind the bars under MISA on the grounds of a complaint filed by our college authorities. Incidentally, the whole Bodas family is a devoted Sangh family. While two brothers were in jail, their mother and father worked silently for their respective Sangh related organizations for women and teachers respectively even at that time. Their only mode of communication in those days was leaving behind small notes on paper about their likely time of coming back home. Such is the dedication of members of the RSS and its associate organizations!

Even the RSS sympathizers and activists who were not active any more were picked up on the basis of CID reports made years back. An illustrative case is the raid police made to search for my elder brother who had long since moved to Surat but his name appeared due to his activities 10 years back. They didn't search for my belongings though I was very active at that time! We used to hear of such humorous mix up from many places.

We in Mumbai were a little lucky and police generally behaved decently with the agitators, realizing that we were very disciplined and law abiding. I suspect that police probably also understood the nature of the struggle and was sympathetic in many cases. Only in case of political pressure did they behave boorishly with volunteers. But, we listened and read about the indescribable horror stories of torture of the RSS activists in police stations and jails, especially in states ruled by overzealous satraps of the Congress like Punjab, Karnataka, Madhya Pradesh and Kerala (where both the Congress and Communists hated the RSS volunteers' guts) etc. But, all the activists bore such insults and tortures resolutely. The tortures if described in detail would shame the infamous Guantánamo Bay Detention Camp of US army.

Just to give an idea to the new generation how a supposedly democratic government and its bureaucracy behave when they get absolute power, I would give you a glimpse of the torture heaped on to these political prisoners including ladies. It is an example of how a fascist state can behave under the garb of democracy. Remember they were not hardened criminals. Simplest thing was to reduce their dignity to tatters by making them lie naked for days, parade them around, make one pee into others' mouth. Or it could become more sadistic like making them do unnatural sexual acts in front of their colleagues and police itself, pushing rods, burning cigarettes into various orifices of human body. It could be plain torture by keeping a person thirsty for days on end, beating him/her, giving aeroplane treatment (tying hands behind back and letting the person hang on a rope with hands for hours, pulling nails etc. etc. Most of these tortures are recorded by the victims with their colleagues while some are part of witness evidence in Shah Commission report. Shah Commission was appointed by Janata Party government after it came to power to probe violation of laws and human rights during emergency. How, the working of this commission was frustrated and disrupted by Youth Congress brigade in with blessings from Smt. Gandhi is also something that a student of contemporary history should study. These are the elements who are top Congress leaders today and lecturing the RSS about rowdy behavior etc.!

My narrative won't be complete without mentioning the incarceration of George Fernandes who was put into jail in harsh conditions along with his brother Lawrence Fernandes and well-known industrialist Viren Shah on charges of planning violence against the state. The case was famously known as 'Baroda conspiracy case'. These people were alleged to have conspired to use explosives to create terror and bring down the government. Lawrence was so badly brutalized with inhuman treatment that he was a physical and mental wreck by the time he was out of the jail and died a sick man. George Fernandes was paraded around in chains and these photographs were printed in newspapers for the benefit of Indian people. The case was closed after the Janata Party came back to power.

The press at that time behaved in a very tame manner except for some great exceptions like brave owner of *Indian Express* G. D. Goenka and journalists like BG Varghese. The government had clamped censorship on the press on the very day the emergency was declared. Everything that went into the papers had to be vetted by an omnipotent censor committee. The press brought up on license quota raj and newsprint doles behaved more timidly than required. In the famous words of LK Advani, "it crawled when it was asked to bend." We were thrilled and inspired by Mr. Goenka, when he left out the editorial column blank as he couldn't write what he wanted to. The government then passed an order that you cannot keep a column blank! But, *Indian Express* didn't crawl throughout the emergency. It fought as much as it could inspite of all kinds of arm twisting by various wings of the government. Goenka was harassed no end under various laws. Then, there was a famous classified in *Times of India* which condoled the death of Democracy in a coded manner. The only way news could travel was through secret meetings, rumours, guarded telephone talks (as even the telephones were tapped), people travelling to carry news or undertake various activities. There were underground pamphlets which were distributed surreptitiously in thousands by volunteers to spread news and information about the pro-democracy agitation.

There were grand courtiers of Indira Gandhi like our famous Sardar Khushwant Singh who wrote sick laudatory articles about great changes that emergency has brought about and how Sanjay Gandhi was a visionary great leader, a wonderful engineer with his 'tinbox' of a small car. Mr. Singh was suitably rewarded with citations, awards and lucrative posting. There were many such worthies in media who curried favours with the Congress party during those days. To round off the car story I may mention that realizing that the car was not going anywhere with its backyard technology, and that the idea of a people's car by itself was not bad all, government finally adopted this project and in collaboration of Suzuki brought out the trail blazing Maruti car. Press including the great old lady of Boribunder, *Times of India,* used to be awash with great stories about how emergency had improved work culture all around (which was a partial truth) and how people appreciated the great disciplined era (which was not that true) ushered in by great leader Indira Gandhi. All this was eerily close to Russian propaganda mills. Any act beyond a point can become counterproductive and leads to excesses. How Indians disapprove of any act to control their freedom was clearly demonstrated subsequently by the election results. I am not expanding on these points as the focus of the book is not emergency but the role of the RSS in the struggle for democratic rights.

On a personal front and even organizational front, this exposure to people from other political streams during the struggle was a great learning experience. There was a clear directive to work with all political and social organizations to fight emergency regime.

We used to meet every evening to play in open grounds but not in a regular way the shakhas worked. We would meet even in the nights to plan out our strategies under the leadership of our local secretary for satyagrah and other modes of agitation, like putting up posters and wall paintings to register our protests.

Fortunately, I was part of the team of volunteers who used to ferry central RSS leaders to different locations incognito for one of the earliest meeting of central committee hosted for three days on three different venues within Mumbai that planned the agitation against emergency. It was funny to see these leaders in western dresses and wigs etc. Not being media figures helped a lot too. They used to stay with families as their uncles, and would be constantly on the move. A colleague of mine, Jagdish Baliga used to move in different attires and facial changes for months before he was finally caught. He was in charge of Dr. Subramaniam Swamy's movements when he attended the Parliament and again disappeared to resurface in the UK. He was hosted in UK by volunteers of Friends of India Society (FISI) a body floated to support pro-democracy movement in India. Founding members of FISI were members of Hindu Swayamsevak Sangh, UK a Hindu community organization registered in UK. FISI played a prominent role in this struggle throughout by lobbying for restoration of democratic rights in India and help spreading the true news about happenings in India.

The big brother was watching everywhere, so there was lot of thrill for us youngsters in underground work. The training we had received in shakhas since our childhood stood us in good stead. Not a single worker tried to stave off an imminent arrest for participation in satyagrah with any excuse. Infact, it was the local leader who would sometimes refuse to allow a person to take part in satyagrah because he knew the person had a serious problem at home or he was required for some other underground activity. It was simply another duty given by the Sangh and it had to be done, that was the attitude. For us, this was an illustrative example of what could be achieved by praying to the motherland daily and pledging to serve her and the society unflinchingly and selflessly. This was also the time when lady members of sister organizations of the RSS, mothers and sisters of the RSS volunteers and young girl students also joined this struggle against dictatorship in good numbers. They also kept the morale of volunteers high by coming to courts during hearings with eatables, sweets etc.

The emergency finally came to an end in 1977 due to various reasons. One of the prime reasons was the political pressure that built up over the issue of nearly one hundred thousand political prisoners in jails. Regular satyagrah or courting arrest that happened all over the country; and large numbers in jails brought enormous pressure on Mrs. Gandhi. Then, there was international pressure built through various channels including the ones used by FISI. A critical factor was Smt. Indira Gandhi's urge to legitimize her dictatorship by winning an election which many in her coterie thought would be a cakewalk. "India is Indira and Indira is India" syndrome was in full flow. That the events proved her and others wrong reflects the greatness of our Indian people wedded to democratic way of life for eons who went to polling booths with different ideas than what their leaders had.

We started off on a very low note when elections were declared, with instructions from the top to work whole heartedly for the victory of Janata Party. There were no resources and people feared coming out in the open even to the party offices initially. Polling booth level plans were devised. It is noteworthy that most of the senior and middle level leaders were in jail at this time, thus, we were nearly leaderless by common political wisdom. The training in the RSS shakhas was useful again. The young volunteers with the help of a few senior workers who were outside the jails soldiered on regardless of the possible outcome. We realized the way anti-emergency wave was building up only in the latter part of campaigning when people started thronging the election offices of Janata Party. We got a shock of our life when one of our simple cycle rally turned into a strong rally of thousands without any major publicity. Even the local meetings would draw unprecedented crowds. It was a heady feeling. We went nuts when we heard news of victory of pro-democracy forces.

I would not like to digress in detail about the dirty politics played specially by Socialist groups within Janata Party to break up the party under the guise of the controversy of 'dual membership' of ex-Jan Sangh members who had merged Jan Sangh into Janata Party. It was not that they did not know of this loyalty issue before the party was created. Infact, there are records of many such leaders singing paeans about the RSS workers for their role in restoration of democracy, their discipline and dedication. Leaders like Madhu Limaye had also gone on record that they had made a mistake in understanding the RSS as they carried a bias within them for years; and that their close interaction with the RSS and Jan Sangh leaders had opened their eyes etc. etc. The fact of the matter was that apart from Communists and Jan Sangh no other political party had a structured organization. They used this organizational power till it suited them. Once they got power they felt that this cadre might capture Janata Party if and when internal elections took place. They had also noted that a big chunk of MPs belonged to erstwhile Jan Sangh. Thus, followed the disgraceful game of back-stabbing, split in Janata Party, its downfall and return of Indira Gandhi.

Regardless of the final political outcome, for the RSS it was an epoch making changeover. From an organization limited to running shakhas and some social service projects and string of associate organizations like Akhil Bharatiya Vidyarthi Parishad, Vishwa Hindu Parishad, Bharatiya Mazdoor Sangh etc, it extended its reach to new directions. In fact, major push for social service projects happened during this time as the volunteers had to find ways of working for society while the RSS shakhas were shut down. This period proved Sangh's mettle as a firm believer in democracy and helped change the rules of the game of elections. Its acceptability reached new levels and newer areas and it grew rapidly after this inspite of massive personal losses to many the RSS and related organizations' workers during this period.

For us, the young volunteers of that time, it was a great learning period. Learning about working underground, going to jails (the earlier generation of the RSS had gone to jail after the ban on the RSS in 1948, but for us it was a new experience), working with people and organizations outside the Sangh umbrella, learning about others' points of views during meetings and in jail. It was also a time to learn closely how other political parties worked in electoral politics and about their ideologies. Till this time our opponents used to ridicule us, but after this era we earned respectability and acceptability in social interactions. Thus, it was a turning point for the organization and its members.

There is a small book in Hindi by the RSS documenting history of the RSS struggle for democracy. Unfortunately, it has not been widely distributed or publicized.

In these days of petty politics of vendetta it is relevant to remember that the then the RSS chief Shri Balasaheb Deoras had exhorted to the political class to let bygones be bygones and not get into any witch hunt against Smt. Gandhi. This was typical of the RSS as it believes in all round growth of nation, animosity towards none and well-being of all.

❑

2

Major Defining Moments in RSS History

The RSS was born in 1925 and is now 85 year old. For an Indian organization, that too of Hindus, to have not just survived as a united entity but thrived over such a time span is indeed a tribute to its tenacity of purpose. The reason for this phenomenon is also scripted in its 'secrets' described in the following pages.

The narrative as it unfolds in the following pages gives one a fair idea that the RSS and its members have done more than the credit they get for their services to this ancient land. One wonders what would have been the state of affairs had it not intervened decisively or persuaded members of the society and leaders to take a different view of things and take right action.

In the life of an organization that aspires to define the innate nationhood for the society and strives to change set pattern of thinking internalized over centuries of foreign domination; there would be some defining moments that would have played a major catalytic role in evolution of the organization.

Of various 'medals' the RSS has received, one most commonly handed out is that of being reactionary and orthodox organization. I would say, slow to respond to various challenges or situations, yes; but reactionary or orthodox definitely never. The birth, the growth, its adaptation to changing circumstances, coming up with newer ways of working through its evolution – all these indicate an organization that is modern, proactive and forward looking. Its urge to reform the society of its ills in its own way and make it progressive is recorded in this book briefly.

Dr. Hedgewar chose to take a harder path of social mobilization when he could have easily stayed on in the Congress, taken up more positions of power in the organization and enjoyed fruits of this power. He chose a novel and innovative instrument of daily shakha for creating this organization. He understood well that it was a long drawn and tough path. The seeds of this thought were sown by Sister Nivedita's call to give a minimum time everyday to the nation if one wished to see its emancipation. Every aspect of organization and its evolution was experimental. All the training processes were freshly designed and implemented. The only thing that carried him through was his abiding faith in the destiny of the nation.

Response to various situations right from the ugly days of partition and various challenges facing the nation saw the RSS take proactive, and many a time, unpopular stance. For example, it opposed reorganization of states on linguistic lines as it could lead to parochialism. People understood the stand taken by the RSS in such cases only in retrospect after the noise, generally created by our comrades and secular-Congress lobby died down. The preceding pages have many such examples. In this chapter, we only look at various milestones in the life of the RSS. It is also possible that you may not connect to some points or views in this chapter till you read the subsequent chapters. Idea of putting them here to give you some reference points as you read on.

The RSS has gone through various trials and tribulations during its chequered history. Given below are bullet points that I consider as defining moments of this organization. Readers may have their own view about the milestones as they understand the organization better after reading this book.

- Partition of Bharat i.e. India
- First ban of 1948
- Vivekananda Rock Memorial
- Second ban in 1975 and Emergency
- Ekaatmataa Yaatraa
- Dr. Hedgewar birth centenary celebrations
- Ram Janmabhoomi movement and third ban

Actually the evolution has been more graded and the growth of the RSS from being an organization to consolidate Hindu society to a virtual social movement over time has gone virtually unnoticed. There have been various campaigns and agitations that it has undertaken directly or with its associate organizations that have defined many a political agenda. I have chosen only the major signposts which have taken Sangh work to a different level.

I have not considered establishment of Vishwa Hindu Parishad, the first Hindu organization in history of Hindu civilization of thousands of years that could manage to bring all the saints, sages, mahants and heads of various religious sects on a single platform in 1965-66 as a milestone in the RSS history. It became a mass organization on its own after initial support from the RSS during its early years. I think it was more an achievement of second Sarsanghchaalak, Shri Guruji who, due to his background as an ordained disciple of Swami Akhandaananda and respect he commanded with his knowledge and humility, could bring them together thus, and persuade all Hindu saints, including revered Shankaraacharyas to declare that 'All Hindus are brothers' and 'No Hindu is fallen or untouchable'.

I have also not taken any social service work like disaster relief, even very large ones as defining moments as they are part of the Sangh's regular agenda. You will get a glimpse about them later in the book.

Some of the points below, specially about Independence struggle, partition and ban have complex background that cannot be mentioned here at this stage as it would not be easily grasped till you have read more about the RSS. So, I have put more detailed notes in the Annexure at the end of the book. There is also a short essay in the annexure on the past Sarsanghchaalaks (the RSS chiefs) and the current one, evaluating their contribution to growth and evolution of the RSS.

Partition of Bharat

British were aware that any delay in declaration of independence could frustrate the conspiracy of partition inspite of the Congress leadership's capitulation, because they understood that the RSS could lead a consolidation of forces opposed to partition. The presence in the RSS shakhas had swelled to huge proportions during pre-partition days. In the later part of the book and annexure you will get better glimpse of the RSS volunteers' sacrifices and death-defying work during the partition days.

The chief of the RSS, Sarsanghchaalak, Guruji had taken up whirlwind tours of various parts of the country including politically sensitive areas like Sindh and Punjab, exhorting the followers to be prepared for any sacrifice to save their motherland from partition. He was in Sindh just one week before the declaration of partition and Independence, while other so called the Congress leaders had already fled the scene to safer places. Organizational skills of its members were tested to the full in the trying circumstances when the members were not only involved in saving families and refugees from death, rape and plunder but also in organizing relief camps. In fact, a dedicated band of the RSS volunteers stayed behind in

Sindh to help safe migration of Hindu families to India under instructions from the RSS Chief and came to India only after accomplishing their mission.

Earlier, Muslim League had waved its 'green flag' for 'Direct Action' on 16th August 1946 and Muslims butchered thousands of Hindus mercilessly, with indescribable cruelty. The Congress was shaken to the core due to this act. The Congress showed total lack of spirit of putting up a fight and not running away from battle ground. Responding its talk of 'non-reaction', the then head of the RSS, Guruji Golwalkar said bluntly, "There is a lot of talk about not picking up arms and not taking revenge. But, I cannot agree with this current language of not reacting; it is not something arising out of bravery. It is nothing but cowardice and about fooling ourselves. It is 'adharma', that is, immoral to inflict pain upon self." Appealing to be ready for self defence, he affirmed unhesitatingly, "It is our firm belief that every individual has a natural right to self-protection and the society made of such individuals also has the same right. I had read a bizarre statement in newspapers which said, 'An individual or society does not have the Right to defend self, only the government has this right, and a person should not take law unto his hands even if he is attacked.' Only Law has the right to defend an individual and society. Does it mean that we should sit quietly and wait for police if somebody attacks us? Should there be no attempt for self- defence? How far can this be justified? Right of self defence is a right endowed by nature to every individual and society."

Hindu brethren, including Sikhs, started coming together with self-confidence in cities and villages of Punjab like Rawalpindi, Lahore, Peshawar, Amritsar, Jalandhar, Ambala etc. Witnessing this atmosphere, English *Tribune* wrote, "Punjab is the sword arm of Hindustan and the RSS is the sword arm of Punjab." Perturbed with this development, mouthpiece of Muslim League, *Dawn*, wrote, "If the Congress leadership wishes to receive cooperation from Muslims, then it must ban the Sangh immediately."

In short, common Hindu populace was not in favour of partition even after Jinnah's 'Direct Action'. Wherever the Sangh reached, Hindu youth power began gearing up for self-defence. Communist Party was also in favour of partition, apart from Muslim League. It had also passed a resolution in favour of partition. At the same time, British rulers and other leaders were stealthily planning for partition of the country in the background. Under a political settlement, a coalition government of the Congress and Muslim League formed a government in Delhi in September 1946. Central Assembly (called Parliament now) went into session with this arrangement. League began throwing tantrums immediately. First day witnessed unruly scenes both inside and outside the assembly. Muslim League exhibited its goonda power to good effect. It decided to play this game with utter contempt even on the second day. But, political leaders decided not to allow the insulting behavior to be repeated. Top leader of Delhi state Congress Lala Deshbandhu Gupta came to the Sangh office in Kamla Nagar and met state prachaarak Vasantrao Oke to see how this could be done. As a result of these talks hundreds of swayamsevaks got busy from early morning and surrounded the Assembly hall to signal a strong response. Smelling the changed conditions on ground, ruffians lost their nerves and assembly could carry on with its session in a dignified manner. Inspite of all this, partition of this ancient land was announced on 3rd June 1947.

The Sangh set up Punjab Relief Committee and Hindu Sahaayataa Samiti. Lahore was the centre of activity for both of these.

In his tours, the then Chief of the RSS, Guruji went to Sialkot and Montgomery after touring Multan. A young volunteer asked Guruji during his tour of Sialkot and Montigomery, "Should we not collect arms to defend ourselves against Muslims?" Guruji asked him, "Have you read Geeta? Geeta says, Atman is immortal. Then what are we afraid of? Collecting weapons is a sign of fear." Quoting a proverb, he added, "A person is afraid of a person who does not terrorize others nor does he fear for self.' Understand this very well that fearlessness is the strongest weapon." The Sangh leadership used to describe the facts of unfolding scenario objectively in their meetings and discussions. But, it was always cautious that it should not result in any disorderly situation. Brief was clear that one was to be ready for self-defence but not be hot-headed or violent.

Situation had deteriorated so badly that even the man of Steel, the home minister, had to admit, "It won't be possible for government to defend everybody. Each person will have to try to defend self." For the Hindu populace these words were but of a helpless cry and worried it no end. The Sangh volunteers took up the job of securing the society at the risk of their lives. The Sangh leaders Guruji, Balasaheb Deoras, Madhavrao Muley, Vasantrao Oke etc. were on the battlefield to guide the self-defence teams, and did not run away to Delhi to safety like proclaimed the Congress leaders.

Defending the valley of Kashmir from aggressors, its merger with the nation, role of swayamsevaks and Guruji in this historic chapter have been recorded with undeniable facts and proofs and dates by Manikchandra Vajpayee and Shridhar Paraadkar in their well researched book *'Jyoti Jalaa Nij Praan Ki'* (Lighting a lamp by making bonfire of one's own life).

It was the first time when the whole of young organization was put to test. Hundreds of volunteers lost their life, families got injured during this period as they were busy with these activities rather than looking after their own families. Though, it succeeded in the limited mission of saving lives and helping refugees reconstruct their lives; the eternal regret of the RSS leadership has been that it was too young and not big enough to stop the partition.

First Ban in 1948

Congress leadership was scared and envious of the growing popularity of the RSS and its organizational muscle. It could not wish it away as it had surrendered its moral authority by agreeing to partition. Murder of Mahatma Gandhi was a god sent opportunity for the Congress to suppress the organization. Guruji was highly disturbed with this tragic incident and had condemned the assassination in unequivocal terms immediately on hearing the news. However, a ban was imposed without any shred of evidence. Guruji was arrested under section 302, as if he had shot Gandhiji from his gun! It reflects poorly on the Congress government that realizing its mistake the government it had to remove this charge within 24 hours. The Congress leaders in various cities, especially in Maharashtra let loose its goons on the RSS and its sympathisers. The RSS volunteers suffered in silence on directions of Guruji who appealed to them from jail to keep their calm in that hour of tragedy as it could lead to serious repercussions for the Hindu society.

It is a reflection of the political games that government under Nehru played that inspite of the investigation report submitted by Mr. Sanjeevi, a respected police official and heading CID enquiry, within 17 days of Gandhi's murder absolving the RSS of any role in Gandhi's murder conspiracy, the ban was not lifted. The report was suppressed for a long time and it came into open many years later. Not only that, in the court case against Nathuram Godse for Gandhi's murder, neither he, nor his accomplice or the judgment mentioned the RSS even once!

It is a sad commentary on our political leaders' petty mindedness that same Congress politicians who had gone to the RSS offices to seek protection during pre-partition times, who had approached the RSS to help them conduct Nehru's public meeting in Sindh peacefully were out to crush the RSS now as they saw it as a rival power centre, inspite of its professed cultural and non-political work of RSS. I have mentioned later about how the RSS volunteers had foiled an attempt to kill all the ministers of newly formed government in September 1947 by reporting the conspiracy with detailed facts to Sardar Patel.

Interestingly, Sardar Patel, was ready to lift the ban on the RSS if it merged with the Congress. There is a sentence in a letter to Guruji during exchange of letters at that time, "I have firm belief that the Sangh people can do justice to their patriotism only by working together with the Congress and not by opposing it or being separate from it". So, an apparently communal organization accused of Gandhi murder and banned could be absolved of all its sins by merging with the Congress! This was contrary to his views about this Gandhi murder episode which he had expressed to Nehru earlier on. It seems he decided to be on the right side of Nehru in this instance and followed his line of not removing the Sangh ban though he did not believe in it as the detailed historical records and correspondence of the time between Nehru, Sangh, Patel shows.

That Nehru had made up his mind about crushing the Sangh was clear from his speech in Amritsar on 29th January 1948, one day before the murder when he thundered that he would see that the "RSS is totally uprooted from the face of India." This was in line with resolutions passed by the Congress committees and its chief ministers in some states demanding a ban on the RSS a few months prior to this as they saw it as the sole possible political competition to their monopoly over power due to its immense popularity based on the work it had done for people who had suffered immensely during partition.

Finally, as the government of the day refused to see reason, a satyagrah was launched. It was one of the largest, biggest and most disciplined satyagrah seen so far by Indians. Around 70,000 volunteers were jailed for coming together in grounds and offering prayer to the motherland. These numbers were more than prisoners taken anytime during freedom struggle including Quit India agitation of 1942. Incidentally, a senior volunteer of Konkan region told me that in his jail, out of 900 inmates, 700 were from agriculture families and rural background. Thus, it is clear that the support base at that time was also widely distributed and not as brahminical as is made out to be.

A large number of its supporters lost government jobs through a vague law that barred any citizen from joining the RSS. (I think, this is a law from British days. This archaic and anti-democratic law is still operational in most of the states and is revived at random to persecute an RSS member!). Many members lost their business and jobs specially in institutions owned by the Congress followers or their sympathisers. Many jails also saw typical police excesses that a fascist state can bear upon its dissenting citizens. The ban and the satyagrah lasted many months. Finally, Kapoor Commission appointed by the government came out with a report that exonerated the RSS of any part in Gandhiji's assassination.

To save itself from further embarrassment, the government raised a flimsy objection that the RSS didn't have a written constitution, not a rare thing in those days. In fact, as Guruji pointed out in one of his letters to the interlocutors during the ban, even the Congress did not have a written constitution for nearly 14 years, from 1985 till 1995! Nor did Sarvoday Mandal and many other voluntary organizations of those times had a constitution. The intermediaries requested Guruji to fulfill this simple condition, the constitution of the RSS was formulated, ending the ban on the RSS. As Guruji pointed out in his covering letter, it was nothing but a written form of how the organization had been running since its inception. On one condition, the Sangh leadership refused to budge, inspite of pressures till the last – that was admitting young non-adult members in the Sangh, as that was the foundation of its work.

For a young organization whose members had suffered grievously in this period, building up the organization was a big challenge. Guruji received outstanding reception all over India wherever he went, showing the Hindu society's support for him and the RSS. He appealed to the volunteers to dedicate at least one year for nation building. His emotional appeal was so great that hundreds of the RSS volunteers left their jobs and businesses to become prachaaraks and vistaaraks to rebuild the RSS. With such a ground swell of support and a renewed sense of sacrifice, the RSS came out much stronger from this trial by fire.

Vivekanand Rock Memorial

Building of Vivekanand Shilaa Smaarak by Vivekanand Kendra in Kanyakumari in 1970 can be considered a defining moment for the RSS. It was a mammoth task for it to take up a project for which it did not have resources and the governments of the time at all levels had no interest in this project at all, even if some of them were not against it. One of the seniormost prachaarak' and leader of the RSS Eknath Ranade was assigned this task and he was freed from the Sangh work for its fulfillment. It was a project that was to become the pride of nation.

It was a historic decision to involve millions of Indians in the noble memory of one of the greatest Hindu saints of our times who led the renaissance of Hinduism in those dark times of nation's history and gave new breath to the urge for independence. The manner of involvement was very simple - a request for donation of only Re. 1/ - (rupee one only) through coupons. It had been resolved that the memorial will not be built with large donations but with small contributions. If I am not wrong, the budget was around rupee one crore, and it was managed through this novel resolve. Collection was done entirely by the RSS volunteers moving door to door without any big hoardings or newspaper advertisements etc. And there was no TV at that time!

That the project faced many other hurdles and it was a difficult engineering feat too, is a matter of minor details.

Subsequently, the central and state governments, except the Government of Kerala then ruled by Marxist Communists, contributed to the general funds. This was the first major mass contact programme of the RSS, much bigger in scope than the earlier big programme like national signature campaign for cow protection and the subsequent agitation in Delhi. In this endeavour, people from the lowest strata of society to the highest were made a stake holder in this national monument and the message of Swami Vivekanand was conveyed to them in a simple way.

Second Ban in 1975 and Emergency

I have dealt at length about this episode in the beginning so I will skip details. It changed the thinking at the level of workers as well as the organization. Its base expanded to hitherto untouched segments of the society. People saw the work and sacrifice of the RSS for restoration of democracy. This period saw the removal of so called veil of secrecy around the RSS to some extent, because media itself harassed by the fascist policies of the Congress government had no choice but to give due publicity and respect to the work done by the RSS. The taboo of virtual untouchability on the RSS imposed by various interested lobbies for decades was truly broken. This was a big gain for the RSS as a movement.

Ekaatmataa Yatra

After the alarming mass conversions of Hindus, primarily Dalit brethren, in Meenakshipuram in Tamil Nadu to Islam, many activities were initiated by the RSS, its affiliates, other conscious Hindu organizations and saints. It activated many religious leaders, heads of various maths to come out into the society and create a sense of oneness amongst the Hindus.

One of the initiatives that the RSS took was to organize a nationwide movement called 'Ekaatmataa Yatra' in 1983. The idea was simple. Trucks carrying image of 'Bharatmata' (sacred motherland) and a huge vessel containing sacred waters of Ganga were to criss-cross length and breadth of the country on four major routes. Holy river Ganga is a symbol of the uninterrupted flow of noble Indian traditions and culture over ages and invokes reverence and respect for our motherland. The trucks were to make various stopovers on way and cover thousands of villages and cities. At these stopovers, some religious functions and presence of local religious leaders was also planned. Holy Ganga water was especially packaged in bottles to be distributed through the yatra to the participants. There were hundreds of other smaller yatras to supplement these main yatras. The idea was to weave a theme of timelessness of our civilization and unity in diversity around one of the most sacred symbols of India, namely, sacred river of Ganga. The most seen iconic image of 'Bharatmata' that you find in thousands of places all over India was created during this campaign.

It is a tribute to the social sensitivity of the senior RSS leaders that they could judge the feelings of the Hindu society about the threat to it from mass conversions. For the first time I could really understand, what is the meaning of having your 'ears to the ground'. Local workers at various places were not at all sure of the reception that this yatra would encounter. Many of us tried to hunt for smaller grounds to avoid the embarrassment of seeing near empty grounds. One of the seniormost RSS prachaarak, Moropant Pingley in one of his meetings with workers said, "This yatra is going to succeed, we are 100 per cent sure. It is up to you to take part in organizing it well and be a part of its success."

We were simply amazed at its success. The turnout of the people, spontaneous welcome programmes on way were as unbelievable as the scenes during the 1977 elections! It was an overwhelming experience that one cannot forget for a lifetime. An estimated 80 million people participated in this programme. For me, this event is defining moment as it was the first RSS programme organized on its own strength with its associate organizations at all India level with really mass participation. It was a programme that brought the RSS and society together as envisaged by its founder. This could be called the precursor the Ram Janmabhoomi movement that saw further consolidation of Hindus at all levels of the society.

Dr. Hedgewar Birth Centenary Celebrations

Dr. Hedgewar's birth centenary was celebrated in 1989 with great enthusiasm and sense of dedication. One of the decisions taken by the leadership was to create a corpus of funds that would help launch large number of social service projects, or seva projects, as the RSS calls it. This focus on seva karya and financial support to such activities through this fund mobilization gave a new impetus to the social service facet of the RSS work.

From an organization focused primarily on organization building, the RSS expanded into another direction with clear focus in areas of social life that were in desperate need of a proper structured approach. This aspect of the RSS activity has become a huge network by itself. You will get a glimpse of some of the seva projects in later chapters. From targeted 1000 social service projects, today the RSS and its affiliate organizations conduct nearly 1.50 lac social service programmes.

To feel the difference they make, one has to actually visit some such projects and understand what they have done for the society. The social changers like Ekal Vidyalay movement, Swasthya Rakshak (bare foot doctors or primary health volunteers) movements and Graamoday initiatives are a spin-off of this initiative.

Ram Janmabhoomi Movement

Enough has been read and seen about Ram Janmabhoomi movement by my generation. However, the current young generation is only aware of demolition of Babri structure and riots that followed, because of the adverse propaganda surrounding this movement. In later part of the book I have covered the intellectual exercise and efforts of the secular-Marxist parivaar to obfuscate real historical issues, defame the Sangh and Hindutva and successfully pushing under the carpet the facts that made the agitation what it was.

Never, in the history of India, has a public movement seen such mobilization of people at large, support of society in general with people hiding and feeding satyagrahis who were hounded by police and railways controlled by secular parivaar during its first satyagrah of 'karseva' or voluntary religious service at Ayodhya for rebuilding Ram temple. Ram has designed the moral and ethical make up of Hindu society since eons. Through migrant Hindus Ram has also reached other societies around the world, had influenced them with his simple message through his life. However hard secularists may try to insult Hindus and make them believe that Ram was only a mythological figure and forward arguments that he is there only in minds and hearts of people, faith of people built on oral history of thousands of year cannot be trifled with.

Never, was a mass campaign sustained and guided through so many phases involving more and more Hindus on a matter that shook their conscience and firmed up their resolve that their dearest Lord Ram must have a temple where it already existed for centuries. For a country where every 5th or 6th person's name from South to North carries 'Ram' in it, it was a natural feeling. Lord Ram is one of the three most popular deities in Hindu pantheon viz. Krishna, Shiva and Ram. One cannot trifle with an eternal faith.

If the secular cabal had been more thoughtful and political leadership more pragmatic, it could have created a deep sense of mutual trust and love by persuading Muslims to give up their claim on a defunct structure that signified all the atrocities and insults Mughal invaders like Babar and rulers like Aurangzeb had heaped on Hindus by demolishing their temples, converting them into mosques and heaping insults on their most revered Gods in Mathura, Kashi and Ayodhya apart from thousands of other places. A section of Muslims had clearly shown an inclination to give up its claim on the Babri structure as a gesture of goodwill for Hindu society and to put balm on centuries old wounds. But, the leadership chose the path of immediate gains, pandering to shallower sentiments egged on by anti-religious, anti-nationalist thinking, goaded by inverse communalism of Marxist parivaar.

The movement helped reach out and connect to all the sections and strata of society throughout India. For the first time, the historians, social scientists and Indologists and journalists got a chance to air their views bravely and honestly. Marxist-secular cabal was exposed for its inability to confront the truth that didn't suit it. It is regrettable that the group of unbiased intellectuals suffered in the aftermath due to vice like grip of the dominant lobby and failure of the BJP, the RSS, the VHP etc. to support them. I will talk about leftist stranglehold on intellectual space in India later.

Koenraad Elst notes in his 'Ayodhya, The Finale - Science vs. Secularism, the Excavation Debate' that "the secularist historians have been bluffing their way through the controversy. In December 1990, the government of Chandra Shekhar invited the two lobby groups involved, the Vishva Hindu Parishad and the Babri Masjid Action Committee, to discuss the historical truth of the matter. Misled by the media into believing that the Hindu claims were pure fantasy, the BMAC office-bearers arrived ill-prepared. They were speechless when the VHP team presented dozens of documents supporting its case. For the next meeting, they invited a team of proper historians chaired by Marxist professor R.S. Sharma, who declared that they hadn't studied the evidence yet. This was a strange statement from people who had just led 42 academics in signing a petition confirming once and for all that there was no evidence whatsoever for a temple. At the meeting scheduled for 25 January 1991, they simply didn't show up anymore. In a booklet issued months later, pompously called *'A Historians' Report to the Nation'*, they tried to save face by nibbling at the evidential value of a few of the numerous documents presented by their opponents (and of course, historical evidence is rarely absolute), but failed to offer even one piece of evidence for any alternative scenario....."

".....During the demolition, an inscription tentatively dated to ca. 1140 came to light. It detailed how it was part of a temple to

"Vishnu, slayer of Bali and of the ten-headed one". Rama is considered an incarnation of Vishnu, and the two enemies he defeated were king Bali and King Ravana, often depicted as ten-headed in recognition of his brilliant mind. This evidence too was locked away and strictly ignored by the secularists until 2003, when *People's Democracy*, the paper of the Marxwadi Communist Party, alleged foul play. It seemed that the Lucknow State Museum mentioned in its catalogue a 20-line inscription dedicated to Vishnu, satisfying the description of the piece discovered during the demolition, and missing since the late 1980s. However, museum director Jitendra Kumar declared that the piece had never left the museum, even though it had not been on display, and he showed it at a press conference for all to see (*Hindustan Times*, 8 May 2003). In spite of many similarities, it differed from the Ayodhya find in shape, colour and text contents."

As we go to press, judgment on the case has been delivered by Allahabad High Court. It has vindicated the stand of Hindus that the place under dispute is, indeed, place of birth of Lord Ram. The judgment has tried to balance facts and faith in equal measure and has tried to achieve what political and religious leaders failed to achieve all these years, i.e. try to bring about reconciliation that can heal the wounds of injustice - festering for Hindus for centuries because of destructions of their places of worship and for Muslims for decades since demolition of Babri structure. It is amusing to see the worthies like Irfan Habib crawling out of woodworks picking holes in archeological findings of scholars of ASI. They forget that this team was appointed by the court and did its work in the presence of judges, experts and witnesses. Each and every finding has been meticulously recorded and presented as expected from such experts. This same group of historians had evaded meetings of historians and archaeologists through good offices of the Central government two decades back when they found that the evidence presented by pro-temple historians and archeologists was overwhelming in comparison to their oft repeated posturing built around British and later leftist interpretation of history.

Another peeve of secularists is that decision seems to have been taken more on the basis of faith than facts, facts that they dispute too. The Hinduism has lived its traditions, culture and religions mostly through oral propagation. Even Vedas - the fountainhead of universal knowledge were carried through generations with oral traditions. It is the tradition of 'Shruti' i.e. oral transmission of knowledge. It is only now that so called myths of Hinduism are being proven through archaeological proofs or, what the law calls corroborative evidence. Limitation is with our current knowledge of research tools, not with Hindu history and its offshoots in the field of science etc. One cannot hold this weakness of Hinduism against it. It is also true that every religion or belief system is basically born out of faith and sustains itself on faith. Going by the same yardstick of scientific evidence, should critics of Islam doubt whether Prophet Mohammad did indeed hear words of God or Allah? Should cynics doubt Immaculate Conception? Should we doubt whether Moses actually received Ten Commandments from the Lord? Should we doubt whether the hair recovered in Shrinagar after its mysterious disappearance some years back was, indeed, Hazrat Saheb's hair? No Hindu would raise such doubts. Nor do our secular friends do so in case of other religions. But, faith of Hindus can be challenged and ridiculed. Only secularists' interpretation of history or faith can be the gospel truth, as if they have a monopoly on truth. It is sad that instead of helping society move ahead with a positive spirit as indicated by the judgment and close this chapter, they are out again re-opening wounds to prove themselves right and satisfy their egos. None of these secular worthies have countered the views expressed by fanatic Indian Muslim leaders who claim that no mosque can be shifted though their land of inspiration, the epicenter of Wahabism, has seen umpteen mosques being demolished or shifted to new places in Saudi Arabia and also in Pakistan. But, they do not tire of spouting 'enlightened noble' views like 'Ram lives in heart, why are you fighting for a temple in his name?' etc. etc. It is but a small example of their biased mindset.

This movement brought Hindutva firmly on the centrestage of national discourse and it became a mainstream ideology. It is not a mere coincidence that the present phase of India's growth story coincides with the new resurgent Hindu society that emerged out of this period of Janmabhoomi movement. A feeling of confidence further strengthened globally by Nuclear explosions conducted by NDA government run by people close to the RSS ideology. This historic cycle also strengthens the premise of the RSS that a society can progress only if its members are confident of themselves and carry a true sense of pride about their country.

I am not sure, though, if the by-product of all this mobilization was as good. The rise of extreme and militant groups like Bajrang Dal could be called a necessity of times when there is a clear scenario of clash of civilizations. I don't wish to talk of lofty ideals of Hinduism to say that this clash is mythical as this clash on the ground is a reality. However, such groups tasted the muscle power for the first time which has seen its manifestation, sometimes, in undesirable agitations and actions. I could sense a departure from spiritual, reformist style of working to a more agitational and militant way of working during those times. This may have led to addition of more people in the ranks of Hindutva movement, but it also led to a dilution of the normal working style of the Sangh. I guess, this is a part of social churning that the society is going through. Ultimately, the constructive style of working in the RSS will succeed and these groups will also channelize their energies in positive social work and reforms.

These years also saw many 'outsiders' getting converted into the cause of Hinduism. Leading Marxists like K. G. Bokare turned Swadeshi and wrote a book *Hindu Economics*. Many leading journalists and intellectuals came out openly against the secular-Marxist parivaar. Some nationalist Muslims like Muzaffar Hussein started working with the RSS related organizations. Many Christians and Muslims joined various organizations of the Sangh to work for national cause. In all, the Sangh grew out of its shakha structure and became a social movement in the real sense.

While studying about various Sangh bans, I find some leftist and 'secular' writers deride 'duplicity' of the RSS in engaging the government in negotiations or launching 'satyagraha' democratically to lift the ban while sustaining its organizational work silently. Ironically, same group of writers go to any extent to ask government to 'engage' violent anti-state Naxalites in talks while decrying any action against them under the garb of human rights! In this case it is a matter of 'strategy' against an 'exploitative state'. It is easy for the reader to judge who plays games of duplicity.

In recent years the RSS has networked with various other organizations working in public domain, religious, voluntary and reforms movements. It believes that it doesn't have a monopoly on nation building or man building. So, it cooperates with various organizations with positive approach to nation building and social awakening wherever possible. It believes that all well-meaning positive forces of national reconstruction must work together, because there is so much to do and speed at which this is happening is too slow. This is the vision that drives the RSS today.

❑

The Spirit

"This nation of ours is Hindu Nation (Hindu Rashtra). We wish to rebuild its paramount status and a sovereign prosperous life for it. We are striving to this end only and this exercise will continue till we are successful in this endeavour....It is true that people try to create confusion about word 'Hindu'. In many places, motivated by selfish motives Hindu is shown as being anti-Muslim, anti-Christian and now even anti-Sikkh, anti-Jain, anti-Harijan. People perpetrating such propaganda do not do so with proper information. They have their vested political interests. It is not that they made these statements after studying dharma, culture and history."

"....Hindu philosophy and systems of living one's life have been present in this country, when Islamic and Christian communities did not even exist in this world. One may ask then, how can Hindu mean to be anti-Muslim? Similarly, Sikh and Jain sects etc. come within purview of Hindu. If one were think about opposing them when one speaks of 'Hindu', it would be akin to cutting one's own limbs. Then, how is Hindu against them? Undoubtedly, these allegations are born out of petty mentality and confusions resulting from it. There is no truth in this. All these are falsehoods. 'Hindu' is not against anybody. This is a completely emotional thought, not against anybody at all."

".....Therefore, we must assert with complete resolve that, yes, we are Hindus. This is our dharma, our culture, our society; and built from all this is our nation. That is all. Our birth is only to build a powerful, capable, grand, radiant sovereign life for it.... Therefore, we must motivate people for this mission. There is no need to be embarrassed or be afraid in declaring this belief."

– M. S. Golwalkar, 1972

Extracts from the RSS Constitution

(Translated from Original in Hindi)

Preamble

Whereas in the disintegrated condition of the country it was considered necessary to have an Organization:

(a) To eradicate the fissiparous tendencies arising from diversities of sect, faith, caste and creed and from political, economic, linguistic and provincial differences amongst Hindus;

(b) To make them realize the greatness of their past;

(c) To inculcate in them a spirit of service, sacrifice and selfless devotion to the society;

(d) To build up an organized and well-disciplined corporate life; and

(e) To bring about an all-round regeneration of the Hindu Samaaj on the basis of its Dharma and Sanskriti

Aims & Objective

The aims and objects of the Sangh are to organize and weld together the various diverse groups within the Hindu Samaaj and to revitalize and rejuvenate the same on the basis of its Dharma and Sanskriti, so that it may achieve an all-round development of Bharat Varsh.

Policy

(a) The Sangh believes in the orderly evolution of society and adheres to peaceful and legitimate means of realization of its ideals.

(b) In consonance of the cultural heritage of the Hindu Samaaj the Sangh has abiding faith in the fundamental principle of respect towards all faiths.

(c) The Sangh is aloof from politics and is devoted to social and cultural fields only. However, the swayamsevaks are free, as individuals, to join any party, institution or front, political or otherwise except such parties, institutions or fronts which subscribe to or believe in extra-national loyalties, or resort to violent and/or secret activities to achieve their ends, or which promote or attempt to promote, or have the object of promoting any feeling of enmity or hatred towards any other community or creed or religious denomination. Persons owing allegiance to the above mentioned undesirable elements and methods or working shall have no place in the Sangh.

Other articles of the constitution define its flag, swayamsevak, shakha, programmes, finances, appointment of Sarsanghchaalak, Sarkaaryavaah, elections - their periodicity and mode of election, e.g. qualifications for voters and candidates, delegates, its set up of its policy making bodies - Akhil Bharatiya Pratinidhi Sabha and Akhil Bharatiya Kendriya Karyakarini Mandal, local kaaryakaari mandals, prachaaraks, and methodology to be followed for amendment to its constitution.

3

What Defines India

Let us just think about what defines India in the eyes of the world. The top Indian brands in the world are:

- Yoga
- Ayurveda
- Sanskrit
- Spirituality
- Matchless ancient literature - Geeta, Vedas, Upanishads, Ramayan, Mahabharat and others.

All the brands and ideas above flow from Hindu or Indic civilization. There is no dispute about it. While RSS was propagating and supporting institutions which supported these ideas for decades, only recently has our establishment intellectual and elite class reluctantly recognised this fact. This probably is the result of late international recognition of these contributions of India to the world civilization!

Today, India is also known as IT power. Behind this too stand our age old knowledge pools of Mathematics, Science, Astronomy etc. A recent book by an American author that tries to decipher the success of Indian Americans that is much out of proportion to their population, notes that robust family system is one of the major reasons for this success. The report of U.S. Census Bureau also comes to the same conclusion. This joint family system also has roots in ancient Hindu traditions.

India is recognized and respected for its non-aggressive way of life. It may have spread its influence far and wide with its philosophies, whether Vedic or Buddhist; but never did it resort to violence, looting, murders to spread its religions or faith. It has an innate inclusive nature that flows from its philosophy "Ekam Sat, Vipraha Bahuda Vadanti" (there is one truth, wise ones speak of it in different ways) that adopts or absorbs other ideas and philosophies over time.

Why should we Indians or Hindus feel apologetic about being proud of these facts? There has been an intellectual exercise for some years to play around with facts that give identity to Hindu society. These intellectual gymnastics of our honourable leftist intellectuals propose that all things good belong to 'ancient Indian heritage' - not 'Hindu' and all things bad (casteism, untouchability etc.) belong to Hindus. Thus, Hindu spirituality is encashed with impunity by well-known media houses professing to be 'secular' by selling mantras, bhajans, yoga CDs etc. as 'Indian culture and Indian spiritualism' and not as priceless Hindu heritage! Yoga is presented as a 'non-religious' discipline though it is clearly a spiritual, rather than a physical exercise, rooted in highly evolved Hindu philosophy. Unfortunately many of such 'secular' media houses also broadcast programmes promoting half baked beliefs that promote superstition. Such programmes are conveniently presented as Hindu belief systems! It is difficult to believe that all this is happening due to lack of understanding of Hinduism, or is it lack of sincerity in understanding ancient Hindu or Indian heritage and history and owning it in its entirety - whether good or even bad.

Prof. D K Chakrabarty of Cambridge University asserts that there is a subtle politics operating in archeology that denies the links between the Indus civilization and Vedic culture. To quote him, "The battle raging these days is whether there can be any relation between the life depicted in the Vedic literature and this civilization. Without trying to pull down this debate to the all-too-common Indian level of 'progressive *vs.* reaction' syndrome which implies that any talk in favour of Veda-Indus civilization relationship is 'right reactionary' proposition (a la Irfan Habib), we note that scholars of the stature of M S Vats, R P Chanda, B N Datta and P V Kane had no difficulty in arguing for a relationship between the two."

It is nobody's case that aberrations in customs and practices of Hindus should be negated. These definitely need to be removed. RSS is foremost in efforts to correcting these wrongs, contrary to popular perception created by Goebbelesian propaganda over years. Problem is RSS does not believe in a confrontationist or propagandist way of resolving problems but follows a reformist path of love and persuasion in silence. I will bring out a few examples of such work later in the book. But, it needs to be understood that both good and the bad are part of Hindu society, Hindu way of life and one cannot play around with this fact to play with Hindu sensibilities.

Oneness in Multiplicity

All our leaders proclaim very proudly that India is a perfect picture of 'Unity in Diversity'. With hundreds of languages, scores of religious faiths, diverse geography, what is the thread which holds together this beautiful garland of diversity denoting Indian identity? Unity in diversity is an expression of a fact. In subjective experience it is 'Oneness in Multiplicity'. The only thread that binds people together from Kashmir to Kanyakumari and from Gujarat to Guwahati is the ancient Hindu civilization and belief system. This deep running sap throughout the nation since eons is what has kept this sense of unity alive. Whatever else we talk of is built over this deep and strong foundation.

According to Shri HV Sheshadri, "Diversity is like leaves, flowers and fruits that grow out of a tree. But, the sap that nurtures all these diverse elements of tree comes from the root of the tree." It is this sap that is the lifeblood of this diverse looking tree. The diverse tree is Bharat i.e. India, this sap is the Hindu way of life. If the sap dries up, the tree will die.

Hinduism is a way of life which happily encompasses so many other faiths and religions. Still, if we talk of this common Hindu heritage, there is a serious problem for secular and Marxist parivaar.

If something other than Hinduness or Hindu culture has bound this nation together for centuries, then why is it that wherever the majority of population in an area converts to another religion, that area cedes or strives to cede from India? Whether it is erstwhile Afghanistan -at one time the cradle of Buddhism, more recently Pakistan or Bangladesh or Kashmir or North East, India keeps shrinking. People who proclaim that this is an alarmist view and there is no risk to Hinduism close their eyes to this fact staring out of pages of history.

You need not invent an artificial logic or reason for this sense of unity. This deep sense of unity amongst Indians just needs to be appreciated if we wish our people to feel connected to their ancient land. Every nation has cultural identity and it strives to build itself around it. It doesn't mean that it should result in a violent or divisive nation. Many newly emerged nations like the USA have forged a common culture successfully. Some like erstwhile USSR and Czechoslovakia failed. We have one common cultural thread running through multiplicity of our national life but we are trying to force an artificial hollow cultural identity based on pop icons - artificial constructs, and negating or trying to bury natural sense of oneness in the name of ill defined interpretation of secularism.

Ancient Geographical Sense of Nationhood

According to political scientists, sense of nationhood arises out of distinct geographical identity. Many modern historians claim that idea of Indian nationhood is a gift of British. But, there are many facts that negate this theory. There are verses in ancient Indian scriptures that describe this land *'aasetu himaachal'* - from (Indian) Ocean to Himalayas. A common chant in many rituals since Vedic times is *"prithviyaayai samudraparyantyayai ekaraat'* (from land stretched up to seas - one nation). Try to hear what your priest chants in the initial parts of a religious ritual or havan. He chants something about, *"Jambu dveepe Bharat khandey"* when he is guiding you through rituals during a pooja. This is nothing but description of Indian nation since centuries.

There are shlokas in our Puranas which were not written during British or Islamic times but much before that. Vishnu Puran and Brahma Puran say:

Uttaraam yatsamudrasya Himaadeshchaiva dakshinam

Varsham tad bhaaratam naama bhaarati yatra santatih'

(That part of land, which is north of the seas and south of the Himalayas, is the great Bhaarata and her progeny are called Bhaaratiya.)

Poet Kalidaasa (the fourth century AD) had also described this country in a similar vein. Chanakya (third century BC) a great authority on political science, stated that the length of this country from seas in south to the Himalayas in north is one thousand yojanaas (an ancient measure of distance.)

Hindu, Indic or Vedic people

At this moment, let us also try to get a few semantics clear as far as possible. This play with semantics by interested lobbies is done to show that there is no entity called Hindu. A general understanding is that the word Hindu is more recent and is a result of Arabs describing people residing around and beyond river Sind as Hindus, because they pronounce 'S' and 'H'. This is true also of many European and Indian languages.

Dr Murlidhar H Pahoja in his article 'Antiquity & Origin of the Term Hindu' says, "In the Avesta, Hapta-Hindu is used for Sanskrit Sapta-Sindhu, the Avesta being dated variously between BC 5000-1000. This indicates that the term 'Hindu' is as old as the word 'Sindhu.' Sindhu is a Vedic term used in the Rigveda. And, therefore, 'Hindu' is as ancient as the Rigveda. *Vriddha Smriti* defines Hindu as,

"One who abhors the mean and the ignoble, and is of noble bearing, who reverse the Veda, the cow, and the deity, is a Hindu."

Similarly other Sanskrit works which use the term 'Hindu' are, *Kalika Puran, Bhavishya Puran, Adbhut Kosh, Medini Kosh, Ram Kosh* etc. Kalidas has used a derivative form 'Haindava.' In *Brahaspati Agam,* the word 'Hindusthan' appears in the following verse –

Himaalayam samaarabhya yaavadindu sarovaram
Tam devanirmitam desham hindusthaanam prachakshate

(This country, created by the gods, that commences from the Himalayas and spreads out till Indu Sarovar – i.e. southern seas or Indian Ocean, is called Hindusthan) Thus, 'Hi' is derived from Himaalay and 'ndu' from Indu Sarovar to create the word Hindu.

The word 'Hindu' carries more of a geographical connotation, though it also has a religious connotation. It also means that people who do not follow traditional ways of worship of Vedic people can also be considered to be in this category. It is well-known convention that people from India irrespective of their faith or religious practices are referred to as Hindustanis or people from Hind by people in Arabic lands. I could quote even from ancient Iranian and Middle East literature, but the central purpose of this book is not to write a treatise on this subject.

So-called modern secular historians try to split hair by claiming that Vedic people were not Hindus. So, what were they? They were not Muslims or Christians or from any other belief systems for sure. The continuity of evolution has unbreakable links from Vedic time to today, so this debate is infructuous and is only meant to create confusion in the discussion about natural Hindu nationhood that we have inherited.

I would like the reader to ponder a minute over why India is called a 'subcontinent' but a much massive geographical entities like Australia and the USA are called countries? You would note that your mind is being conditioned subtly to accept that we are not a natural country but have been brought together by British through legislative efforts.

In essence, etymology of the word gives it strength but at this stage in history, it is not so important how the word was derived. It is a word that has come to identify people living in this land spread from Himalayas to Indian Ocean.

Many people feel that more appropriate word is Vedic or Indic civilization. There has also been lot of debate that RSS should substitute 'Bhaaratiya' for 'Hindu' and 'Bhaaratiyataa' for 'Hindutva' or 'Hinduness'. It would kill the whole case of Hindu bashing. I raised this query during a Q&A with a very senior RSS leader. He explained that the fight is not about the word, as Bharatiya is older than Hindu. It is nothing but hair splitting and typical intellectual subversion to obfuscate the main argument of the antiquity of our nationhood. The fight is for a unique identity of the soul of Bharat which the west educated dominant intellectual class abhors as it goes against the grain of what they have learnt in the laps of British historians. They would find fault with this word also just because it is promoted by RSS. The problem seems to be with the promoter of the concept and not with the content!

Cultural Sense of Nationhood

Another condition for a group of people in a given geography to be called a nation is a common culture or sense of identity. I would like to give a few examples that connote a common cultural identity. These are things that we experience in our daily lives and simply take them for granted without appreciating their significance.

We have 'Kumbh Melas' once in 12 years from time immemorial where Hindus from all the corners of Bharat come in millions on a preordained day without any posters or marketing support. All the saints of India come together at this time to exchange notes about their thinking, discoveries on spiritual plane, social issues and also to propagate their philosophies to the common people. These Kumbh melas are celebrated in four centres spread over India - Prayag (Allahabad), Haridwar, Ujjain and Nashik. It has no director or promoter, nobody knows when and how it started apart from some Puranic tales. Thus, there is a sense of common identity for eons. Vishwa Hindu Parishad did not invent these massive gatherings.

Adi Shankaracharya set up four maths (or centres of learning) nearly 2800 years back - Shringeri (South), Dwarka (West), Joshimath (North) and Jagannathpuri (East) to stress the geographical spread and unity of Bharat. Fortunately, His holiness was not indoctrinated by the RSS or VHP!

Hindus have a custom of taking Ganga waters to Rameshwaram for abhishek (offering of water) of Lord Shiva there. There is no known source or time frame about this custom. But, we all recognize that it is there for ages. It has not been propagated by the RSS/VHP.

Hindus worship same Gods with different regional variations from South to North. Anybody who has travelled different parts of Bharat, i.e. India can vouch for this.

There are same festivals all over India with different names with minor variations. Bihu, Baisakhi, Vishu, Cheti Chand, Yugadi, Poila

Baishakh – all signify the beginning of new Hindu year with harvest. The customs are similar in various communities with some local flavour. Vijayaadashamee is celebrated in different styles in different places. Worshipping of weapons and tools of livelihood is not the insidious invention with fascist designs of the RSS as some critics claim, but a well-entrenched practice in various parts of India on the occasion of Vijayaadashamee or Dussera. Nine days preceding Dussera, Navaratri, are one of the most pious days in different parts of India celebrated in different ways - in Bengal (Durga puja), Gujarat (garba and fasting) and whole of North (Ramlila plays and fasting), in Tamilnadu and Karnataka (Golu).

While North celebrates Diwali as the day when Lord Rama killed Ravana and returned home, in South it is celebrated to commemorate the killing of demon Narakaasur by Lord Krishna. Central theme is victory of good over evil. Makar Sankranti is the day when enters the sign of Capricorn and marks the end of winter. It is celebrated as Makar Sankraman in North and West and as Pongal in Tamilnadu. Other regions celebrate it with different names. Holi is also celebrated in major parts of India in different ways as Holi or Basant Panchami.

Shri Ranga Hari, a senior RSS prachaarak and central leader, once gave an interesting example of a few of common traditions and cultural practices we share across this vast geography called Bharat. All over India, the shopkeeper adds a little amount over and above what he weighs for the customer before packing. The idea is, "if there is an error, let it be corrected from my side." This custom has different names in different languages but it is prevalent right from South to North and East to West. I know that it is called 'runga' in North, I am sorry that I couldn't make note of the words for this practice in other Indian languages.

Even if you look at a very simple expression, in English a devout person is called 'God fearing' but in Hindi and other Indian languages, he is called 'Prabhu Premi' or lover of God. Undercurrent of this word play is that a Hindu loves and reveres God, but in Abrahamic or Semitic traditions God is feared. Ranga Hari ji gives another example that gives very interesting and revealing insight into Hindu traditions. In English we say, "think of the devil and he is there"; but in Indian tradition, we say, "you will live for hundred years, we just remembered you." This expression is same across any region and any language in India.

I just recounted a few examples to underline some unique features of our national life which are common to all citizens living in India, whatever be their faith or religion. Such traditional practices all over this land define the Hindu culture. Thus, it is not a matter of religion. It is part of dharma of the individuals, the society and the state.

Ramayan talks of Ram's visit to jungles and staying with tribals. It talks of Ram's deep love for his brethren of all denominations and regions. Indians understand that language and customs change every ten miles and they accept it happily. Therefore, they are habituated to variations in language, behaviour and still feel one as Indians. A true Hindu looks at commonalities and does not lay stress on differences – till politicians and people with vested interests violate this innate thinking process.

We have Common Ancestors

Does this sense of inherent unity exclude any group from celebrating the essence of Indianness? Certainly not. Nearly 95-98% of Islamic and Christian converts in India are so from only a few generations, and have Hindu roots. There need not be any problem in their acceptance of the culture of their ancestors even while they profess different faiths or ways of worship. In fact, we all know that Christians in Kerala or Muslims in many Rajasthan areas do not find it difficult to blend their native or ancient beliefs with their new religions or faiths. People in North East still worship their ancient tribal Gods though they also go to Church. We know of Indonesian people who still take pride in their ancient Hindu culture though they are now Muslims. Indonesian currency notes have Lord Ganesha imprint on them; but God forbid, if that happens in India, it will spell doom for our secularism! This acceptance that we are all one and we haven't changed our forefathers or our traditions can end all emotional and physical turmoil being foisted on them by the so called protectors of their faith.

In any of the above proposition I see no communalism as it is based on well-known historical facts and realities of our nation accepted consciously or unconsciously by nearly all the citizens of India. So, when RSS says that India is a Hindu nation, it is only stating the obvious without malice to anybody or any sense of negativity. We should, rather, celebrate this as a unique country in the world and the historical fact that Hindus don't fight wars or kill others to impose their faith or way of life on others. Right from times of Chalukyas to Ashok the Great, message of Dharma and religious faith has been spread with love and not sword.

Question of Secularism

Not once, in its eight decades of history has RSS advocated a Hindu theocratic state. The political philosophy of secularism was invented to keep Church off its ambitious designs about political control in Europe. So, the textbook definition of secularism is separation of state and religion. Even this definition does not prohibit the rulers or the governments from professing their religion. So, Britain and the USA can be secular though their Queen, prime ministers, presidents swear by God and Bible.

It is interesting that the founding fathers of Indian constitution did not feel the need to have the word 'secular' in the preamble of the constitution. Not that there was no debate on it, but this word was not mentioned because in their wisdom they must have seen it as a part of Indian or Hindu tradition with no need to stress it further. Picture of Lord Ram is displayed in our constitution. Remember that the Indian leadership of the time had steadfastly refused to call India a 'Hindu' nation inspite of agreeing to partition on religious grounds and Pakistan declaring itself a 'Muslim' nation state.

The word 'secular' along with another 'use-and-throw' term 'socialism' was inserted in the constitution with the help of steam roller majority during emergency that Smt. Gandhi enjoyed at the time, further helped by absence of opposition ranks stuffed into jails.

Secular in India has come to mean irreligious state which translates into 'adharmi' or 'nidharmi' (non-religious) state, as the term 'dharma nirapeksha' translated in constitution implies. This is against Hindu or Indian ethos. We talk of Dharma as per Hindu tradition as 'rule of law'. RSS has only affirmed that India cannot be an irreligious state in the name of secularism. Other suggested term, 'sarva panth samabhaav' (equal respect for all faiths) is more close to Indian or Hindu ethos and should ideally be the conceptual framework here.

I can do nothing better than quote highly respected scholar and second Indian president. S Radhakrishnan, quoted in *Times of India,* 27th June 2009, in this respect: "It may appear somewhat strange that our government should be a secular one while our culture is rooted in spiritual values. Secularism here does not mean irreligion or atheism or even stress on material comforts. It proclaims that it lays stress on the universality of spiritual values that may be attained by a variety of ways... three ellipses. Religion is a transforming experience. It is not a theory of God. It is spiritual consciousness. Belief and conduct, rites and ceremonies, dogmas and authorities are subordinate to the art of self-discovery and contact with the Divine. When the individual withdraws his soul from all outward events, gathers himself together inwardly, strives with concentration, there breaks upon him an experience, sacred, strange, wondrous, which quickens within him, lays hold on him, becomes his very being."

"..... Even those who are the children of science and reason must submit to the fact of spiritual experience that is primary and positive. We may dispute theologies but we cannot deny facts. The fire of life in its visible burning compels assent, though not the fumbling speculation of smokers sitting around the fire. While realization is a fact, the theory of reality is an inference. There is difference between contact with reality and opinion about it, between the mystery of godliness and belief in God. This is the meaning of a secular conception of the State though it is not generally understood..... This view is in consonance with the Indian tradition. The seer of the Rig Veda affirms that the Real is one while the learned speak of it variously. Asoka in his Rock Edict XII proclaims: "One who reverences one's own religion and disparages that of another from devotion to one's own religion and to glorify it over all other religions does injure one's own religion most certainly. It is verily concord of religions that is meritorious."

The endless breast beating of secular-Marxist parivaar about RSS wishing to impose a Hindu theocratic state is nothing more than a falsehood repeatedly propagated over decades to deride Hindu philosophy of 'many paths -one truth' and tarnish RSS.

Composite Culture vis-a-vis Dynamic Culture

Another term bandied about is 'composite culture'. Argument being that Indian culture is not essentially a Hindu culture but made up by adding many other elements. My simple submission is, Ganga remains Ganga even as hundreds of streams merge into it. It doesn't become a 'composite' river. A silk coat remains a silk coat though it may be embellished with golden embroidery. English remains English even as it absorbs hundreds of foreign words, because the inherent spirit of the language remains English.

Thus, essential innate quality uniting the Indians is deep running sense of Hinduness or Hinduism, and is shared consciously or unconsciously, knowingly or unknowingly by all Indians. It, in no way, deprecates the contribution of other cultures and traditions that embellished it later on.

Ideal word for the Indian society should be 'Dynamic culture', rather than "Composite culture". Composite denotes a patchwork, how so ever colourful. Dynamic denotes culture that is always on the move in a positive sense, not held back by fossilized ideas, or not open to new knowledge. A culture that is open to assimilating new ideas and thoughts, shown dynamism in moving with times, reinvented itself based on changing times. While going through this process, the core essence doesn't change. The rainbow becomes more colourful, more inclusive. This dynamism is the inherent Hinduness of our culture.

Some Distinguishing Features of Hindu Thought

Hindus believe that all roads lead to absolute truth and that they have no monopoly over this route. None of its belief systems, avataars or gurus say that unless you follow my path you will go to hell nor do they enjoin their followers to save the 'non-believers' from hell by converting them. There is no concept of 'non-believers' and their deliverance through either conversion or elimination. It doesn't say, 'my way alone' but says 'your's too'. Such a frame of mind rules out any chance of bigotry or hateful persecution of 'others'.

Osho (Rajneesh) points out that Hinduism is the only belief system in the world that worships not just God of creation but also the God of destruction. It has created a symbol of a Supreme as Trimurti (an idol with three heads) signifying different aspects of the Divine - Brahma - the creator, Vishnu - the sustainer, Shiva - the destroyer. It believes destruction to be an integral part of creation just as death is the other side of birth. There is no separate concept of 'Satan' who disrupts the scheme of things created by God. Good and bad are part of human life.

In prophetic monotheist religions, understanding is that God creates human being in his own image, while in Hinduism, we believe that human being creates God in his own image. Since God has no form, we try to see him or her as per our inner nature. So, someone loves to see Supreme being in the calm continuance of Lord Buddha, someone sees it in loving and dancing Krishna or in another one sees it in just and moral king Ram while a devotee sees that supreme being in fiery Goddess Durga. Any stone can be consecrated as God. We worship God in different forms to help us focus better in this exercise of reaching the Supreme being.

Hindu sages and gurus never forced their opinion onto their disciples. They encouraged questions and gave answers till the doubts of the disciple were removed. Take the example of Geeta where Lord Krishna himself goes through an elaborate exercise to satisfy Arjun in as many ways as possible till he say, "All my doubts are clear and I am ready to fight for dharma." In all the Upanishads, the most complex knowledge is passed onto the disciples through question and answer. God himself doesn't ordain blind faith; sceptism and questioning is welcome. Compare this to monotheist religions brought up on a single book. One is supposed to follow it totally and not question any of its premises. This is one of the reasons why the Hindu philosophy stands up to newer discoveries of modern scientific age much more easily and doesn't have to get into convolutions of explanations to get out of tight situations created by science. Nor did its followers or religious leaders ever had to apologize for persecuting scientists for heresy when their discoveries went against a 'book'.

Vedas and Geeta talked of millions of Brahmaand (universe) eons back when it was a blasphemy for others. Now it is an accepted fact. It would surprise readers if I were to suggest that the famous shlok, '*Poorna midah, poorna midam, poornaat poorna mudachyate, poornasya poorna maadaay, poorna mevaavashishyate*' (That is Absolute, This is Absolute, Absolute arises out of Absolute, If Absolute is taken away from Absolute, Absolute remains) is the best possible enunciation of Einstein's famous formulation, $E=mc^2$ (Total of energy in the universe remains constant, whatever you produce, transform or destroy - to summarize this greatest scientific formulation.) Think it over!

Fritjof Capra in his book *Tao of Physics* notes with amazement, the similarity of experience of ancient sages at micro level and the experience of scientists studying both at sub-atomic level and level of the universe. He says, "Later came the experience of Dance of Shiva which I have tried to capture in (a) photomontage. It was followed by many similar experiences which helped me gradually realize that a consistent view of the world is beginning to emerge from modern physics which is harmonious with Eastern wisdom."

In a book in 1990, Prof Klaus Klostermaier wrote: "Hinduism will spread not so much through the gurus and swamis, who attract certain number of people looking for a new commitment and a quasi-monastic life-style, but it will spread mainly through the work of intellectuals and writers, who have found certain Hindu ideas convincing and who identify them with their personal beliefs. A fair number of leading physicists and biologists have found parallels between modern science and Hindu ideas. An increasing number of creative scientists will come from a Hindu background and will consciously and unconsciously blend their scientific and their religious ideas. All of us may be already much more Hindu than we think."

A philosophy so much in tune with scientific thinking can never be anti-modern, nor can an organization which strives to strengthen such a society can talk of going back to medieval times. Medieval times are a gift of our history of enslavement, not of Hindu civilization. We need to move away from the dominating thought that being modern is being 'western' and a critique of 'western way of life' implies that one is 'orthodox' in a negative sense.

Some thinkers have drawn together a few strands of thought that run through all the faiths born in Bharat. They are - Theory of Karma, immortality of soul, principle of rebirth, worship of nature in all its elements, remembering and worshipping elders and forefathers, the belief that all paths lead to one God and that God is beyond gender (i.e. God can be He, She or even It), ultimate goal to achieve Nirvana, Moksha, state of Shunya etc., and treating entire world as one family.

A seer in Atharva Veda declares: " *Maataa Prithvih, putroham prithvyaah.*" (The earth is my mother, I am her son). On the same lines, an ancient Dakota tradition in Americas proclaims, "Mitakuye Owasin" (All are my relatives or We are all related)

Worship of nature logically means that one must preserve environment, using it only to the extent that is necessary for self preservation. This alone can lead us to sustainable development based on sustainable consumption, a more practical model that can preserve both nature and mankind. This thought leads to chanting of shaanti mantra (mantra of peace) at the end of any prayer which proposes not only of peace for the mankind but animal kingdom (dwipaada and chatushpaada - two legged and four legged creatures) other elements of nature i.e. environment as well as mother earth.

I would like to add at this juncture that all pre-Christian and pre-Islamic traditions and cultures, dismissed as animist and pagan religions, also have similar philosophy about nature, integral view of human beings and nature, sanctity of nature and forefathers. They too do not have tradition of conversions or proselytisation like Hinduism, because of their firm belief that 'all roads lead to one supreme truth.' This universality of enlightened traditions needs a separate treatment so I will leave this part of discussion incomplete and leave it to the readers to explore it further.

This stress on self-restraint has led to the model of consumption unique to India where every item is recycled to its death and not thrown away. We all have enough examples to it in our own homes, right from recycling a packing thread to each and every thing that can be reused to it simply gives way. This principle goes against the avowed consumerism of the West. The fact that 8% of world population in US consumes nearly 33% natural resources, tells us its own story of bottomless hunger for consumption driven by capitalist thirst for profits and more comforts. This endless longing for more is the source of 'greenhouse gases' and 'global warming'. We are now well aware what happens when there is unbridled avarice to acquire things at any cost. The collapse of US economy and domino effect on other economies has reminded us that there is still time to go back to our own traditional mode of living life satisfactorily with only sustainable consumption.

At personal level, Hindu philosophy talks of fourfold aspect of a successful and fulfilling life 'purushaartha chatushtaya' - dharma (living moral life as per one's innate nature and responsibilities), artha (economic well being), kaam (personal desires), and ultimately nirvana or moksha or liberation by following the path of dharma. It talks of four phases in an individual's life. The broad division of a human life in brahmacharya (period of learning and personal discipline and restraints), grihasth (worldly duties, raising the family), vaanprasth (getting detached from the family affairs even as one follows worldly affairs and moving one's attention towards God) and sanyaas ashram (giving up worldly affairs and focus totally on one's spiritual life). It is very difficult to find such a clear enunciation about one's way to live life as a normal family and social person in any other culture or religion.

When a Hindu uses word like 'dharmic' or 'adharmic' he or she means a person who follows just laws of the society or his own duties as 'dharmic' and a person who acts contrary to what is his duty as per his nature or social customs is 'adharmic'.

At a personal level, the dharma is that which is as per his or her nature or duty. So we talk of 'pitri dharm' (duties of a father), 'matri dharm' (duties of a mother) or 'putra dharm' (duties of an offspring). At a societal level dharma is that which holds society together with just laws. Dharma of fire is to burn, dharma of a tiger is to attack a prey for satiating his hunger and dharma of a merchant is to provide products and services honestly. Conduct at social level as per set norms and laws of a particular society are dharma at social level. It helps create systems that would allow a person to attain his full potential. Word 'dharma' in social context is more close to 'ethics'. Raj dharma is the rule of law. So, the dharma of a school is to impart good education, dharma of government is to provide righteous rule of law in which citizens can live a dignified life etc. etc.

These are just a few illustrative ideas with which we can easily identify, and feel happy and proud that we belong to such an enlightened culture born in this land. Hindu society is even comfortable with an atheist philosopher like Chaarvaak and calls him 'rishi'. One of his shlokas (paraphrased) says, "You should drink ghee, even take loan for it if required. Who has seen next birth?" It can adjust deviants in its society much more easily than other civilizations. It may be the only place in the world with a district named 'Kinnaur' denoting a place where 'kinnars' (people of alternative sexuality) resided. It adopted the path of foster motherhood or fatherhood thousands of years back without any stigma attached to it. There are many Puranic stories and stories in Mahabharat talking openly about such practices.

There are volumes written on this subject by learned sages and scholars. When a Hindu says that India is a Hindu nation, it encompasses all these thoughts mentioned above, which in no way can be compared to the theology driven nations like Islamic nations of Middle East, where any person not following Islamic religion has a secondary status. The way a professed Islamic country suppresses or oppresses non-followers is well known right from Saudi Arabia to newly Islamized countries like Malaysia.

Thus, Hinduism connotes national entity of Bharat not merely religious faith - but identification with national mainstream - that is Hindu. Hindutva means policies and practices based on this spirit of Hinduness.

Addressing the Ills of Hindu Society

Hindu society is facing lot of problems and lot of self-correction is waiting to be done. It is a society split on basis of regionalism, sects, caste and language. There still are social ills like untouchability which plague us. Some community specific customs like child marriage also need to be ended. The inhuman customs of dowry is common to all communities in India, whether it is UP or Kerala, it is there irrespective of the religion they follow. Casteism is so deeply rooted that it runs deep even in Christian and Muslim communities. It is well known that 'high caste' Muslims don't easily marry into 'artisan' castes. Many people who convert to Christianity hoping to get out of this vicious cycle often complain that they cannot get away from the discrimination even after conversion.

It is a stratification of society not based on economic conditions but also on political power of various groups in the society. This division of societies is common in different societies world over in different names and different guise. Koenrad Elst proposes that "castes and caste systems have developed in very divergent parts of the world, e.g. the originally ethnic division in Hutu and Tutsi in Rwanda, or the endogamous hereditary communities of blacksmiths, musicians and other occupational groups in West Africa. The European division in nobility and commoners was a caste system in the full sense of the term: two endogamous groups in a hierarchical relation. When the Portuguese noticed the Indian *jaati* system, they applied to it the term *casta,* already in use for a social division in their homeland: the separate communities defined by religion, viz. Christians, Jews and Muslims. In practice, these were virtually endogamous, and there was a hierarchical relation between the top community (first Muslims, then Christians) and the other two."

Various Hindu scriptures including Geeta talk of caste being based on one's profession, mental and intellectual inclinations (prakriti) and not based on birth. They also talk of possibility of vertical movement from one caste to another. Even the critics of Hinduism agree about it. It is unfortunate that this system got corrupted and decayed into a label by birth. It requires a much more patient approach driven by heart to overcome such divisions and not agitational and vote bank politics which exacerbate the difference and create fissures. The current politicians' approach has done precisely that. Mandalization is the most known example, but this game has been played subtly and not so subtly for many years in India now since independence by short sighted and cynical politicians. It is ironic that parties based on caste are secular but parties talking for Hindus are communal. Muslim League of partition fame is secular, sharing governance with Congress but BJP is communal! The bitter truth is that any attempt at splintering Hindu society is considered 'secular'.

Dr. Hedgewar and every chief of RSS have consistently criticized caste system. There are sterling examples of total absence of caste system in the RSS and its associate organization without any big talk or show of egalitarianism. National leaders like Mahatma Gandhi and Dr Ambedkar wondered about this achievement when they visited the RSS camps. Only thing is that it doesn't make a song and dance about reforms it carries on silently. Balasaheb Deoras, the then Chief of the RSS had, decades back, declared, "If untouchability is not bad then nothing is bad in this world. Untouchability must go - lock, stock and barrel."

RSS has been working silently to remove inequalities in Hindu society and bring about a sense of brotherhood. We shall come to the work done by the RSS in this area in subsequent chapters. The guiding principle of the RSS is: concentrate on unifying factors, ignore differences. India and Hindus cannot be subject to constant hammering and sanctimonious lectures on such issues beaten to death by the so called liberals. It is job of Hindus to solve its problems and also its privilege to celebrate its contribution to civilization.

Dharampal on Pre-British India

Before we proceed further, I would like to digress a little and bring on record certain facts about the all round deterioration in social, economic and scientific field that Indians suffered with arrival of the British. Dharampal, a renowned Gandhian, has done remarkable research work in this field. His research is jaw dropping for the new generation brought up on the staple discourse about India being held back by archaic, backward and caste ridden Hindus before British rescued this country from its downhill journey. His works suggest that the harshness of caste divisions and resulting social deterioration that crept into India were actually the gift of British.

S Gurumurthy in his tribute to late Dharampal recalls his discovery that, "Before the British rule in India, over two-thirds – yes two-thirds – of the Indian kings belonged to what is today known as the Other Backward Castes (OBCs). "It is the British," he said, "who robbed the OBCs – the ruling class running all socio-economic institutions – of their power, wealth and status." So it was not the upper caste which usurped the OBCs of their due position in the society.

By meticulous research of the British sources over decades, Dharampal demolished the myth that India was educationally or economically backward when the British entered. Citing the Christian missionary William Adam's report on indigenous education in Bengal and Bihar in 1835 and 1838, Dharampal established that at that time there were 100,000 schools in Bengal, one school for about 500 boys!

Gurumurthy quoting from Dharampal's works tells us that, during 1822-25 the share of the Brahmin students in the indigenous schools in Tamil-speaking areas accounted for 13 per cent in South Arcot to some 23 per cent in Madras while the backward castes accounted for 70 per cent in Salem and Tirunelveli and 84 per cent in South Arcot. The situation was almost similar in Malayalam, Oriya and Kannada-speaking areas, with the backward castes dominating the schools in absolute numbers. Only in the Telugu-speaking areas the share of the Brahmins was higher and varied from 24 to 46 per cent. Dharampal's work proved Mahatma Gandhi's statement at Chatham House in London on October 20, 1931 that "India today is more illiterate than it was fifty or hundred years ago," completely right.

In his celebrated book, *Indian Science & Technology in 18th Century* Dharampal notes that based on the documents of East India Company that the British found the Indian education system of the time far superior to that of Britain.

Dharampal's major works were published in 1971. Infact, he started his research on the subject only in 1965-66. I cannot understand why discovery of these achievements and their acceptance took so many decades in independent India. Even now it is difficult to find his books in shops or academics. It is a tribute to the control that secular-Marxist parivaar has over academics that these facts have been successfully hidden from Indians and have never got a respectable place in official publications or textbooks on humanities. This kind of information actually would give our youth a great sense of pride in our nationhood, a sense of patriotism based on solid knowledge.

That India had a grand past, that Indian sages and teachers had done a wonderful job of research and discovery in various sciences and arts is a well-established fact now. Many of us would have read that many of the scientific theories named after Western scientists were already known to Indian achaaryas (or teachers) and established by them much earlier. The theories in Trigonometry, Algebra, Physics, highly accurate calculations in Astronomy, achievements in Chemistry, Medical sciences are being brought out with painstaking rediscoveries and proofs from various old texts, and accepted worldwide. We don't have to go far back and can talk of scientists like J. C. Bose who were not given due credit till recently. If India were to raise claims against MNCs and research organizations for various IPRs that rightfully belong to her and damages for their violations, all of them would go bankrupt!

Dharampal quotes Col Kyd, "It appears that Indian medical men (with whatever names they may be termed at the end of the eighteenth century) made considerable use of surgical techniques in different parts of India. In 'Chirurgery (in which they are considered by us the least advanced) they often succeed, in removing ulcers and cutaneous eruptions of the worst kind, which have baffled the skill of our surgeons, by the process of inducing inflammation and by means directly opposite to ours, and which they have probably long been in possession of."

British talked in awe of the indigenous medical system that included inoculation against smallpox. They refused to believe the advanced astronomy of 'Brahmins of Varanasi' or acknowledge that the algebraic and geometric theorems that they claimed to be their discovery may have found their way from India.

Contrary to what we have been taught for years, Dharampal's study indicated existence of a functioning society, extremely competent in the arts and sciences of its day. Indians' interactive grasp over its immediate natural environment was undisputed and praiseworthy. This was reflected in both agricultural and industrial production. Till around 1750, together with the Chinese, India was producing some 73 per cent of the total world industrial production, and even till 1830, what both these economies produced still amounted to 60 per cent of world industrial production. In a moderately fertile area like that of Chengalpattu (Tamilnadu), India's paddy production in a substantial area of its lands around 1760-70 amounted to some 5-6 tonnes per hectare. This is nearly equal to the production of paddy per hectare in present day Japan, the current highly productive region in the world. The critical feature of the set-up was the elaborate fiscal arrangements made for its upkeep in perpetuity, if required. From the gross produce, amounts were allocated by tradition for the upkeep of the system, from the engineers who looked after the irrigation tanks and channels to the police and school teachers. In technology, we produced steel that was superior to Sheffield steel. We also produced dyes, ships and literally hundreds of commodities.

Says Dharampal, "By their methods of extortion and other similar means, the British were able to smash Indian rural life and society by about 1820 - 30. Around the same period, the extensive Indian manufactures met a similar fate. Because of deliberate British policy, the famed Indian village communities so eloquently described by Thomas Metcalfe around 1830, and by Karl Marx in the 1850s, had mostly ceased to exist."

Voltaire considered India 'famous for its laws and sciences', and deplored the mounting European preoccupation (both individual and national) of those in India with the amassing of 'immense fortunes'. This quest for riches intensified the struggles, plunder, etc., during his own time, and made him remark: "If the Indians had remained unknown to the Tartars and to us; they would have been the happiest people in the world."

Imagine our economists demeaning Indians by talking of 'Hindu rate of growth' for a country that suffered worst economic slowdown and exploitation after British overran India and later when our government chose half baked Nehruvian Socialist policies! We have witnessed the fact that the day Indian genius was unshackled, we have seen boom time and growth. Thus, what was derided by economists as 'Hindu rate of growth' was actually 'Nehruvian socialist rate of growth' and what you see now is the real 'Hindu rate of growth.' Poverty in India is a legacy of British rule and earlier phase of mixed-up socialism much against the innate genius of Bharat i.e. India.

Even if we go by only the available data, about 2800 years back Indians had overcome the basic issues of hunger, day-to-day rules of social behaviour like Ten commandments and were discussing the metaphysical issues like purpose of life. Lord Buddha and Lord Mahavir were amongst us to further refine thoughts on living and liberation from the cycle of life and death. At that moment in history Christianity and Islam were not yet born, and Western civilization was comparatively primitive. One gets wonderstruck when one thinks of the antiquity and maturity of this civilization. Osho reminds us that a society leans towards spirituality only when its basic economic and social requirements are met. Then, the members of that society say, "what next?" We can see the current quest for spirituality in West against this background.

When I state this, I am not talking of superiority or inferiority of different civilizations. I am just setting up terms of reference for any informed debate. Dattopant Thengdi used to term these historical cycles in different civilizations as 'kaal chakra' (wheel of time). We also need to acknowledge that due to various historical reasons, some of which arise out of the pacifism of Hindu culture, the same West took lead in the next cycle of economic progress and geographical dominance while we were left behind.

I cannot hold myself from paraphrasing Claude Alvares, "All histories are elaborate efforts at myth-making. Therefore, when we submit to histories about us written by others, we submit to their myths about us as well. Myth-making, like naming, is a token of having power. Submitting to others' myths about us is a sign that we are without power. After the historical work of Dharampal, the scope for myth-making about the past of Indian society is now considerably reduced. If we must continue to live by myths, however, it is far better we choose to live by those of our own making rather than by those invented by others for their own purposes, whether English or Japanese. That much at least we owe ourselves as an independent society and nation."

RSS does not talk of going back in times, but wishes our society to move ahead with confidence born out of knowledge that we belong to a civilization and a country that should lead the world not in negative connotation of domination but with positive power of knowledge and spirit of 'vasudhaiva kutumbakam' (whole world is one family). It has been famously said that those who do not learn from history are condemned to repeat it.

"We have to discard the status quo mentality and usher in a new era... There is no need to cling to past institutions and traditions which have outlived their utility," Pandit Deendayal Upadhyay wrote in his exposition of 'Integral Humanism'.

❑

4

Need to Organize Hindus

Critics of the RSS and many others in India who have developed a great sense of comfort with existing status quo, feel there is no reason to organize, unite or consolidate Hindu society. If this society has survived eons of material and spiritual plunder and still exists due to its innate strength as signified in the previous chapter, it will survive and thrive. They claim that the RSS is only creating fissures in society with its agenda.

Hindu society has a fatal disease of collective amnesia, which has been aided and abetted by the secular Marxist axis of historians and sociologists. There has been a systematic, sometimes, brazen attempts to castrate history to such an extent that facts become myths and new myths are created. In West Bengal, even the school history books have been sanitized to cover up history of pillaging of Hindu temples by earlier marauders and Mughals like Aurangzeb. To make history palatable, their textbooks project Jaichand as a better person than Prithviraj!

What our present generation reads is a neutered, amoral if not immoral version of history. The effect of all the moral posturing of the dominant intellectual elite is that our people seem to treat partition as a bad dream of our own making. They fail to note that whenever Hindus become a minority in a region, that region cedes from India, thus we see an India which has shrunk considerably over centuries. I, for one, would not like to see Hindus and Hinduism reduced to museum pieces like aborigines of Australia, Red Indians of USA or ancient pagan communities of Europe, Canada or Latin America to be dusted and brought out on special occasions in all their fineries.

We just have to look around us in very recent history how once avowedly secular countries Malaysia, Libya, Iran, Bangladesh and Sudan have become Islamic theocratic countries. Once Islamists have become a majority there they have got control of the ruling apparatus, the liberal secular laws have been given a silent burial and Shariah resurrected that treats 'non-believers' as second class citizens with very limited rights. The disappearance of Hindus from Muslim in most of the areas in Bangladesh, Pakistan from a minority of 20-30 per cemt to mere 1-3 per cent within 50 years of their existence and even our own Kashmir is too recent a history to be forgotten or brushed under the carpet.

If we prize our heritage, we need to nurture and preserve it and see it flourish to offer the world a truly universal thought. This requires some organized efforts. Nurturing one's heritage can, in no way, mean destroying somebody's else. This thinking doesn't fit into the Hindu ethos as we have noted.

Uncomfortable Questions that Seek Answers

Some uncomfortable questions always bother me as a Hindu lectured about secularism and tolerance. Whenever I feel a little distant from jingoism of Bajrang Dal types, ruckus raised by secular fundamentalists over some supposedly communal issues, their barely camouflaged hatred for assertive Hinduism and some resulting uncomfortable thoughts drive me back to a firm reaffirmation of my Hindu faith. A friend of mine in Chennai told me that he was grateful to 'card carrying' N Ram of The *Hindu* (what an irony of name calling!) for berating and condemning Hindus to such an extent that a typically carefree 'secular' Hindu has become a conscious and insecure Hindu!

As I raise just an illustrative list of questions, I would like to remind readers that the RSS was born only in 1925 and was strong only in select pockets of India even till 1947, while VHP was born in 1964.

- What factors led to Indian partition and who led this move? Should we subscribe to the new theory being subtly promoted through various fora of Marxist-Islamic historian parivaar that the Congress was perceived to be a Hindu party and Muslims felt that they will never get justice from it; so they chose partition of the motherland rather than live under Hindu hegemony of Gandhi, Nehru and Patel? It is well known that Communists gave strong theoretical and political support to Muslim League in its quest for an independent nation for Muslims. This separatist movement had started even before the RSS was born. Clearly, the RSS didn't influence this politics.
- Gandhiji supported Khilaafat (1919-1924) movement in India to restore Caliphate in Turkey to promote Hindu-Muslim unity, and Hindus participated enthusiastically in this movement. But, when the movement fizzled out with some clever handling by British,

why did Moplah Muslims turn against Hindus and perpetrate indescribable atrocities on Hindu brethren including murder, rapes and forced conversions of nearly 20,000 Hindus? There was no RSS to foment this so-called 'revolt'. (Marxists don't call it a communal pogrom).

- Direct Action of Muslim League to force the partition of India on 16th August 1946 that led to thousands of deaths in Bengal had no element of Hindu provocation. Why did it happen? Did the Congress of that time force it upon the hapless Muslim League supporters?
- Kashmir was a virtual paradise for centuries and a centre for sages and saints. With aggression from Central Asia, it slowly converted into Islam. But, there is still enough history to connect it deeply to India and Hindus. With strengthening of separatism, Hindus have been driven out of their own homeland. There was no provocation from them, they were a peaceful minority. The RSS had hardly any presence in Kashmir at the time this tragedy overtook Hindus. Who provoked this exodus? It is alleged by separatists, ably supported by secularists, that the then governor of J&K Jagmohan is the culprit! Did he send threatening messages over loudspeakers, through newspapers and pamphlets to Hindus to vacate the homes of their forefathers? (One can read his side of the story in his book *Kashmir My Frozen Turbulence* on the subject for better insight.)
- I am always troubled to read about 'communally sensitive areas' in matters of policing and law and order issues. At what point of inflection does an area become 'sensitive' and why? Why no Hindu majority area is 'sensitive' What kind of politics dominated by 'secular' politicians has created this sense of isolation in minorities? Obviously in Muslim dominated areas the RSS would be weak, so it cannot convert such areas into sensitive areas.
- If Muslims or Christians are treated as minorities in various states, why are Hindus not given special status in states like J&K, North Eastern states where they are in a minority? Any sense of natural justice would assume this uniform application of laws.
- Why can Hindu religious institutions be taken over with impunity and even allowed to have trustees from other religions. But, no government touches any so-called minority institution or tries to take over the working of places of their worship? How does our secular polity justify diverting funds of these trusts donated by pious Hindus to other communities rather than use it for the betterment of the followers of that religion. His Holy Highness Shri Shri Ravi Shankar ji has got the data on this issue compiled and brought it to public attention.

- Why is it that Hindu community can get its grievances like wrongful presentation of its faith heard and force the education department to involve it in the new textbook writing exercise in US (California), but it has no voice in India about the way it is presented on all possible platforms in a negative manner and why is its universal philosophy is not presented at all in educational syllabi or presented in a shabby manner?
- Why a law like 'Freedom of Religion Bill' becomes a 'controversial' issue? This bill is nothing but a reassertion of Indian philosophy that a person is free to choose his or her belief system, as one among many paths. Such bills only say that it cannot be done through lure or misrepresentation of facts. (Interestingly, it was the Congress government of Madhya Pradesh decades back which first saw the danger of such mass conversions to exclusivist monotheist religions and appointed 'Neogi Commission' to establish the seriousness of this issue.)
- Why a call for Uniform Civil Code is communal in a country being run on the basis of a secular constitution containing it in its directive principles?
- How come according to critics of the RSS, 'semitization' of Hindu society, allegedly tried unsuccessfully by the RSS is bad; but these same critics very smugly certify the 'semitic' religions as good? If 'semitization' is bad then how can the religions running on supposedly negative semitic principles be good? Is it purely a case of intellectual dishonesty or diabolic argument to keep Hindu society always in state of internal conflict?

Idea here is not to list grievances of Hindu community, nor is it an attempt to promote a 'divisive agenda'; neither is it a exhaustive list. I had to resort to this negative way to bring out the hypocrisy that has been internalized into our polity in the name of secularism, thus promoting a polity charged with negativity. For some, this way of relooking at many issues through a different looking glass may bring better clarity. Answers to such issues are obvious but reasons behind them are not so obvious.

A truly secular government should assert that all citizens of this free country have equal right to its resources, or that all deprived sections of the society should get a priority in distribution of resources. An atmosphere has been created that any pro-Hindu talk or any opposition to policies of appeasement of minority automatically becomes anti-minority, hence communal. The present political discourse has an in-built bias which is promoted by negationism of Indian society.

Negationism of Hindu Society

Koenrad Elst, the renowned Indologist, has written an illuminating book, *Negationism in India.* He gives examples about how Hindu society wishes to forget bitter past of being victims of violence, killings, rapes, pillage etc. How it avoids the bitter truths and hence lessons of history to avoid pain; in the process inflicting more pain on self. I am quoting below, extensively from Koenrad Elst's essay on negationism, though in fractions. You are welcome to read his scholarly works from the Net and through his books.

"Negationism means the denial of historical crimes against humanity. It is not a reinterpretation of known facts, but the denial of known facts. The term negationism has gained currency as the name of a movement to deny a specific crime against humanity, the Nazi genocide on the Jews in 1941–45, also known as the holocaust (Greek for fire sacrifice) or the Shoah (Hebrew for disaster). Negationism is mostly identified with the effort at rewriting history in such a way that the fact of the Holocaust is omitted."

".....Leftist negationism regarding the Nazi holocaust is, of course, only a footnote in the much more general negationism practiced by most leftists, hard and soft, regarding the crimes of Communist regimes............."

It would be educative to note that number of people killed by the Soviet regime between 1917 and 1985 is estimated at between 34 million (on the basis of official figures), while Alexsandr Solzhenitsyn puts the figure at 67 million. Around the same time, Mao Zedong's number of victims to be some 30 million, during the Communist takeover, the Great Leap Forward and the Cultural Revolution. Over a million Tibetans have died because of Communist massacres and organized famines; forced sterilization on large scale. These numbers are hotly debated or denied by its supporters.

About Indian negationism, says Elst, ".....In my study of the Ayodhya controversy, I noticed that the frequent attempts to conceal or deny inconvenient evidence were an integral part of a larger effort to rewrite India's history and to whitewash Islam. It struck me that this effort to deny the unpleasant facts of Islam's destructive role in Indian history is similar to the attempts by some European writers to deny the Nazi holocaust. Its goal and methods are similar, even though its social position is very different: in Europe, Holocaust negationists are a fringe group shunned by respectable people, but in India, *jihad* negationists are in control of the academic establishment and of the press."

".......A section of the Indian intelligentsia is still trying to erase from the Hindus' memory, the history of their persecution by the swordsmen of Islam. The number of victims of this persecution surpasses that of the Nazi crimes. The Islamic campaign to wipe out Paganism could not be equally thorough, but it has continued for centuries without any moral doubts arising in the minds of the persecutors and their chroniclers. The Islamic reports on the massacres of Hindus, destruction of Hindu temples, the abduction of Hindu women and forced conversions, invariably express great glee and pride. They leave no doubt that the destruction of Paganism by every means, was considered the God-ordained duty of the Muslim community. Yet, today many Indian historians, journalists and politicians, deny that there ever was a Hindu- Muslim conflict. They shamelessly rewrite history and conjure up *centuries of Hindu-Muslim amity.* Now a growing section of the public in India and the West only knows their negationist version of history. It is not a pleasant task to rudely shake people out of their delusions, especially if these have been willfully created."

The American historian Will Durant summed it up thus:"*The Islamic conquest of India is probably the bloodiest story in history. It is a discouraging tale, for its evident moral is that civilization is a precious good, whose delicate complex of order and freedom, culture and peace, can at any moment be overthrown by barbarians invading from without or multiplying within.*"

Suppressing and Negating Historical Facts

Sitaram Goel has written some thoroughly researched books on Indian history. One of the books, *Hindu Temples – What Happened to Them* would shake up your views about history, or rather the falsification of history being perpetrated by the lobby of historians who are controlling the academia for years now. Whenever such evidence is discovered or brought to light, it is ridiculed by established lobbies, if not possible then it is hushed up as being 'sensitive'. In the previous chapters I have quoted Dharampal and Claude Alvares extensively and noted how historians controlling the establishment try to brush aside or hush up such information.

The first volume of the *Hindu Temples: A Preliminary Survey,* was published in 1990 and played an important role in the political debate over the controversial Rama temple in Ayodhya. It contains a competently compiled list of about 2000 mosques in India that forcibly replaced Hindu temples. This list is not complete, and does not cover Pakistan and other countries where temples have been violently replaced with mosques. Moreover, the number of temples of which material has been used in these 2000 mosques far exceeds 2000. For the single Quwwat-ul-Islam mosque in Delhi, as an inscription at the entrance proudly proclaims, 27 Hindu temples had been destroyed. These 2000 are only the tip of an iceberg. Muslims have raised a hue and cry over the demolition of the Babri structure (which they had not used since decades), but few people seem to realize that destruction of the religious places of minorities is a routine affair in Islamic states.

This book also contains articles by Ram Swarup, Jay Dubashi, Prof. Harsh Narain, and Arun Shourie. Ram Swarup, like editor Sitaram Goel, traces the facts of Islamic intolerance and iconoclasm to the exclusivist theology of the Quran and the Sunnah (tradition). He also deals with the role of Marxism in recent negationist efforts: "Marxists have taken to rewriting Indian history on a large scale and it has meant its systematic falsification.....The Marxists' contempt for India, particularly the India of religion, culture and philosophy, is deep and theoretically fortified. It exceeds the contempt ever shown by the most die-hard imperialists... Marx ruled out self-rule for India altogether and in this matter gave her no choice... Marxism idealizes old imperialisms and prepares a people for a new one. Its moving power is deep-rooted self-alienation and its greatest ally is cultural and spiritual illiteracy... No true history of India is possible without countering their philosophy, ideas and influence."

The second volume of Sitaram Goel's book, subtitled *Hindu Temples: The Islamic Evidence*, and published in May 1991, goes much farther with its revelations of the grim facts of the Islamic campaign to destroy Hinduism. It deals with the controversies over Krishna's birthplace temple in Mathura (UP) and the Rudramahaalaya temple complex in Sidhpur (Gujarat), both forcibly replaced with Islamic structures and exposes the negationists' machinations to distort or conceal the facts. The chapter 'From the Horse's Mouth' gives full quotations from Muslim documents that describe and glorify the destruction of Hindu temples very explicitly. Elst feels, "It is only an anthology, and the already very impressive material collected in this chapter is again only the tip of an iceberg."

We know of Ram Mandir agitation and how Hindus are eternally shamed for the destruction of Babri structure. But, the facts are being glossed over. It was agreed that if the structure below Babri is found to be a temple, it will be handed over to Hindus. But, when the research resulted in a report that pointed to a large number of properly laid out pillars of typically Hindu designs discovered under the mound that proved the existence of a temple, the report was quietly buried by media till it was resurrected with the Allahabad High Court judgment on the matter.

To quote Elst again, "It is worth recalling that the negationists have also resorted to another tactic so familiar to our European negationists, and to all defenders of untenable positions: personal attacks on their opponents, in order to pull the public's attention away from the available evidence. In December 1990, the leading JNU historians and several allied scholars, followed by the herd of secularist pen-pushers in the Indian press, have tried to raise suspicions against the professional honesty of Prof. BB Lal and Dr. SP Gupta, the archeologists with impeccable credentials, who have unearthed evidence for the existence of a Hindu temple at the Babri Masjid site."

We need to accept Koenrad Elst's criticism that there has been very little intellectual exercise by major sections of Hindutva school to counter the leftist secular onslaught on history and creating a negative image of Hinduism. Nor have there been enough efforts to sift truth about its so-called myths and reality. It has not been proactive and has not been able to support people bringing out historical and scientific facts about ancient India, Hindu contribution to the world in various fields, wholeheartedly.

The acceptance by the ruling group of historians of evidence of ancient city of Dwarka has been rather reluctant. Doubts were raised about the academic qualifications of S R Rao too, who did the research. Even now, it has not been accorded the importance it should have been in revalidating Indian history through ancient Indian texts. When researchers like Dr S Kalyanaraman and N S Rajaram have tried to do original research on subjects like Saraswati river and studies countering the theory of Aryan invasion as these hold special significance to Vedic period, they have been thwarted by leftist and secular historians. If nothing, they found their scientific background objectionable!

In fact, one of the first acts of Arjun Singh on his appointment as HRD minister was to stop grants to Saraswati river research. What is this Marxist parivaar of historians afraid of that they sought support of the government to suppress it? There is, now, enough new historical evidence to suggest that the story of Aryan invasion may not be true account of history. It is ironic that US academics give alternative viewpoint about Aryan invasion theory etc., but Indian history books remain monochromatic.

As Elst asserts, the evidence available so far on which the edifice of this theory is built, can equally be used to provide convincing arguments why this violent aggression theory is flimsy. The latest study done by Indian scientists from Centre for Cellular and Molecular Biology in collaboration of Harvard Medical School,

Harvard School of Public Health, Broad Institute of Harvard and MIT about common genealogy of Indians from all parts of India negates racist theory of Aryan aggressors from Europe *vs.* Dravidians from South totally, thus demolishes with one scholarly stroke the mythical North South divide.

We are aware how the Central government stonewalled a suggestion by Supreme Court of India to do an archeological survey of 'Ram Setu' and the possible ecological disaster it might entail. Compare this to the utter sense of supplication of the Central government and West Bengal government with which they agreed to change the alignment of new Kolkota airport runway as it had a small makeshift, hardly in use, masjid on way. They spent crores of rupees to change the alignment and also change town planning of new upcoming buildings which came in the way of the new alignment. The problem is not with this realignment but the difference in approach to problems which are similar in nature for the respective communities, in fact, much more emotional for Hindus, like Ram Temple. Will any intellectual of substance simply refuse to allow new facts come to light? Why does government want to steamroll an issue like Ram Setu very close to Hindus' hearts without any application of mind?

Only those whose bread and butter depends on regurgitating the information created by colonial mindset, and who are now full of inertia, lack intellectual objectivity and integrity would oppose such exercises. The simple reason is that such discoveries would bring down their citadel of construct built on outdated theories that the whole Vedic and Puranic literature is cock and bull story, or at the best, a bundle of mythical stories. It would open a floodgate of new truly Indian view of history that would spell 'finis' to their cosy careers built painstakingly through JNU kind of networks.

Many friends of my generation will recall how casually our college lecturers would tell us that 'people consider Kalidas as Shakespeare of India' forgetting that Kalidas was born nearly 1000 years before Shakespeare when English language was not even born. How we were given to understand that *Mahabharat* was probably influenced by Greek classics *Iliad* and *Odyssey,* forgetting that antiquity of *Mahabharat* far exceeded that of *Illiad.* In fact, both are classics in their own right. This mental slavery went to the extent that it used to be hinted that the Hindu concept of Trinity (Brahma, Vishnu, Mahesh - signifying the supreme forces of birth, sustenance and destruction) was borrowed perhaps from the concept of 'Trinity' in *Bible,* conveniently overlooking the fact that Hindu civilization was born thousands of years before the *Bible* was written!

A French journalist Francois Gautier has been pointing out, insistently, the deep scars that Hindu society carries because of its nearly 1000 years of subjugation under Mughal and British rules, has resulted in an inferiority complex about their religion and nationality. They wish to put up a show of being a 'good boy', whatever the cost to the society or nation. This sense of guilt has been perpetrated by western historians and the so-called Indic scholars, most of whom had never referred to original Sanskrit texts or learnt Sanskrit, but depended on secondhand translations by a very few people who had studied a little Sanskrit and did some half literate translations.

Unless we face the bitter truths of history and then move on, we shall only be talking of cosmetic unity and not unity of heart. Francoise Gautier, points out, "The argument that looking at one's history will pit a community against the other does not hold either. French Catholics and Protestants, who share a very similar religion, fought with each other bitterly. Catholics brutally murdered thousands of Protestants in the 18th century; yet today they live peacefully next to each other. France fought three wars with Germany in the last 150 years, yet they are great friends today." Countries like Germany, Great Britain, the United States of America, Japan – all have faced the bitter history, learned lessons, apologized to people, nations or communities where required and moved on together."

Recently, Pope has apologized to a few nations for the difficulties they faced due to evangelization drives of the Church. Our avowed liberals applaud these moves but any demand for sense of regret for Hindus, who faced genocides for centuries, the persecution and wanton killings of Goan Hindus through inquisitions by Catholic evangelists abetted by Portuguese colonialists, is called digging the past or resurrecting ghosts from the past! Unfortunately, we wish to simply negate facts and talk of superficial rhetorical unity based on myths and not facts.

"No nation can move forward, unless it squarely faces its past. The courage to remember helps us not to repeat the same mistakes and to build a better future for our children" says HH Shri Shri Ravi Shankar

An Organization for Hindus

With this historical background, let us appreciate the fact that the RSS is an organization wedded to the wellbeing of Hindu society. And since Hindu society forms nearly 80 per cent of the population, it is equally true that unless Hindu society reforms itself and organizes itself in a positive way, India as a nation cannot grow and develop into a vibrant country. Incidentally, many people believe that the figures are flawed and Hindu population, actually, could be much lower than this, already. And if we go by 'secular' definition of Hinduism then these numbers would be much lower.

Koenrad Elst points out, "But for Hinduism, there would not have been an Indian Union. Suppose that, as some foresaw a century ago, all Hindus would have been converted to Islam or Christianity. What would happen then, can be seen from such happy Muslim-Christian bhai-bhai countries like Lebanon, Cyprus, Sudan, Kosovo (Yugoslavia), Nagorny-Karabakh. The country would have been split at the very least into a Muslim North and a Christian South. In the sense that Hinduism is the cultural reason for India's very existence, India cannot exist but as a Hindu Rashtra."

There is no reason why Hindu society needs to be apologetic about this mission or why self-styled secular thought contractors and critics of the RSS should certify it as communal because it professes to work for Hindu community. If a Christian organization working for Christianity or Muslims holding various congregations for nurturing their religion are not communal; or for that matter any organization working for a particular community is not communal or casteist; then this communal stamping on any person or organization which talks or works for Hindus is nothing but hypocrisy and double standards.

Elst mentions a Hindu-friendly India-watcher of the Foreign Broadcast Information Service, a parastatal world-watch bureau in Washington DC, remarking that this alleged semitization, which is but a pejorative synonym for self-organization, may simply be necessary for Hinduism's survival. He points out that in Africa, the traditional religions are fast being replaced by Christianity and Islam precisely because they have no organization which can prepare a strategy of self-defence. African traditionalists are not denounced as 'semitized fundamentalists' because in effect, they submit to the liquidation of their tradition by mass conversions.

Dr Hedgewar's Objective behind Establishing the RSS

Having covered various angles about Hindu society, its mindset and the political implications of such a mindset, let us go back to the reasons behind establishment of the RSS by Dr Hedgewar.

Dr Hedgewar was a staunch nationalist who worked with organizations associated with revolutionaries, Anusheelan Samiti while he was in Kolkota to study medicine. He was so hot-headed as well as clear-headed about independence even as a young boy that he was rusticated from the school for inciting his classfellows to refuse sweets distributed on the birthday of Queen Victoria.

After completing medicine, he returned to Nagpur, turned his back to the medical profession and started working in the Congress, taking up different responsibilities as an office bearer at various stages. He was senior office bearer of regional Congress committee including the committee that organized the Congress plenary session in 1920. He took part in freedom struggle through various satyagrahas and agitations and was imprisoned. His association and activities continued even after he had begun the RSS work. Many of his colleagues in Congress also became members of the RSS and worked for both organizations. Many of the swayamsevaks also went to jail with him. These facts have been documented well by Rakesh Sinha in his biography of Dr Hedgewar.

Having gone through this whole gamut of activities and being a serious student of history, Dr Hedgewar realized that Hindu society was deeply divided on various counts like caste, region, language etc. He saw a total lack of self-discipline, social commitment and lack of self-confidence and found that Hindus were driven by self-interest and not by love of motherland. He realized that unless this society was organized into a well-knit and disciplined patriotic society with selfless members ready to do anything for the nation, the freedom that was imminent would be useless. It would only mean change in the rulers and not the rules. The common man may not enjoy the fruits of this independence and public discourse would be devoid of meaning as it would be driven by self-interest and not national interest.

Dr Hedgewar had firm conviction that Bharat i.e. India had a unified national consciousness, that freedom is indivisible and society is an organic integrated body. Guruji, his successor saw the society as, "Viraat Purush, single unified colossal personality by organic relationship, where each individual is the limb and arm of this Viraat Purush." Just as the whole body reacts to a problem in any cell of the body, society should feel the pain and respond to it without any discrimination.

Dr Hedgewar envisioned an organization that would look beyond immediate gains, which would be non-political and its only job would be to create extraordinary human beings out of ordinary members of the society, who would be selflessly dedicated to the cause of nation building and service to the society. People who would lead a highly disciplined life based on high thinking and simple living that is moulded with great character. He knew it was not an easy job and nor was it a job which could be done with only preaching or propaganda. Moulding of character and human beings and filling their heart with passionate love of motherland is not a matter of short-term training sessions, but requires regular nurturing. His goal was Hindu unity and creation of a self-confident Hindu society. It was a long haul.

In the dark days of British rule when calling oneself a Hindu was an embarrassment for the educated class, Doctor Hedgewar stood up in 1925 and said, "Yes, I, Dr Keshav Baliram Hedgewar proclaim that I am Hindu and this is a Hindu nation."

Thus, was born the RSS shakha, vehicle for propagating this philosophy. He started off with half a dozen school going kids on a playground. He was already a middle aged man at that time. He had decided to remain unmarried because he knew from the beginning that he would dedicate his life for the nation and thought family had no place in it. It was an arduous task. He put in his all.

He worked so hard that a person of his wonderful physique and health burned out within years and died of extreme exhaustion in 1940. Within this short period of 15 years, he had already laid foundation of the RSS in all the states. The last training camp he attended had representation from all the states. The participant of that year's third year Officers Training Camp (now called Sangh Shiksha Varg) in 1940, for the first time, represented every state of India. In his last speech before these young people, the ailing founder of the RSS said, "... I see before me a miniature picture of Bharat today..." Rest is history.

Minorities and the RSS

Contrary to common belief, there are many examples of Christians and Muslims becoming members of the RSS and being active for many years. It is also a sad fact that most of them leave the organization because of peer pressure of their society to give up their 'wayward' behaviour, so to say. There are large number of so-called religious minorities in the normal sense of word who are sympathetic to the RSS ideology.

The RSS has been running disaster relief camps during each and every disaster or natural calamity. It has been well documented that not a single disaster centre has ever discriminated against minorities in those camps. In fact, such people have been offered facilities for namaaz and Ramzan fasting etc. No relief camp organizers supported by the RSS have tried to convert people to Hindu faith. In places like Jammu where Seva Bharati is running residential schools for orphans of terrorist violence, young Muslim children remain Muslim with no compulsion or persuasion to change their faith.

None of the social service organizations run by people inspired by the RSS has ever discriminated between the beneficiaries of those schemes, whether it is a dispensary, hospital or a micro-finance scheme or a school. An RSS volunteer has learnt offering namaaz and helps patients in ICU in Dr. Hedgewar Hospital in Aurangabad to offer it to boost their morale. These are recorded facts. Thus, working for Hindus does not mean working against some other people.

The stories of Parsis and Jews settling in India with full support of local people are well known. Syrian Christians landed in Kerala centuries fleeing persecution in Persia before Portuguese brought in the worst violent form of inquisitions and persecution for conversions in the sixteenth century. They have lived and thrived for hundreds of years without any persecution from local kings and populace. There is the story of professed Hindu king like Shivaji who saw his mother in a beautiful Muslim lady captured by his forces and gave full freedom of worship to people to whichever faith they belonged. There was no religious persecution. Shivaji is one of the biggest icon in the Sangh' pantheon of great Indians.

The RSS and other Hindu organizations have no problems with Christians and Muslims. Hindu society's problem is with the institutionalized efforts by their evangelist leaders who try to convert their members by devious means and seed their hearts with hate and embarrassment by misinterpreting their Hindu faith.

At policy level, the RSS view has been that all citizens must be treated as equal and public policies should not be biased against or in favour of any particular community or religion. India can be secular as per Indian ethos, but not irreligious or non-spiritual. The RSS offers terse opposition to policy of appeasement and the cult of inverse communalism that passes off in the name of secularism. It believes that minorities should own the ancestors and ancestry of this land as it is a common heritage, though method of worship may have changed. In no way, does it wish to throw or crush minorities out as alleged by its critics.

Elst believes that spirit of Bharat is Hindu, though other streams may have enriched it. Unless, policies and public discourse on various issues take this basic reality into account, we shall have arid rootless policies producing rootless citizens who may be flag waving kind of patriots who know pop patriotism in a jingoistic manner, but with no idea about the spirit behind it.

Leftist Secular Fascism, Hindutva and the RSS

It is not a finely kept secret that an academic or a media person not conforming to leftist and secular lobby's ideas is simply shut out of the whole system. The person doesn't get a job easily. If he or she gets it, his/her career prospects are totally blocked till the person drops out of the system with sheer frustration. Their works are not allowed to be published easily. If they manage to get it published they are blanketed out of academic discussions, various fora and censored in every possible way. If nothing there is character assassination, ridicule and isolation. There is a very interesting e-mail that is under circulation that gives the internal networking of this lobby across print and media journalism. Though, not wholly correct, it has a big grain of truth in it. All this in the name of liberal thoughts!

This began right from the days of independence. For example, scholars, especially in humanities, like Sita Ram Goel, Ram Swarup and many others could not get employment in colleges and universities. As mentioned above, if a scholar got into some academic job, he or she would be blocked or hounded out if there was suspicion about his or her loyalty to the Red cause. JNU lobby is a well-known fact in academics and media. Scholars like BB Lal and others can be insulted and doubts raised against their antecedents built over years of hard work if they change their views which are not in conformity with their friends' established views. Journalists can reach the level of bureau chief or assistant editor but can never become chief editors. Editors like Girilal Jain, developed sympathies for Hindu cause and were squeezed out. This is just a very very small glimpse of the vice-like grip these groups have over these two institutions of democracy.

This suppression of opposing views is nothing but intellectual fascism. Use of force to enforce your viewpoint and suppress other's viewpoint is the first sign of fascism. This network is intertwined in very complex personal and professional relationships. Here is most recent nugget. I am quoting part of a report in *Times of India* dated 10 October 2010 titled 'HC exposed Waqf board experts (in Ayodhya case)' – "To the court's astonishment, some who had written signed articles, found themselves withering under scrutiny and the judge said they were displaying an ostrich-like attitude to facts. He pointed out how the independent witnesses were all connected, one had done a PhD under the other, another had contributed an article to a book penned by a witness. Some instances underlined by the judge are: Suvira Jaiswal deposed whatever knowledge I gained with respect to disputed site is based on newspaper reports or what others told (other experts) (sic)". Once you understand this networking, you will understand why supposedly independent media houses act in near unison on question of so-called secularism. A prominent Congress leader during a TV interview had boasted recently that the Congress and its supporters owned 159 newspapers all over India!

When theses lobbies are in power, they don't mind using state apparatus to silence their critics. Emergency was a manifestation of the same mentality. Attacks on commoners by Marxist goondas in Singur and Nandigram is another sign of this fascist way of implementing one's ideas. Attacks on the RSS volunteers and their murders in hundreds wherever Communist and Naxalite monopoly is threatened is indicative of this intolerance. Tragedy is that in places like Kerala where the RSS volunteers have suffered most, the sufferers are members of underprivileged or weaker sections of the society, the people who Communists claim to be working for.

As I write this book, I am reading about the new wave of violence in West Bengal. It is amusing but sad to see the late realization by the Congress that Communists have been practising Lenin's terrorizing policies of killing their opponents for last 17 years and they have killed more than 30,000 (thirty thousand) of their own volunteers. These same seculars closed their eyes conveniently when they slept with these fascists for five years at the centre. Communists have, in turn, called the Congress and its supporters fascists. We need to realize that Naxals and Maoists belong to Marxist parivaar, a fact that that media has shied away from mentioning. The way Marxists have criticized the ban on Maoist outfits in Bengal clearly shows which way their sympathies lay. Clearly, big brother is trying to shield the errant and violent younger brother, current violence against each other being only an aberration. Thus, fascism is no more than an invective which can be hurled at anybody at will, nothing more.

And what does the RSS have to show for its so-called fascist designs? Inspite of numerous enquiry committees, not one report could blame the RSS for any riot. If there were firm allegations or proofs, I am sure it would have been permanently banned. Though, there have been unproved allegations against the RSS again in Gujarat riot, it would be relevant to recall that the worst riots in Gujarat took place in the Congress regime when there was a continuous curfew in the cities for days.

Petty violence by a fringe group, criticized by the RSS leadership in unequivocal terms, becomes the face of Hindutva to defame the RSS and Hindu society but when Muslim turns out to be a terrorist, it is an aberration not representing true Islam! Rightly so, but why are there different yardsticks? There has been lot of breast beating about attack on MF Hussain's painting by Hindu groups as being against liberal values of artistic freedom. Interestingly, Hussain's same artistic freedom becomes coy when depicting Mother Teresa, his mother or other Muslim women! The stark contrast in his artistic impressions can be seen through various presentations of Hindu gods and goddesses. You can see these images floating around on the net. Many of them are so obscene and hurt our sensibilities so deeply that I can't even describe these. Same liberals also are in the forefront for banning Salman Rushdie and Taslima Nasreen. They keep quiet when extremists force Taslima out of India. They are quiet when a Muslim lecturer is terrorized and stopped from taking lecture without burqa in West Bengal, supposedly a bastion of secularism of Marxist variety. They wish to paper over ruthless burning of unarmed pilgrims in Godhra but are not tired of breast beating about post-Godhra riots. They are stung into silence when their stories of rape of nuns in Jhabua turns out to be a case of rape by followers of Church or when their arch secularist like Teesta Setalvad turns out to be a past master in tutoring the witnesses to implicate some people. But, inspite of all this, the RSS is the sole claimant to the title of being fascist, courtesy our honourable liberals.

The RSS has always tried to use opinion building, a valid tool of democratic way of life to put forward its points. It has launched mass agitations on various issues of national importance. It has not retaliated with violence even under worst of provocations; on the contrary it has been a target of persecution by the government and Communists at different times. It has not burnt offices of press or killed leaders or intellectuals who have insulted its leaders, or degraded Hinduism.

Leftist-secular lobby has been repeatedly quoting two paragraphs of Guruji's views on minorities for last 60-70 years from a book which was published in 1938–39 before he held any important position in the RSS. This book was discontinued after 1947 and disowned by the RSS and Guruji many years ago. After this, the opponents have not been able to find a single other quote from Guruji that could support their claim of Guruji being a fascist. Imagine, these verbal terrorists and secular fundamentalists could not find anything even remotely fascist in the speeches of the head of an all India organization for 33 years inspite of tracking and poring over his each and every public interaction and writings.

Worst charge that they could put even based on his quote of 1938–39 is that he advocated that no group should have any special privileges (which the leftists translate as the minorities be given a status of second class citizen). Even if this view is taken at its full face value, it is not in anyway, different from the stated Islamic rule (evident in all Muslim majority states) that gives status of second class citizen to 'non-believers'. If this proposition is true, then are they accepting that Islamic rule is fundamentally a fascist rule?

Even when these invectives are thrown at the RSS and its associate organizations in general, we must remember that both the Hindu

Mahasabha (born in 1906) and the RSS (born in 1925) came into existence before anyone in India knew of Hitler. Savarkar's *Hindutva* (1923) was published three years before Hitler's *Mein Kampf*. He was inspired by the sacrifice of Chaphekar brothers who were hanged in 1899. His views about modern nationalism were moulded by Italian revolutionary Giuseppe Mazzini. His Hindutva was inspired by Shivaji and activism for social equality and fight against casteism was moulded by thoughts of Sant Tukaram and Samarth Ramdas. Clearly, the inspiration to organize and defend Hinduism at the political level does not stem from Hitler, and it did not need any outside impulse.

If we look at the way Doctor ji developed tbe RSS and its philosophy, we can surmise that Doctor Hedgewar's methodology was more close to and influenced by Lokmanya Tilak's Hinduism and its symbolism to channelize and organize the Hindu society, than by Savarkar's Hindutva.

Koenrad Elst asks, "Have they sided with Hitler ? Have they (Savarkar, RSS) even called on its followers to follow Subhash Bose and join the Axis war effort against the British? .....But of course, since the Hindutva people are at the receiving end of all the blame, their non-support to Hitler is being turned against them.... The Communists opposed the British in 1940 (under Stalin's pact with Hitler) and supported them after 1941, yet after independence they have not been branded as collaborators with either fascism or colonialism. They can get away with it, while the Hindu parties are covered with abuse regardless of the stand they take. The RSS has not glorified Hitler when he was successful in any larger measure than most Indians at that time (the facts of the extermination camps were not known until 1945, and for the rest most Indian were skeptical about the British propaganda)."

I was too young to understand Guruji's lectures when he was alive. But, I was involved in translation of summary of Guruji's complete works of nearly 320 pages, called *Guruji – His Vision and Mission*. I have also gone through the complete works on and off. I was unable to trace any speeches or writings that smell of fascism. So, this bogey of fascism needs to be buried along with all the invectives thrown at the RSS. The conduct of Marxist parivaar and the secular lobby vis a vis conduct of the RSS during all these years is much better testimony of the RSS's faith in democracy than the certificates issued by these self-appointed guardians of democratic traditions.

A Christian Priest's views on the RSS

To Fr. Kundukulam goes the credit for being the first Christian priest to do a doctoral thesis on the Rashtriya Swayamsevak Sangh, that too in a foreign university. He is also the first clergyman to author a book on the RSS titled *RSS: Enthu Engott?* (What is the RSS and Where is it headed for). In fact, a former clergyman, Anthony Elenjimittam, had published a book titled *RSS: Bharathiya Samskruthiyude Kavalsena* (RSS: Watchdog of Indian Culture) way back in 1951, but he had ceased to be a priest and had taken to social service when the book was published.

The phenomenal growth of the RSS in post-Independent India, firmly rooted in all walks of life, all nooks and corners of the country kindled his curiosity. In Madhya Pradesh, he came across a European who had been doing a doctoral thesis on 'Hindu nationalism' in the Sorbonne University.

In an interview in Pontifical Seminary, Fr. Kundukulam confesses that when he broached the idea of writing a book on his research findings on the RSS, some of his co-religionists cautioned him that the RSS men would beat him up if he wrote something against them. He submits that he has tried to remain as objective as possible in his assessment of the RSS. He was pleased that it was well-received in the church and the RSS circles.

In his view, the RSS is a multifaceted organization which is political, cultural, religious and voluntary in nature and approach. Different facets gain upper hand at different times depending on social and political exigencies.

At the same time, Fr Kundukulam argues against branding the RSS ideology as fascism, Nazism, fundamentalism and communalism. He said the terms fascism, Nazism, and fundamentalism are much abused terms in India. They have a distinct connotation in the European context that can hardly apply to the Indian milieu. The term fundamentalism was first coined in the context of the emergence of the Protestant movement in the Christian church in America in the twenties.

According to him, the ideology of the RSS and the way in which it is interpreted by the Sangh leaders borrowing modern terminology have no comparison to the sense in which the term fundamentalism was used in America. So also, fascism and Nazism do have distinct meanings in the socio-political contexts that prevailed in Italy and Germany which have no bearing in the Indian context.

Fr. Kundukulam feels that BJP, the political arm of the RSS, during its rule at the Centre had not committed any acts that could truly be described as fundamentalist, fascist, or communal. He notes that one of the first acts of A B Vajpayee after taking over as prime minister last time was to call on Mother Teresa and Delhi Archbishop.

One admirable aspect of the RSS, Fr Kundukulam says, is its flexibility to move with the times and to adopt the best from other sociocultural-religious movements. It learnt the rudiments of social work from the missionary organisations of the church and mass mobilization techniques from the Communists. He admires the RSS for the dedication and discipline of its cadres, the simple life style of its prachaaraks, the moral teaching it imparts to the younger generation in its daily shakhas, and the voluntary labour put in by its cadres at critical times such as natural calamities.

Indian society, Fr Kundukulam feels, is in a "vicious circle" with the majority Hindu community suffering from a "psychological inferiority complex" on account of its failure to have a proportionate say in the governance of the country in spite of its numerical superiority and the minorities are always suspicious of the majority community. The growth of minority fundamentalism would only strengthen the RSS. "India can prosper only by strengthening the forces of democracy and secularism and ensuring economic justice to the people," concludes Fr. Kundukulam, who is now busy working on the second edition of his book.

Need to Organize Hindus

After going through the preceding two chapters, one would come to a conclusion that the RSS has filled in a vacuum in the thought process at political and social level. When the whole establishment, under the influence of Nehru's Fabian thoughts and impractical political ideas tilted towards an alien leftist ideology and wrongly interpreted secularism, the RSS stuck out as an organization rooted in Indian thoughts and traditions. It was the period of internationalism providing cover to the Communist designs of international hegemony. At such a time the RSS kept the flame of nationalist thought and faith in indigenous genius alive when it was fashionable to ridicule it.

It gave a sound underpinning to the feeling of patriotism which was based on positive pride for the motherland, founded on its heritage and knowledge and not on airy ideas. It gave muscle to the nationalist ideology in politics which Nehru had once threatened to crush while speaking in Indian parliament. We shall look at the other aspects of its organizational methodology, systems of building a good human being and the manifestation of its ideology in various social dimensions later in the book.

❑

5

RSS Prayer and its Meaning

Prayer that the RSS volunteer recites daily in the shakha is the essence of the RSS mission and a daily reaffirmation of how a swayamsevak should act in personal and public life. Its daily invocation strengthens the resolve of the volunteer at spiritual level.

I am giving below the prayer in original form i.e. Sanskrit and its simple English translation.

Namaste sadaa vatsale maatrubhoome
Twayaa Hindu bhoomey sukham vardhitoham
Mahaamangaley punyabhoome twadarthey
Patatwesh kaayo namaste namaste II1II

Prabho shaktiman Hindurashtraang bhootaa
Imey saadaran twaam namaamo vayam
Twadeeyaaya kaaryaaya baddhaa kateeyam
Shubhaamaashisham dehi tatpoortaye
Ajayyaancha vishwasya deheesh shaktim
Susheelam jagadeyna namram bhavet
Shrutam chaiva yatkantakaakeerna maargam
Swayam sweektritam nah sugam kaarayet II2II

Samutkrash sanishreyasasyaaikamugram
Param saadhanam naama veeravratam
Tadantah sphuratvakshyayaa dhyeyanishthaa
Hridyantah prajaagartu teevraanisham

Vijetree cha naha samhataa kaaryashaktir
Param vaibhavam netumetata swarashtram
Samarthaa bhawatvaashishaa te bhrisham II3II

II Bhaaratmaataa kee jay II

English translation

I forever bow to thee, O loving Motherland!
O, motherland of us Hindus,
thou hast brought me up in happiness.
May my life, O great and blessed Holy land,
be laid down to thy cause.
I bow to thee, again and again II1II

We, the children of this Hindu nation,
bow to thee in reverence, O Almighty God.
We have girded up our loins to carry on thy work.
Give us thy holy blessing for the fulfilment of this purpose.
O Lord, grant us such might
that no power on earth can ever challenge,
Such purity of character
as would command the respect of the world,
And such knowledge that would make easy the thorny path
That we have voluntarily chosen II2II

May we be inspired with the spirit of stern heroism,
which is the sole and ultimate means of
attaining the highest spiritual bliss,
with greatest temporal prosperity.
May intense and everlasting devotion to our ideal
ever inspire our hearts.
May our victorious organized power of action, by thy grace,
fully protect our Dharma and lead this nation to the
highest pinnacle of prosperity and glory II3II

II Salutations to Bhaaratmaataa II

The prayer is inspiring, humbling and arouses the most noble and selfless thoughts to serve the motherland and dharma. It is not against any one, and doesn't have a single line or word that ignites hatred or any negative feeling is equally clear. It is a positive prayer.

But, to me, the most important line which is embedded in the heart of a RSS worker and influences his day-to-day thinking and style of working is - "I have taken up this task voluntarily and I know that it is full of thorns (not easy)." Therefore, no volunteer can claim or assume that he is doing anybody any favour by working for the society and the nation. This reaffirmation every day persuades him to take everybody along without fear or favour, be open to others and work together with people, regardless of difference of opinion, for a supreme goal – that of making his motherland prosperous and strong. It is his bounden duty which he has accepted. This is the spirit of selfless service. And he repeats this prayer everyday till his death.

In every training camp, special sessions are earmarked for explaining the prayer in depth and detail. These are the sessions an RSS volunteer doesn't forget easily.

Last act of Guruji before he finally breathed his last was to recite this prayer even though he couldn't stand due to intense weakness from terminal illness. Active Sangh volunteers feel that this is the ideal way of walking into the sunset of one's life.

❑

The Form

Secret of the RSS Work

"There are only two secrets of our work – First is that there is no secret. And, second is, Kabaddi. This programme, even today, has the same character. Motherland beneath, God created skies above, and Hindu society all around us – based on these elements, Kabaddi has been successful. So much power was generated by this kabaddi; power that saved lives, honour and wealth of lacs of people during partition of Punjab."......From where did we get this power? Did we have manifestos at that time? Did we have rosy pictures of the future? Or did we organize conference or publicized our views? We only played kabaddi. This is absolutely true. The foundation of our unified soul in that kabaddi came to signify 'organization'. We need to understand this well."

– Shri Guruji Golwalkar, 1948

6

RSS Shakha

Shaakhaa (shakha or local branch) of the RSS is the public face of the RSS. It is the powerhouse that energizes and powers ordinary people to successfully carry out extraordinary feats and create pan-India organizations.

People often wonder how a small group of 10-20 people who come together for an hour and while away their time in playing games, doing some physical drills, singing some patriotic songs or discussing some social issues, singing and praying together can build together an organization with 50,000 shakhas all over India with a daily attendance of nearly half a million. If you consider approximately 100 members per shakha who don't attend it everyday this figure would come to nearly 50 million regular members. This network is spread up to district level all over India and in most places to tehsil level. You can find village level shakhas in most of the states. Incidentally, Kerala has the highest density of shakhas in Bharat. Then, there are a large number of people who are not directly involved in the Sangh shakha but are active in its other social organizations motivated by the RSS ideals, these figures run into multi-millions. For example, today there are around fifteen hundred thousand (1.50 lac) social service organizations inspired by the RSS working in different parts of India; and there are associate or sister organizations that fall outside this count.

Thus, one is talking about millions of people fired with selfless urge to do something for the nation and ready to leave the comfort of home for the organization and the country. You can also realize why our secular-Marxist parivaar is so frustrated and mouths all kind of political profanities and throws wild allegations at it. These people realize that they cannot match this organized force with mere talk and misuse of propagandist machinery at their command.

The thought behind this unique set of tools or working style of the RSS through daily shakha is that a person should willingly dedicate at least one hour in every day for the nation. Once, this thought becomes a part of his personality he will, willingly, increase his participation as the nation demands. Ultimately he reaches a state of mind reflected in a Sangh song that says, *"tan samarpit, man samarpit, chaahata hoon maan, tujhe kuchh aur bhee doon"* (i.e. I have dedicated my body and soul to you, O' motherland, I long to give you something more).

A shakha runs on daily basis for one hour divided into various periods that include games, physical drills or yoga, songs, some intellectual inputs and prayer. All the activities ultimately tend to create a team of fun loving, hard working people who share common ideas and ideals, and a sense of oneness. A volunteer is reminded time and again that the values learned in this one hour should reflect on his conduct in balance 23 hours of his day. There have been some modifications to this system as times change. There are weekly shakhas and even monthly get-togethers for people who find it difficult to attend this daily programme.

Any person who has grown through this shakha culture can become a successful manager. A management thinker, Sandeep Singh, submits that a well trained RSS worker could easily qualify for Social MBA as enunciated by management guru, Mintzberg.

Induction into RSS

We have heard a lot about the need to "Catch 'em young". Educationists and social scientists confirm that you can educate young people and inculcate good value systems (a much richer word in Sanskrit is "sanskaar") in them more easily which they carry through their life. The Sangh has internalized this lesson right from day one.

Doctor Hedgewar, the founder of the Sangh was 35 year 'young' when started the first branch (or shakha) of the Sangh with a group of young boys on an open ground where they played some interesting Indian games together. Even today the most common mode of recruitment in the RSS is the open playing field. The common theme running through any of these games is importance of team or working together apart from the sportsman spirit. The young boy slowly gets involved into this fun loving group without realizing it. He also ends up learning importance of discipline, time management and physical fitness. All this happens on daily basis, thus reinforcing good habits regularly.

Throughout this induction process, never is a member asked about his caste, his faith and social status etc. I had with me students belonging to Marathi, Gujarati and Marwari communities from various castes and religious groups which I found out much later only as a general gossip material. Our teacher was Sindhi. I had in my group, boys belonging to slums, small chawls as well as higher middle class. We would have simple snacking together on the ground once a week consisting of 'chanaa kurmuraa' (gram and puffed rice). We would visit each others' homes and be equally at ease whether we were together in a chawl or in a big apartment. This intense mixing together with all strata of society without any feeling about high and low castes, high and low economic layers has helped me throughout my life in working with any kind of person at any level without any problem of ego and superiority or inferiority complex.

Through all this, we would be guided by one or two simple, loving teachers or instructors (shikshaks) who could be working or studying during the day and spending their entire evenings with us virtually all days of the week. We never felt the need to ask them how they managed their other worldly affairs or kept their families happy! I know of my teacher, Mahendra Shringi, lovingly called Mahiji, who opted out of promotion in his bank for years as that would entail transfer to a distant branch and he would not be able to give enough time to his young wards. Incidentally, he was a film freak and would see a cinema every Saturday with one or the other young member of his shakha.

Thus, the very process of induction is so simple and fun that before one realizes, he is brought into saffron brotherhood. The intellectual inputs come much later and they are not anywhere near, say, dialectic materialism, let me confess. Since, these inputs are based on Hindu ethos and ancient traditions, understanding and appreciating them is much easier. They strike a chord immediately in one's heart. I don't know of many people who joined the RSS as active volunteers after getting convinced about its philosophy and ideology. Such numbers are minimal. In this era of the Internet, I do find more people asking their friends about how to join the RSS. In Vile Parle in Mumbai, where I got inducted into the RSS shakha, I can count such examples on finger tips. Yes, there are huge number of sympathizers who are late converts, but I am talking of active participants who work on field daily.

I once asked a very senior prachaarak of the RSS Bapurao Moghe during emergency period, "No other country in the world has such mass level social organization just to provide cultural values, inculcate a positive sense of patriotism and selfless love for the society. Why is the RSS carrying on such an activity in Bharat?" His answer was, "World over these values are inculcated in schools but they are amiss in our schooling system due to perverted ideas about secularism and moral education. Thus, the RSS is fulfilling a social obligation. If and when these duties are taken up by the government and schools, there will be no need for the RSS."

Physical Training

Though, the stress on physical drills is declining slowly over years, it is an integral part of the RSS training methodology. The RSS is on a man-building mission. i.e. nurturing ordinary human beings into a disciplined and cultured, socially dedicated citizens of India who would go to any extent to serve their motherland, help build the nation even at the cost of personal discomfort and harm. These drills are used as means to nurturing the basic qualities like discipline and 'falling in step' to march together and work together. When we see mass physical drills in various game opening ceremonies it is sheer thrill and everyone wishes to see it live. For example, the sheer logistics of bringing two columns of march past from two parts of the city to match steps and merge into one at a precise minute with a band that could match the best in the world is something that should earn respect from any person. It is a thrilling experience to witness it. It is equally exhilarating when one performs or sees mass yoga, surya namaskaar, physical drills for the sheer finesse of it. Funny enough, when done by the RSS, such drills become paramilitary activities!

The teachers or 'shikshaks' themselves are generally very proficient in the drill or game they teach. If they are not, they are encouraged to gain that skill from experts or through workshops and camps. Idea is to lead by example. We had excellent instructors or teachers - some in games, some in physical drills. My first teacher, Shivram Ghate, lovingly called Ghateji was an ever smiling relatively short, lean and sprightly gentleman who was a champion in *kabaddi* as well as mock sword fight. He could exhibit a drill with swords in both hands. He is in his eighties now and still moves around on cycle with same alertness with same loving smile on his face.

Many critics are not happy that 'offensive' martial arts like exercises with wooden stick (dand) or niyuddha (adapted from Kalaripayattu of Kerala - the mother of all martial arts) are taught to the members of the RSS. Incidentally, Kalaripayattu was taken to China and there onwards by a Buddha bhikhu Bodhi Dharma where it evolved into other forms of martial arts. It would suffice to say that even ordinary citizens go to learn martial arts for self-defence and more importantly to gain self-confidence and improve concentration.

Many of my liberal friends are mighty scared of the semi-military drills that are undertaken in the RSS shakha and its other programmes. They feel the RSS uniform indicates a regimented mindset. They find simple wooden sticks or lathis as intimidating as AK-47s. For them, this semi-military activity puts the RSS into paramilitary organizations bracket.

Critics also look rather derisively at the Indian games that are preferred over western games in shakhas, considering them 'backward'. All the games played in shakha hardly use any resources, thus can be played by any person irrespective of his or team's financial condition. Most of the popular games being played in shakha like kho-kho, kabaddi and other similar games inculcate team and sportsman spirit. They also help build strong body and endurance. There are hundreds of such games and there are small booklets available to physical instructors of shakhas that explain these games.

An important lesson during the games is that once the instructor says - Stop - one must stop, howsoever interestingly the game may be poised. So, even here, instilling discipline is of prime importance. One of the tricks taught to the teachers is to stop the game when it is at its peak and not when it was really over!

One hour of shakha is divided into periods which may be of 3 to 10 minutes, based on the subject. Following the time table and one's appointments to the minutes is the hallmark of the RSS and its members. Utilization of 60 minutes in small sections of minutes trains a swayamsevak to use every minute of his time productively and efficiently. This self discipline and time management skill is one of the most important lesson one learns in a shakha.

Intellectual Training

Truly speaking, there is not much of a stress on intellectual training at shakha level as the RSS is more action oriented and a volunteer is supposed to become an activist working on ground, interacting with people most of the time and spreading the good word through personal contacts. There are sessions for intellectual training with activities like imparting training in patriotic songs, singing together, learning and understanding The RSS prayer, discourses on Indian history, culture and social issues. These sessions have an important place in creation of a swayamsevak or a volunteer and are given lot more time during workshops and camps.

There are other regular rituals like reciting 'Bharat Bhakti Stotram'. It is meant to recall and pay homage to the great Indian souls and the greatness of this land. An 'Ekaatmataa Stotram' comprising a single Sanskrit shloka or verse was introduced a few years back which reminds one of diversity of faiths in Hindu civilization and gives a message to respect them all, as all of them lead to one ultimate truth.

Songs (called Geet in the Sangh parlance) invoking patriotism and reminding of one's duty to the society are an integral part of the Sangh shakha. There are hundreds of such songs, some can be sung in unison as group songs while some are more classical music based and are sung by somebody who knows his music better. These songs can be broadly categorized as songs for march pasts, energizing songs of patriotism, songs about devotion to motherland, songs about social harmony etc. Some songs are composed for a specific occasion and people remember an occasion through a particular song for years. Many volunteers, enamoured by such classical music have got into serious music training and become accomplished artists. For volunteers well versed in such songs, there are enough 'geets' to have regular 'antaakshari' competition that can last hours!

It is interesting to see a subtle shift in themes of the songs over years as national and social issues emerge and evolve. Most of the songs are written by some RSS activists or a prachaaraks while a few are adopted from existing literature. They can be Sanskrit, Hindi or local languages. As is practice in the Sangh, names of poets are not known. Only once in a while one comes to know that a particular song was written or composed by a particular activist.

There is another small activity of narrating a 'subhaashit' i.e. great words or saying. Generally, they are shlokas from ancient scriptures, or speeches of great leaders. Most of them are in Sanskrit. These are pithy commentaries about Hindu philosophy, principles of ethical living for individual and society etc. relevant and contemporary even today. A volunteer is supposed to learn it by heart and also speak out its meaning in local language. Having heard many of them over years, one wonders why the newspapers in their 'quotable quotes' rarely find such shlokas or words of wisdom but quote mostly from Western scholars.

Honestly speaking this intellectual training becomes tiringly repetitive as one grows over years. I don't recall many sessions where I was told about scientific strength of Hindu philosophy that makes it a unique living faith even with passage of 5000 (or is it 10000 ?) years. For example, I do not remember any lecture on the deep philosophy behind Hindu symbols and figures of Gods ; nor were many references provided for scientific or technical achievements of our ancient scientists and sages. Such things were to be discovered by self. Yes, we were told about greatness of our scriptures, our heritage, our civilizational values etc. but for anything deeper, an activist had to find his own path.

However, recently there have been serious efforts to generate literature of Hindu thought on the scientific basis, its rituals and mantras, and well documented literature with critical references on achievements of Hindu civilization in science and technology since ancient times, that would appeal more to today's generation.

A participant is encouraged to study various subjects and if he is good at it, also give lectures after proper preparation. Many of the RSS workers are very well read and write well too, but since they are very busy running a shakha or taking care of multiple activities of the localities they don't get time to write or study really in depth. Sometimes I feel unhappy that in case a person is really good at intellectual studies and exposition and active on field too, preference is given to field activity. There are some good examples, on the other hand, of some volunteers I know, who became established writers due to influence of their seniors who persuaded them to study certain subjects.

When I reflect upon this training, I would say it is not just intellectual training but it is also a sustained exercise in raising the emotional quotient that makes a volunteer sensitive to his society, his nation and his fellow beings, sensitizing him about the problems of people around him that make a society. For example, during various lectures an activist is explained about the Hindu philosophy of a human being incurring various kinds of debts (rin or ruun) when he is born on this mother earth. e.g. debt of his mother (matri-rin), father (pitri-rin), teacher (guru-rin) etc. and debt of the society (saamaajik rin) that contributes to his or her growth in personal as well as social sphere. Thus, when a person does something for the society, he or she is only trying to pay back that debt as a duty, and is not actually doing any charity or favour to anybody. A volunteer brought up on songs that say, 'I will not be adorning the pinnacle of the temple, I am just a small stone in the foundation of the temple of motherland', will not forget his moorings easily.

Various intellectual exercises strengthen one's conviction that only a united and disciplined Hindu society can take care of its ills that can result in all round growth of the society and country. Lessons of history taught to the members stress the fact that Hindu civilization faced reverses primarily because the society was not united, people fought about petty issues and differences, and withdrew into a shell under assaults from outsiders rather than face them unitedly. Since, 80 per cent of the Indian society is Hindu, unless it takes care of its ills, its divisions and subdivisions, and stands united one cannot dream of a prosperous India. The focus through all this exercise is more inward looking to understand weaknesses of Hindu society rather than find scapegoats for its decline. In these sessions it is explained that if foreign invaders have weakened this country and corrupted its systems, it is a historic fact that it was allowed to happen by a disunited Hindu society. Similarly, if caste system weakens Hindu society, it alone can correct this historic distortion of its social structure.

Many prachaaraks have been great thinkers and analysts. Their understanding of the Indian society is astounding. I have heard some of the most perceptive and dispassionate analysis of social issues that confront Hindu society from such thinkers. Generally, the approach is not to get into confrontationist barren arguments or debates, but concentrate on an inclusive approach to all. Interestingly, highly revered Guruji M S Golwalkar, the second RSS chief who built up the RSS over his 33 years of stewardship from a young fledgling organization to an all India powerhouse drew attention to the limitations of intellectualism, pointing out that you may score some debating points with a person who opposes you with intellectual debate but you cannot win him over. He himself was a towering intellectual who had a photographic memory and tremendous spiritual depth. He had, probably, cautioned his followers to be more concerned with actual work rather than get bogged down by fruitless debates. One of the favourite sayings of all the senior leaders is, "Every Hindu you meet is a prospective swayamsevak, so try not to antagonize him or her. Listen, even to your opponents with open heart and be ready to learn." We have seen many examples of such diehard opponents joining the RSS later on.

The most important part of regular intellectual, or rather mental, training is the prayer that is written in Sanskrit. It asks for Mother India's blessings so one can dedicate one's life for motherland's glory and prosperity. It reminds the participant that it is He who has chosen this difficult path of sacrifice for his society on his own volition so he seeks her blessings to make him strong to bear difficulties in his path with equanimity. Daily invocation to Motherland creates an emotional bond which clings to one's heart throughout life and always guides one's actions.

U R Anandmurthy has noted somewhere that Hindu militancy is more political than spiritual. Though, nearly all the RSS volunteers are religious and spiritual, I doubt if most of them perform regular rituals that go with visible Hindu practices. There is no training about Hindu rituals and practices or pressure to follow the so-called brahminical sanskaars, though the RSS is supposed to be a citadel of orthodoxy that is ready to take Indians to middle ages! Guruji was a saint in normal worldly clothing. He even carried the typical pitcher of a sadhu given by his guru, and followed regular rituals of pooja, meditation etc. But he would admonish people that putting tilak on forehead, reciting shlokas or Geeta blindly and garlanding the statue of your god is not true religiosity or spiritualism. To him, all this was of no use, if the person did not take care of his fellow human beings and society. For him patriotism, surrender of self for motherland and service to fellow human beings were the highest form of spiritualism.

Remembering National Heroes Regularly

For a person to feel inspired or motivated, he needs a role model. It is important that he thinks positive and works in any adverse circumstance. To keep up this spirit of nationalism and selfless work, the RSS through its shakha programmes, reminds volunteers about various great personalities that Mother India has produced.

'Bharat Bhakti Stotram' which is also called 'Ekaatmataa Stotram' – a hymn of national integration – is a virtual roll of honour that recalls all such great sons and daughters of India, starting from Vedic to contemporary times. They include ancient sages like Valmiki and Ved Vyas, the mathematicians and scientists from antiquity to modern time like Bhaaskaracharya, Charak and J C Bose, inspiring women like Gargi, Laxmibai and Channama, patriots and freedom fighters like Gandhi, Dr Ambedkar and Bhagat Singh, holy places of pilgrimage, our rivers and mountains etc. Famous poet Ras Khan also finds a pride of place in this recitation. It is recited every day in some shakhas or periodically in some. A volunteer is encouraged to recite it every day to get inspiration from these personalities and the greatness of this land. Enlarged version of this set of shlokas in form of booklets also gives brief information about these personalities and places and their significance.

The personalities that generally adorn the stage during a programme are Shivaji, Rana Pratap and Guru Gobind Singh. All three dedicated their lives to fight for Hindu dharma and protect it. Though stories are recounted about various great personalities to impress upon the young members the contribution countless great sons and daughters of India made for its progress, these three occupy the pride of place.

The person most quoted is Swami Vivekanand, who revived Hinduism at a critical juncture in history and gave it a modern perspective. He exhorted thus, "Too much of inactivity, too much of weakness, too much of hypnotism, has been and is upon our race. O' ye modern Hindus, de-hypnotize yourselves." Swami Vivekanand can be considered the pioneer of Hindu missionary work. His Guru Swami Ramakrishna Paramhamsa saw God in every poor and he called the poor - 'Daridranaaraayan'.

Sowing the Seeds of Leadership

The earliest responsibility that a young person is entrusted by the time he reaches his teens is to be a 'gat naayak' or a group leader. This group could be staying in the same area, or it could be from similar age group, but never on linguistic or income basis. From these early days of life he is supposed to bring this team to shakha every day, lead it in shakha activities, visit homes of its members, talk to their parents, ask about their studies – in general be their coordinator and lead member, at an age when other boys simply enjoy their funs and games.

There could be another person planning and executing games in the shakha while someone could concentrate on learning and singing patriotic songs, reciting the daily prayer and training others for it. A senior member may be asked to do some study and present a talk on some social issue or even narrate some instructive story to the members of that shakha. A person may be given a temporary responsibility of managing a picnic. So, you are being groomed as a disciplined team leader, in a very unobtrusive way, who can handle multidisciplinary activities naturally. And this is just a beginning.

As a member matures, he would be asked to be in-charge of a shakha as mukhya shikshak (chief instructor or teacher) or kaaryavaah (secretary) who looks after the whole group and is the guardian for all the members of that shakha. Mukhya shikshak is in-charge of physical education, games etc. while kaaryavaah is expected to guide all the team leaders and also attend meeting with other volunteers of other shakhas in the vicinity for planning programmes. The two together are responsible for running the shakha.

Unity through Purpose

The secret of unity in an organization is unity of purpose. An ingrained respect for consensus based decision making comes to every volunteer through his experience in the organization. Right from the day a young volunteer starts attending a meeting in the RSS, he experiences consensus building. I have seen real hot-heads who could easily lose temper on minutest things, finally calming down and coming to a common decision. This decision making is also tempered with respect for seniority in the hierarchy as an organizational discipline.

You find a 50 year old saluting a young instructor half his age. In fact, sometimes it may happen that a father could be saluting his son, or a teacher in school saluting his student in shakha. There are jokes abound in shakhas about a son getting more respect than the father because he happens to be a responsible member of the RSS. This training through simple acts in shakha results in respect for any person who has been given responsibility and who holds a higher post in the organization. Since, nobody is promoted out of favour or fear, members respect the authority and not the individual representing that authority. This mutual respect for each other and admiration for the work a person is doing filters down to a vibrant consensus based decision making process.

Though, this style of working leads to delays many a time and many activists crib about it, this is a small price that an organization has to pay to take everybody along. Once in a while, many impatient members complain that there are too many meetings and less action. But, this is a hallmark of the RSS way of working, for better or worse.

We had a very senior activist, Rajabhau, in our local district level team that I headed. He is still active at 85. At that time, he might have been nearly two and half times my age. He had been a full time worker (prachaarak) in his youth and a very accomplished activist. He could do handstand and walk on hands even till the age of sixty-five. His neat notings in his diary and follow ups, his relentless social work over and above shakha work even at his advanced age, his own databank maintenance would be a lesson for anybody in running an organization. One tough and emotionally draining social work he keeps doing year on year without fail since the age of 16 is to guide a family about various funeral rites whenever he gets to know of a death. I believe he may have guided thousands of such unfortunate families in their hour of distress. Such a Rajabhau would put forth his views very strongly in meetings. If they were overruled by others or me, so be it. There would be heated arguments too. But, after the meeting was over, he would come to me and pat my back, saying, "Son, very good. You are doing a great job!" I have not seen such dispassionate and objective working in any other organization that is basically fuelled by passionate hearts inspired by philosophy of personal sacrifice.

Respect for Honest Work

One important lesson I learnt in the RSS was to always respect a person if he is performing genuine work, regardless of the ideological background of that person. This is the reason an RSS worker can cooperate and work with any organization or person if situation demands. There is no concept of any kind of 'intellectual or organizational untouchability' that plagues many of our social organizations. The RSS workers are asked to interact with local social organizations and good social workers regularly and have good relations with them. The open discussions that take place in meetings also encourage one to keep an open mind for different way of thinking. Having interacted with extreme left to centrist and socialists, I dare say that they are more fundamentalist in their beliefs and closed to hearing other ideas than a Sangh activist. They shy away from any interaction for the fear of being stained by saffron!

Even a leader of the stature of late Jai Prakash Narayan had to be persuaded very hard by a person like Sitaram Goel to meet the RSS leaders and attend an the RSS programme late in life due to his biased mindset built over years. But, after attending one such meeting, his apprehensions were totally allayed and he was all praise for the RSS and its members. During his interaction with the RSS volunteers in one such programme in 1977 he said, "The RSS is a revolutionary organization. No other organization in the country comes anywhere near it. It alone has the capacity to transform society, end casteism and wipe the tears from the eyes of the poor." He further added "I have great expectations from this revolutionary organization that has taken up the challenge of creating a new India." It is his greatness that he admitted to his earlier unfounded bias and also like a true Gandhian changed his views with courage, at the risk of being ridiculed by his erstwhile colleagues.

Bringing the Best Out of a Person

Personality development and character building through all these activities happens effortlessly, unconsciously. One learns to sing, give speech, discuss issues, work together, relate to and talk with people at various levels in age, social status or education. In a few years, he comes out a better person from this system with a well-honed personality. Traditional Indian values like respect for womanhood, holy men, elders etc. are ingrained by the atmosphere, visits to each others' homes and various lectures and examples given during shakha. "Let us not forget character building in this new pious era of reconstruction, let us not forget about the upliftment of mother earth in this mad rush of self aggrandizement", says one of the Sangh songs.

I have seen keen students from socially and economically deprived strata being trained lovingly by their more fortunate friends and senior colleagues going on to become successful engineers and doctors. I recall young friends like Manik and Deepak who rose from slums and went on to become engineer and accountant and leading a much better life today. Some have become successful political leaders. I have seen the son of a humble so-called low caste tailor, Ramesh Patange, who used to be our senior in shakha in a neighbouring area and secretary of a much larger area later, maturing into a leading thinker and writer. I had a young school going colleague deputed as my junior for running a shakha. It turned out that he was a compulsive liar and also indulged in petty thefts once in a while. He generally cleared his examinations in second attempt. His family was fed up of him. To my surprise, he not only gave up such practices within months of taking up new responsibilities, but also managed to clear all his subsequent classes in single attempts without a single lecture from me. It just happened!

There is a Marathi proverb which is repeated often, lest an activist forgets it - "Accept a person as he is and mould him into what you want him to be." A great lesson for any human resource manager too. It is easier said than done, but I have seen large number of lives being moulded this way. Daily renewal of his faith, his social commitment is the cause célèbre of shakha.

Many successful business people, like Shri Rameshwarlal Kabra, Chairman of RR Kabel ascribe their success in business and social life to the art of recognizing a person's abilities and his character through the practical experience they had gained in meeting and handling various kind of people in their days in shakha. Dr Ravindra Khedekar in Mumbai, a renowned orthopedic surgeon always credits his rise from a very average student to a successful surgeon, without falling into the trap that many people fall to rise fast in the profession, to his training in the Sangh. In his long career, he has never charged fee from any RSS volunteer, his friend or his family, whatever the pressure from the beneficiary. A person like Dr. Vinay Sahasrabuddhe has risen from a typical middle class family to be a prachaarak of ABVP and now heads Rambhau Mhalgi Prabodhini, never ever taking advantage or boasting of his close relations with high and mighty in political arena. I am talking of examples around me. Needless to say, at all India level, such examples would multiply in thousands and if compiled, could lead to volumes of print.

Simply put, it is all about simple living and high thinking, following high values and traditions. All efforts are to build character of the swayamsevaks or volunteers through easy to absorb ideas. These values imbibed in the years in shakha are so strongly embedded in one's heart and mind that a person that has come out of this system will sooner or later come back to his roots and beliefs, and devote his energies for nation building.

Moropant Pingley, one of the earliest prachaaraks, a remarkable organizer with keen understanding of Hindu society's psyche and one of the senior most ideologues used to conduct 'laugh a minute' kind of meetings He used to say, "Work of the RSS is serious but we must do it light heartedly, full of laughter."

Thus, this humble shakha is the training ground for future social leaders who can take up any job with natural ease and is the powerhouse of the RSS. All this happens in open grounds without any bamboo curtains or secrecy. Reading about this man making programme run through the shakhas of the RSS, you would agree that my friend was not too far off the mark when he suggested that a well trained the RSS worker could easily qualify for Social MBA.

❑

7

Supremacy of Mission over Self

Right from his entry into the RSS fold through a shakha, each volunteer or swayamsevak has clear understanding that the mission and the organization are bigger than the individual. And, that nation is bigger than the organization. Work is organization oriented, not person oriented. This message comes through time and again in meetings, decision making and conduct of individuals.

There was a camp a few years ago. A senior activist and head of a Juhu area, Vasudev Valecha, a successful industrialist and also a major supporter for local organizations in many ways, was to participate in the camp. He came one hour late due to a traffic jam while he rushed from the airport. He was disallowed entry. His junior colleague went to the seniormost incharge of the camp, Bhaskar Rao, and requested him to make an exception for this gentleman, trying to buttress his argument by mentioning his dedication and benevolence etc. etc. He was unmoved, saying, "How does it matter? Discipline is discipline", and Valecha ji was sent back. To top it all, he returned back all the way back to city without raising a ruckus and never did he complain about this incident, but went on working with full energy till his last breath.

There are such examples at all levels. The activist is trained throughout to sublimate his ego for higher goal of nation building for which organization is the medium. It is not easy to ingrain this state of 'egolessness' or genuine humility in an age when even the friend's friend of a nephew of a municipal corporator can threaten a policeman on duty with "don't you know who am I?" I know of friends like Milind and Ravi who gave prime 4–5 years of their lives to RSS work and are on backslapping terms with many ministers, but are back to their humble lifestyle and keep on working selflessly for the society, not expecting anything for the years devoted for nation building. This overall simplicity and humility of the activists from young to old is a humbling experience for any person.

When the ego of a manager becomes bigger than the purpose of the organization, even commercial organizations fail or suffer badly. Case of Lehman Brothers is too new to be recounted here. The ego of the CEO in not agreeing to terms of rescue of the beleaguered corporation led to the collapse of not only Lehman but the whole financial system of the US, leading to an unforeseen major global disaster.

Social organizations split or become dysfunctional because of this curse. Ego is further boosted by propaganda or personality promotion. This is the reason why the RSS people shun propaganda and media consciously. Though, this has affected its image as its critics' comments have gone unchallenged, it has also resulted in sustained growth of organization, human resources and a sense of joyful brotherhood which is envy of its critics.

Subsuming One's Personal Choices to Organizational Goal

I have seen people giving up on their pet hobbies due to their preoccupation for a responsibility the RSS has given to them. I can cite endless anecdotes about such change in a person's priorities. I will just recount one interesting story. A renowned art director of Raj Kapoor era, Shanti Dev tells us that he refused to go to shakha in Lucknow as it clashed with his flute classes. One day his prachaarak late Deendayal Upadhyay jokingly told him, "Shanti, don't listen to your shikshak and carry on with your music lessons. After all, when the country is on fire, you can play your flute!" This was prior to independence. Young Shanti dropped his flute lessons from that very day and resumed his attendance in shakha.

Most of the prachaaraks, generally, have great academic credentials and could have been great professionals had they not given up these worldly pursuits. Many a talent of senior activists are subdued towards the greater goal. There are very few exceptions to this philosophy and such people have done very well in the fields they have gone in. I can talk of late Sudhir Phadke, a highly respected music director and singer from Maharashtra as an example. Though, I for one, do not agree with this approach. I believe that such talents should be allowed to grow and make a place for themselves in the society. Let them serve society in a different way. But, if such people heed to a higher calling, well I am in a minority! And one has to admit that unless there is focused devotion to nation building exercise and readiness to sacrifice self interest in any way, it is not an easy task. Call of a higher goal will ultimately override all other considerations.

A volunteer is reminded that service to motherland cannot be a 'time pass', to be taken up at a 'suitable free time'. Things will happen only when this service itself becomes the prime goal and every other pursuit is tailored to that end. An evocative the Sangh song reminds one that, "it is easy to be a moth and burn oneself over the glowing flame of love, but it is very difficult to be a lamp that burns self, atom by atom, to give light to others. Path to dedicated services is, indeed difficult."

I recall a gentleman, Vijay Swami, an engineer with a decent job and good life in Pune. He went to hear a talk by a prachaarak of Vivekanand Kendra. After hearing him talk about Arunachal Pradesh and Vivekanand Kendra's work there, he felt that there was a higher calling than the mundane life he was living. He left his job and went there. He is living there for more than a decade now and is more like a citizen there, working with locals, running schools, dispensaries etc. Now, he is heading a new project for a university there specializing in ancient traditions and tribal cultures.

Nurturing and Promoting Talent

One of the secrets behind sustained growth of the RSS as an organization is recognizing a talent and nurturing it. The promotion of a volunteer through the organizational ranks as an activist and a senior worker is strictly based on performance and his dedication. A senior activist (kaaryakartaa or worker) of a particular locality or region is supposed to keep a watch on the work being done by junior activists and recognize their talent on different parameters. The next job is to persuade that person to take up a responsibility. It is amusing that the RSS is the only organization where a promotion is dreaded by an activist! Reason is that he would have to work harder and dedicate more hours of his day-to-day life for this work.

Never in my experience, have I found a person being promoted due to his closeness to a senior. Nor have I found a deserving person being overlooked because of his social or economic status. Yes, there can be some mistakes when an unsuitable person is picked up. But, all concerned people understand that it is human to err. When something like this happens, the affected person jokes that "he was falsely accused of having a quality which he didn't possess!"

It is possible that a person may be given a responsibility sometimes because there is nobody better available at the time. But, it is striking that the person 'accused' of having a particular quality, then works hard to acquire that talent and deliver results. It doesn't surprise anybody when a physical instructor is promoted to be an intellectual trainer; or a good singer is entursted with food arrangements of a camp. The underlying lesson is that if a person has decided to dedicate a major part of his life for the organization and the society, he will surely work hard to acquire any talent that is required to fulfill his mission. This horizontal movement across the different disciplines is not very common in other organizations though there may be exceptions.

Shunning Organizational Politics

Sometimes, two people in a team don't see eye to eye on many issues, nor does their style of working match. They may have heated arguments during meetings which sometimes carry outside too. One is amazed when a worker proposes the name of the same person, with whom he has serious differences, for an important assignment. This is because he feels that he is best suited for that responsibility. I have gone through such moments myself. Organizational politics is firmly eschewed. As a Sangh poem says, "The ultimate goal of this path is not rising to higher positions of power."

There are cases where a person was removed from a post if he was found to be behaving in a way contrary to expectations from his position. The case of late Vasantrao Oke, prachaarak of Delhi during and after partition is well known in the Sangh lore. He was one of the most powerful public figures in those times. He had an imposing personality. But, when it was felt that his ego was getting better of him and he was treating himself as bigger than organization, he was transferred by Guruji, the then the RSS chief, to another position. He was so incensed that he resigned and left the organization. The reconciliation happened after decades.

According supremacy of organization and the mission, conquering personal ego for higher objective, promoting talent irrespective of personal likes and dislikes has led to a robust organization and a team of workers difficult to find in any other social organization. Shri Balasaheb Deoras in the third Sarsanghchaalak of the RSS, used to call swayamsevaks, 'Dev durlabh' team of workers, i.e., a team that even gods would find difficult build.

❑

8

Human Relations and Management Training

Beginning from the rank of a 'gat naayak' – group leader – a volunteer goes through HR and management training all through his working life in the organization at different levels. After all, RSS is built on 'Human Relations' in the purest sense of the term. The young volunteer gets the basic lessons in interpersonal skills, communications and also dealing people from diverse cultural backgrounds right from his first responsibility.

He learns to overcome his own personal likes and dislikes, even modify his basic personality traits to have better relations with people. He learns to work with people from diverse backgrounds. As he moves up the ladder of hierarchy, he learns more lessons. He learns to coordinate between different teams and work without bias and prejudice with different kinds of people.

How the human relations can be maintained through heartfelt but effortless behaviour is illustrated by an incident that was narrated by a budding singer Sanjay Pandit in 1980s. He was supposed to sing the main song during the valedictory function of a state level camp in Maharashtra held in Pune in 1983 with an attendance of 10,000+ volunteers. Naturally, he put in painstaking efforts for one of the most memorable events in his life with active help from a senior prachaarak, late Nanarao Dhobale. However, just a day before this event, a message came that Sudhir Phadke, highly respected music director and singer of Maharashtra, would be coming to the camp and be on stage in full uniform to sing the song. Naturally, since renowned swayamsevak had made time for this event, the seniors asked Sanjay to stand back. Sanjay was heartbroken, but as a swayamsevak he too understood the importance of the event and took it in his stride. Anybody else could have forgotten this small incident in such a massive three-day event, but, not Nanarao. Sanjay received a letter within a week from Nana, sharing his pain, apologizing to him for this last minute change and heartbreak that he must have felt, blessing him with a great future. Sanjay used to say that an incident that could have embittered his heart, turned him into a lifelong swayamsevak with this simple heart to heart communication.

Dr. Hedgewar, himself, was the best example about a person moulding his or her personality to suit his or her goals. He had a fiery temper that was a gift of his genes. The whole family was known for its temper. His testimony in the defence of his act as a satyagrahi in front of a British judge so alarmed the judge, that he said, "Your defence is more seditious than your speech!" But, once this Doctor decided to build an organization like the RSS, he changed himself so much that nobody ever heard him shout or lose his temper with anybody later in life. He could joke and play with people one-third his age and also work with the most respected leaders of those days in political and social arena. He spoke simply, without any flourish, but effectively as his words came directly from his heart.

This self-driven motivation for a mission leads one to modify one's own personality traits to work with other people. I was an introvert who would move to the other side of the road to avoid getting into some acquaintances just to avoid chatting. But, the compulsions of working with people led me to open up, force myself to talk to people and greet them even if it meant crossing over to the other side of the road.

Personality Development

A volunteer learns to recognize inherent skills in his colleagues and nurture them. As a swayamsevak becomes a kaaryakartaa (more active volunteer or activist), giving more time and energy to organizational work, he hones his skills further. From being a member of a local shakha he graduates to being a senior worker who handles the coordination of various activities of the RSS. He may look after physical training, intellectual training or special workshops, meet renowned people in his locality and so on. This interaction with people of varied backgrounds, sensing their problems or their likes and dislikes, taking them along, persuading them to work for a cause by dedicating his time and effort builds up his managerial and HR skills.

Purushottam, my friend who joined the RSS at a comparatively older college going age during emergency, was a typical carefree young man playing street cricket, getting into arguments or street brawls; having a team of friends who would play and gossip at street corners. Once, he plunged into Akhil Bharatiya Vidyarthi Parishad work (ABVP was not banned during emergency) and later became its prachaarak, his transformation was amazing. Initially, it was not easy for him, he admits. But, as he settled down, his skills were channelized into aggressive but disciplined act of organizing students, meetings and networking with teachers, professionals and industrialists, and generally being helpful to people. His same skills made him a successful businessman. I rate him as one of the best PR man today in our circles.

A highly respected teacher, Prof. Mohanrao Apte, is another name that I can recall with awe for his sheer energy and a great eye for talent. He may have brought in more young people into social arena right from national level to local level on the strength of his inspirational personality. He finds time to write highly researched books on foreign affairs, defence and science inspite of being busy on field with his students with something or the other. Such is his impatience with any kind of lethargy that all his students humorously recall his oft used word, "useless" for anybody, any activity that drops in pace.

The most difficult part of working for an organization which has nothing to offer but, on the contrary, which demands more out of you in terms of time, efforts and even money; is to motivate people to work harder for a cause that doesn't offer any personal rewards in any way. To motivate people to do something in which there is no self interest is the biggest challenge a volunteer faces and this changes his whole perspective about life, people and work. Anybody in social field will vouch for this. He learns these persuasive skills as he learns to manage people.

Immaculate Planning

Apart from regular shakhas, there are other programmes like six regular Hindu festivals that are celebrated with much more organized effort, with larger numbers of the Sangh volunteers and members of public. There are occasional local or regional programmes that don't fall under these six all India festivals, say a picnic, a social gathering for a lecture, organizing sports events from different shakhas or a larger territory, organizing workshops, being part of a team that organizes camps. This camp arrangement can mean putting up tents, surfacing the playground, organizing the space for different units of volunteers, plumbing, electrical job, looking after kitchen including cooking, cleaning of utensils, preparing for intellectual and physical programmes or even digging ditches for toilets.

A young member who is graduating to be a worker, or kaaryakartaa in the RSS terminology, finds it extremely exasperating the way his seniors pore over each and every detail of a programme or an event, delegating the smallest to critical responsibilities to different team members as well as work out a backup procedure. No detail is too small for the seniors. Right from the arrangement of flowers, flag, chairs, lights, sound to taking care of chappals – nothing is left out. While working on the book, I met a very senior activist. He took out an old sheet of paper casually from his carefully maintained files with minute detailing of the arrangement to be made for a RSS festival (utsav). This detailed arrangement is called 'vyavasthaa' in the RSS parlance. The senior colleague or co-worker guides the organizer of any programme to chalk out details of each programme from start to finish, each person told about his role diligently.

The effect of all these exercises can be seen in everything a volunteer does. I was wonderstruck when I was shown the stores management of a huge relief camp by a young man, who seemed to be hardly a school pass out, after Gujarat earthquake in Raandhanpur in Kutch. Same approach is true of every event or programme a swayamsevak manages. More a worker rises in ranks, more people he is supposed to interact with. It is not a surprise that an RSS trained person can organize any programme in a very systematic way and with a calm efficiency as if he were trained in it. Having organized so many events, he becomes an effortless event manager who takes up such jobs as a fish takes to water, whatever be the situation.

This immaculate planning is the hallmark of 'RSS School of Management'. Naturally, you hardly find any press coverage of the RSS programmes as there are no gaffes, no stampedes, no scuffles, nor complaints of leaders coming late or programme stretching beyond yawns and disorder! Our media, afterall, is trained only to report negative news.

Consensus Based Decisions

All decisions in the RSS are taken through consensus, even the election of the General Secretary at the top is based on consensus. One wonders how come this 85 year old organization has not split even once, contrary to Indian traditions of a social organization. In a lighter vein, one can say that till RSS launched its mission of uniting Hindu society, four Hindus would look in the same direction only when the fifth one was on their shoulders! In our young times, the joke on Socialist groups used to be that three socialists can have four opinions and they can split like amoeba.

Normally, each activist or worker having a record of selfless public service should have ego which should be more than that of a housing society secretary or local social worker. Since he is under nobody's obligation and is entirely self-driven, there are more reasons for him not to listen to another colleague or senior. But, the RSS working ethos defy this conventional logic. This lack of personal ego is one reason why decisions can be taken with consensus.

The stress on consensus based decisions does not mean there is no democracy in the RSS. In fact, I have yet to come across a social organization which has more internal democracy than the RSS. But, it is tempered with an organizational culture – respect for consensus arrived through a very high majority in a given situation, with firm belief that no one in the discussion has a vested interest and that everybody is thinking and working for the society. There are heated debates and discussions that may end up in a unanimous decision or even being put on hold for lack of consensus.

A person brought up and trained in such an environment can definitely manage a group or a team of colleagues and bring them round to a consensus based decision where everybody feels that he is a part of it and that it is a win-win situation for all.

Evolution of a Manager

Thus, a swayamsevak or volunteer gradually gets involved in management, managing team and building teams right from his teenage years as he matures into an activist. He learns how to motivate his team members and get tasks done with a sense of joy. He is trained to identify a problem, study it and resolve it. He learns how to manage things by taking people together.

Review of the work done by each activist is done regularly in periodic meetings and also informally. Final review is once a year when he may either be asked to continue, or shifted to another responsibility based on the reading of the seniors about his talents or promoted to higher responsibilities.

Sanjay Hegde, founding director of a social service organization, Sewa Sahayog Foundation and Executive Director of Price Waterhouse Cooper India, attributes his rise from a humble village home in Goa to the select 'who-is-who' of the corporate world to the readiness for hard work, discipline and character he imbibed in the RSS and training he received in managing various jobs or duties given to him from time to time by his seniors in most trying personal and social circumstances.

This is the training that has produced a highly efficient administrator ministers like Nitin Gadkari who could build more bridges, flyovers and highways in five years than the Congress ministers could build in 50 years. This system produced chief ministers like Manohar Parrikar (Goa) who put a small state like Goa, known only as a beach destination till then, firmly on growth path through industrial development and by plugging loopholes in the system; Shivraj Singh Chauhan (M.P.), Dr. Raman Singh (Chhattisgarh) whose welfare schemes for lowest and neglected strata of society are being keenly watched and replicated by other states. Narendra Modi rose from a humble beginning as a canteen boy to be a prachaarak and then become a chief minister to launch so many innovative schemes for social and economic development that it has won him national and international accolade and governments from other states send their officers to study them. Media may deride and demonize him, but his hard work and vision have made him darling of the people. Atal Behari Vajpayee, one of the best and the most popular prime ministers of India, gave a vision to planners that resulted in National Highways network and rural road network schemes that changed the way men and material move in this vast country and gave new push to economic development in untouched areas. I recall that the so-called progressive economists had laughed derisively at Atalji's vision and called it a scheme for rich for which there would be no funds. Only an Atal Behari could explode the Bomb, face sanctions, motivate people including PIOs and NRIs to contribute liberally to India's funds to face those sanctions bravely and finally bring USA to a situation where it would look at India as a friend and an ally. All this happened because these fiercely proud nationalist people trained in this disciplined organization were close to people, to the society and have had a dream of a well-developed, prosperous India that they visualized everyday in simple shakhas where they smelt and rolled in Indian soil.

Probity in Public Life

An RSS volunteer, nearly always has a striking experience when he approaches people for any cause. It is the implicit faith people have in the Sangh and its volunteers about financial probity. Swayamsevaks are conditioned from day one to deal with each other in total faith. Each and every penny is accounted for very transparently. This habit is fortified further as a volunteer graduates to higher posts and takes up more responsibilities. The amounts may change over years but there is never a doubt that accounts will be handled scrupulously, with complete honesty.

When we used to go door to door to collect funds for various disaster relief programmes, people would openly say that they give funds to the RSS unquestioningly because they have full faith that money would be utilized properly. It would not be out of place to note that the share of administrative cost in percentage terms of any RSS run social service organizations is the lowest, or zero in many cases, as compared to other designated NGOs. From the beginning, an activist has been trained to spend out of his own pocket for any activity, right from refreshments to picnics and camps. So, it does not come easily to him to get his expenses reimbursed or spend lavishly on himself. He has been trained to be frugal with himself as well as the organization.

There is an instructive incident that I can't help sharing. Ram Ratna Vidya Mandir School was coming up in Keshav Srishti near Mumbai. Rajju Bhaiyya (Shri Rajendra Singh) was the chief of the RSS at that time. Since, he had laid the foundation stone of the school he would enquire about its progress whenever he visited Mumbai. He was told that the school would open in June 1997. But, on this occasion he was told by the concerned trust member that the committee had decided that the opening will be shifted to next year as there were some practical difficulties. Rajju Bhaiyya was highly perturbed. He gave an earful (in his own soft loving way) to the trustee on the importance of accounting of public money and its cost; which is not just interest on funds but the public trust in you about sticking to your promises. Naturally, trustees took the lesson to heart and worked very hard to start the school on a near impossible original schedule.

Lead by Example

One of the most important secrets behind the success of organizational management of the RSS is that a person is expected to lead by example. People listen to a person who puts into practice what he preaches. A person is not trained by mere talks, but with live examples of his leaders and colleagues. Respect in the organization is commanded by conduct and not demanded by position in the hierarchy.

One of my senior colleagues, Bimal Kedia took a conscious decision the very first day he joined his family business that he would devote only 8 hours out of the 24 hours of a day to business and nearly every other waking hour will go for the Sangh work. I have not seen this conduct change in 35 years that I have known him, come what may. In fact, the actual time contributed to business has only gone down over years. Even when the family demanded more from him to promote the booming business further since he was a qualified engineer as well as the best public face, he firmly refused. Such is his moral influence on his colleagues that nobody can say no to him, whatever responsibility he requests a person to take up.

Each and every teacher (shikshak) and prachaarak is a living model of this code of conduct. This is what makes an ordinary person into an extraordinary achiever in social field.

I am not convinced with the argument that today's generation is not motivated to do selfless service because it doesn't find role models in political or social leaders. One could find such role models around one's own homes or institutions if one were to look carefully. Media can also play a positive role by giving important place to such personalities in its coverage. We do not forget a very good teacher from our school days, or a social worker in our neighbourhood etc. afterall.

Before I close this chapter, I will talk of another instance of setting example with one's own conduct. Mr. Valecha, about whom I talked earlier also, decided not to move to the new plush bungalow in Juhu the family had built for all the brothers. He explained, "If I move into such a fancy home, my young friends from shakha from poor families may feel shy to come there. So, I better stay in my old flat." In earlier years, he had allowed Vidyanidhi School trust to run its initial classes from his garage and drawing room! I am deliberately quoting from my next door colleagues and friends so you realize that any ordinary person can become an extraordinary soul when he goes through the unobtrusively simple training through live the Sangh work.

I have noticed that cadre based organizations, be it RSS related ones or others, cannot retain all the brilliant members because they are too fast or too impatient for an average member. The RSS has generally been an exception though I have seen some such brilliant people drifting away. However, it is equally true that organizations are generally built by average and steady persons and not by a brilliant few. Building an organization requires patience of a farmer. Even Jim Collins, author of *From Good to Great,* has come to the conclusion that it is not brilliant individuals but the average steady hardworking guys who take the organizations to greatness. This unsung ability of the RSS style of working that brings out the extraordinary achievers out of ordinary individuals is the biggest source of its strength.

RSS Volunteers through the Eyes of a Management Theorist

Dr. Sadhana Satish Modh, whom I also know now as a managing committee member of the Sangh inspired Vidyanidhi group of educational institutions in Juhu in Mumbai, did her research for Ph D on *Understanding Human Response in Organizations: A Study of Rashtriya*

Swayamsevak Sangh with a Management Perspective. The research concept drew its inspiration from the theoretical work done by Dr S K Chakraborty (IIM, Calcutta) which provides a normative framework of Gunas (Satwic, Rajasic and Tamasic) in his book *Human Response in Organisations*. Her conversion from a research student to an active member of an RSS inspired educational institution was, to an extent, also the result of this study.

Her research was inspired by a study by celebrated management guru Peter Drucker on the famous international movement of scouts. Peter Drucker lists the reasons why one should study non-profit organisations for advancing knowledge in organization theories:

1. Non-profit sector is one of the largest influential factors in society,
2. Non-profit sector is growing at a much faster pace.
3. Effective endeavour of 'non-profit' is commitment to their management who is dedicated to "doing good".
4. As a rule, 'non-profits' are more money conscious than business enterprises but they do not base their strategy on money. They start with the performance of their mission.
5. Mission is one the most important parts of any non-profit organization. It has clear-cut implications for the work its members have to perform.

She says, "The RSS has over 140 frontal organisations and they are the front-runners in their respective fields... What keeps the saffron brotherhood together? The answer lies in the crucial fact that it has evolved a unique style of operation. When many organisations copied the western style of functioning, the RSS developed its own system, which is indigenous. Many may differ on the Sangh's world view and its solutions to problems but no one can question its organizational skills, ideological rectitude and unequaled discipline."

Her research questionnaire was designed after initial response to a pilot study with 25 selected RSS workers in Mumbai. Based on more inputs, the final questionnaire was sent to more than 1500 senior activists by mail in Madhya Pradesh and Mumbai; and 351 of these responded. The age group wise distribution from the received responses was 62 per cent between the age group of 26–55, 15 per cent below 25 and 23 per cent above 55 years. Similar care was also taken in distribution in terms of occupation.

Characteristics of the RSS Volunteer as per Data Analysis

Dr Modh had devised the questionnaire that would lead her to draw her conclusions objectively about the behaviour of an RSS worker at personal level and analyse his personality. For example,

Is the RSS worker, really, a devoted Hindu? Does he believe in doing Puja/Meditation? The RSS claims to work for uniting Hindus. It would be interesting to find out whether those who work for the RSS are Hindus, doing Puja or meditation regularly or just using this platform for some hidden agenda as the critics allege. It was found that almost 65.8 per cent of the RSS workers in the sample were religious by nature.

How dedicated is an RSS worker? One touchstone for a dedicated worker is how much time he dedicates to his social work. It came out that almost 47.8 per cent workers devoted more than two hours daily. Nearly 24 per cent said that they were able to do so sometimes. Quarter of the workers in the sample (28.2 per cent) found it difficult to devote so much time regularly.

Is the RSS activist a staunch 'Swadeshi'? Would he buy 'Swadeshi' products even if inferior in quality? More than half the workers in the sample (53 per cent) agreed that they would.

A Unique "Micro Unit Management" System: The Shakha

Dr Modh observes, "The RSS has evolved a management system where the smallest unit gets the maximum attention. The organization structure of the RSS is created in such a way that it facilitates the smooth running of a "Shakha". Even during its Annual General Meeting of 'Pratinidhi Sabha' the focus is on the number of shakhas, its average attendance and the issues associated with its functioning."

".....Various functions of Shakha are distributed, and for carrying them out there is an arrangement. There are no officers, there are office bearers ('kaaryakartaa' with responsibilities). Each responsibility is structured to carry out some task during Shakha hour. Bereft of that, all are equal, all are friends, all are brothers. This unique feeling of comradeship is the characteristic of the RSS and it is the outcome of the RSS methodology of running a Shakha."

Continuous Training for Teamwork and Leadership

Continuing with Dr Modh's analysis, "The RSS believes that there are no such things as 'leadership traits' or 'leadership characteristics'. May be, some people are better leaders than others. By and large, though, we are talking about skills of leadership that can be learnt by most of people. There are continuous programmes throughout the year which keep on honing the organizational skills of a Swayamsevak. There is also an opportunity for organic development of the RSS and its workers. When, the kaaryakartaa is going through planning and organizing such events, year after year, he keeps on acquiring leadership skills, without his knowledge."

Empirical Testing of Guna Framework

To me, the most interesting part of this research was analysis of the RSS workers on the parameters of Gunas to explain the human responses as expounded by Dr SK Chakraborty. These Gunas are: Dull (Tamas), Passionate (Rajas) and Balanced (Satwa). A classification of factors (obtained from factor analysis) was carried out by Dr. Modh based on prior characteristics of Gunas, that is: *(a)* Satwic Guna: commitment to mission and ethical; *(b)* Rajasic Guna: passionate, authoritarian, motivated and *(c)* Tamasic Guna: inflexible, indolent, distracted, disinterested.

She noted that that the RSS workers scored more than average on Satwic and Rajasic Guna variables and much less than average on Tamasic Guna variables. In conclusion, she says, an RSS worker can be called a "Satwo-Rajasic" type personality according to Guna theory.

Conclusions of the Study

To paraphrase her conclusions: "Philosophy of the RSS covers Hindu value system and the need to organize the entire Hindu society..... the RSS uses the synthesis of religious construct, Hinduism and Nationalism in its philosophy and has crystallized it as Hindutva." To my mind this use of religious construct is more close to Tilak who directly linked it to nationalism than Gandhi.

She believes that Dr Hedgewar's major achievement was that he succeeded in changing certain deep-rooted wrong conceptions in the people's mental makeup prevailing about social work at that time. She writes, "An ordinary person thinks that it is sufficient for him to provide some financial assistance to one or the other social cause, or when he has free time he should participate in social programmes. Majority of people would either keep themselves entirely unconcerned or are contented with only expressing sympathies. Dr. Hedgewar had designed and organised Shakha programmes to overcome such mental blocks about social activities and to unhesitatingly participate in them."

Importance of Mission

To quote Dr. Modh, "A non-profit organization exists for its mission. The mission of the RSS is to unite and rejuvenate Indian nation on the sound foundation of Dharma. This mission can be achieved by a strong and united Hindu society. Therefore, the RSS has undertaken the task of uniting the Hindus. Rejuvenation of the Hindu nation is in the interest of the whole humanity... From Dr. Hedgewar's time till today, Hindu Unity has been the sole, unfaltering mission of the RSS."

She concludes that "Lesson to be learnt by organizations is that the mission statement should be simple, clear and direct. A mission statement has to be operational, otherwise it is just good intentions. A mission statement has to focus on what the institution really is trying to do and then do it so that everybody in the organization can say; this is my contribution to the goal. The mission is forever; the goals are temporary."

❑

9

Organizational Structure

Physical structure

The RSS has a highly federal structure that is defined clearly in its constitution. Though the policies are controlled centrally, the execution of different ideas and plans is left to the regional, state or local level depending upon the scale of the plan.

An RSS volunteer is the basic cell of this huge network of the organization. A 'gat' or team is the smallest unit of operation in a shakha. Shakha is a complete local level unit by itself headed by a mukhya shikshak (chief instructor or teacher) and kaaryavaah (secretary).

Various shakhas are organized at the level of 'tehsil' in villages and 'mandal' that form part of a 'nagar' in case of urban areas. The next level is District (jilaa) level committees, followed by State (praant) and Region (kshetra). The final organizational block is Central Committee (Kendriya Kaaryakaarini) that is chosen from its Akhil Bharatiya Pratinidhi Sabha (All India Delegates Council) that is an elected body.

Organizational units from Tehsil or Mandal to Central level have Kaaryavaah (secretary) as the executive head of the team and in-charge of overall activities. The guide and philosopher at each level is 'Sanghchaalak' (closest you can call this post is, Chief of the RSS organization of a particular area). He is akin to Chairman of committee with high dignity but no constitutional executive power except the moral authority to persuade the team to take a certain view or help bring around consensus for a policy decision. He does not take part in day-to-day functioning or decision making of the organization; this falls under a kaaryavaah's domain. His most important role is to be like a guardian to all the volunteers and workers. He is the public face of the RSS in the locality. Sanghchaalak commands high respect and his word carries weight. Though, he does not have executive powers his word, as and when he puts it, is taken as final word about a matter.

Committees at all the levels have other members for physical training, intellectual training, social service, coordination for other associate organizations and a few other members assigned to some responsibility depending upon the size of the organization in that area.

Regular elections are held every three years for the central body where local delegates in different geographical regions vote for members to the national committee (pratinidhi sabha), and these members vote for the post of General Secretary (Sar Kaaryavaah). The delegates need to have a good record of organizational work to qualify as delegates. The post of Sarsanghchaalak (Chief of the RSS) is non-elective. As a convention and part of its accepted constitution he is nominated by his predecessor after due discussions with the most senior members of central committee (Kendriya kaaryakaarini). So, it is not a one man's decision though he carries the final responsibility of this nomination.

Resolutions passed in the Pratinidhi Sabha truly reflect the RSS views on various issues facing the nation and Hindu society at a given time. A serious student of the RSS should read these resolutions which are made public immediately and sent to media for publication. He or she will, then, be able to appreciate the clarity of thought and fiercely assertive views on various national and social issues which are guided more by long-term vision of a great nation rather than short-term political exigencies of the times. For example, the RSS opposed reorganization of states on linguistic lines as it could prove to be divisive though most political parties were in favour. It has supported any government wholeheartedly in case of any foreign aggression through resolutions and on ground. Similarly, the RSS has opposed inclusion of caste for the current census underway. I hope against hope that its fears about its fallout are proven incorrect.

Communications

A special feature of the RSS is that all its commands are in Sanskrit. The senior workers of the RSS who sat down to give a formal shape to day-to-day working of the RSS after a few years of its inception, decided to opt for Sanskrit to overcome the problem of multiplicity of languages all over countries. Sanskrit being the mother of all these languages was the ideal choice. It is a different matter that even this integral approach is a grudge point for its critics. Though, Hindi is the most spoken language, The RSS gives equal respect to all languages. This has resulted in a harmonious growth of the RSS and a sense of oneness between the volunteers of different regions.

There is a structured way a communication or an instruction passes from HQ to a local shakha or from a state level or district level to the local level organization. It is an unwritten protocol that any directive or information must pass through the designated hierarchy. There is no short cut from top to bottom or bottom to top.

There is formal and informal system of information sharing that flows both ways. This two-way flow of information and feedback helps organization and its leaders firmly grounded about social and political issues from local to national or international level.

Communications in any particular region generally happen in the local language. Even English is not abhorred where required. Patriotic songs that are sung in shakhas are either in Hindi or in the local language. There are a few Sanskrit songs also.

The daily prayer is in Sanskrit that is recited as the concluding activity of a shakha.

Personality Neutral Organization

A unique feature of the RSS is that the 'Guru' i.e. the supreme teacher of the RSS members is not a person. It is 'Bhagwaa dhwaj' or 'saffron flag' (like we see on the temples). Doctor Hedgewar realized through his long social career that no person can be perfect. A Guru has to be as perfect as possible. Even a perfect person can make mistakes and fall from grace. There are enough examples about such fall from grace right from Sage Vishwaamitra to modern times. The supreme guru needs to be above reproach. A human being as a Guru can also lead to personality cult and where a person becomes more important than the purpose.

The Guru must also reflect all the qualities that the organization wishes to imbibe and remind one of its lofty ideals. Considering all these factors, Dr. Hedgewar decided that 'Bhagwaa Dhwaj' should be the supreme teacher or the Guru of the RSS activists. It symbolizes all that is noble, all the qualities worth imbibing, glorious heritage of Bharat, spirit of sacrifice as well as courage. From time immemorial, this flag has had a pride of place in India, whether used on the chariot of various warriors since the times of *Mahabharat* to Swami Ramdas (Guru of Shivaji) and worn by great saints from ancient times to current times. Most inspiring of these in modern times is Swami Vivekanand, named 'the Saffron Monk from India' by the mesmerized Americans. Saffron reminds one of all that is great and noble about this country. In that sense, 'saffronization' of country is a desirable objective!

This far-sighted idea of Doctor Hedgewar has stood the test of time. Every time its illustrious leader passes away, press and critics write obituary of the RSS. But, organization keeps growing irrespective of the person who heads the organization. The activist is so clear about his mission that it doesn't matter who is heading the organization. If he has a problem with any pronouncement of the chief, he will criticize or crib or talk to his seniors or colleagues, but will keep working nonetheless, knowing that mission is bigger than any person. No person is bigger than the organization or the ideology.

Self-Financing of the Organization – Guru Dakshina

The RSS has a unique system of financing the activities of the organization at all levels of operations. It has been criticized and targeted for legal action many a time by many governments that are envious of the smooth working of the organization. It is the only organization which has not asked for donations or grants to run its organization in its more than eight decades of existence. It is the only organization where members spend out of their pocket to enjoy any activity or face any hardship of winter camps or training camps and even social work. For any activity, the members contribute the moneys themselves, 'going Dutch' as we would say in today's parlance. If a member cannot pay for his camp fee, another member may help him out without any other people in the group knowing about it. It is like a family.

There is an annual function (or festival or utsav) named 'Guru Poojan and Guru Dakshina' (worshipping the Guru) which takes place on the auspicious occasion of 'Guru Purnima' a festival dedicated to worshipping and expressing one's gratitude to one's teachers and is celebrated all over India since time immemorial. In this programme, all the members bow before the Guru – Bhagwaa Dhwaj, offer flowers and dedicate their own contribution for the organization in an unmarked envelope. There is no discussion afterwards about who donated what amount. There is no distinction between a rich and poor member; nor are the organizational posts offered on the basis of one's financial clout or this once a year contribution. This contribution is deposited with the local branch and is used for various activities of the RSS and sometimes offered for some other activities where there is requirement. It is also used to support the 'prachaarak' who works in that area. Thus, the RSS is a totally self-financed organization.

Training Camps and Workshops

There are annual winter camps of two to three days for all the volunteers – from as old as 10 years to as young as 80 years.

Participants in these camps are supposed to be members who attend shakhas regularly. These camps have physical as well as intellectual sessions. These are intensive, highly exhausting and physically challenging camps which act as refresher courses and renew the energies of hundreds of volunteers who come together. This coming together of similar minds creates very positive vibes for the attendees. The atmosphere is of military-like discipline with similar command structure and creates an exhilarating experience, even though facilities are very sparse.

There are monthly or periodic workshops for the budding activists and young workers who have taken some responsibility already. They generally take place on weekends and are conducted at local level, tehsil or district level, depending on circumstances and organizational strength in the area. These have emphasis on skill enhancement in dealing with people and situations, intellectual training and physical drills.

Sangh Shikshaa Varg

The most important training that an activist goes through is the Sangh Shikshaa Varg (or the Sangh Training Workshop). These used to be called OTC (Officers' Training Camp) in earlier days. These workshops are conducted in summers and last for four weeks. They are held, generally, at state level as making various arrangements for such a long period is not an easy task nor is it easy to get training faculty for nearly one month. The whole physical and intellectual training faculty is voluntary. People take special leaves to attend or contribute to arrangements (called prabandhaks) or as instructors. I know of a volunteer, Apte ji who left for one such camp on the very next day of his marriage!

The participants need to qualify for training camp through a primary training workshop of one week which takes place once a year at state or district level. The attendee also needs to have some responsibility within the organization i.e. he should be an office bearer. There is also age bar and young activists below 16 years are not allowed as the person needs to be mature enough, and also because they are very strenuous.

The training is done over three such summer camps. They are called Pratham varsh (first year), Dwiteey varsh (second year) and Triteey varsh (Third year). The final training or third year training is conducted centrally at Nagpur. This is the ultimate qualification for an activist, referred to, in lighter vein, as postgraduation.

For all these workshops, the physical instructors are supposed to be third year trained activists and intellectual training sessions are generally conducted by senior workers and prachaaraks. The senior all India office bearers or prachaaraks travel relentlessly for at least two months as the training camps have to match with local summer vacations of colleges, making it necessary to spread them over this period. These camps are very challenging with very tough time-table. The sessions are divided into physical activities and lectures with discussions. The mornings and evenings consist of tough physical regime while the balance part of the day is devoted to intellectual training.

Activists who attend these one month camps or workshops remember them long after passing out. Even the duration of one month is not easy for the members of a family as one has to manage vacations and sacrifice all the fun of holidays. The very fact that not many people go beyond first year underlines this difficulty in managing to make time for it. People who come for third year are, of course, very well seasoned. The third year being central, meeting people of all regions right from Kerala to Bengal and Jammu to Gujarat is an experience itself. People who reach this stage are said to cherish this experience through life. For people who come from outside Nagpur, it is like a pilgrimage to visit the place of its birth and place of birth of its founder.

Thus, the image that blind critics of the Sangh create - that of lumpen elements, riotous mobs and blood-thirsty fanatics is far removed from the reality of enlightened, highly trained, dedicated, selfless activists who sacrifice their most loved interests to work for the society, their motherland. By virtue of this kind of training over years, they can never be irresponsible street fighters or ruffians.

I have already explained the working of shakha which is the basic building block of this humungous organization. It is through whole lot of activities that the future managers and activists are trained in all aspects of organization, management, creating and sustaining networks besides being trained in personal values of integrity, patriotism, spirit of sacrifice, selfless service to the society and burning urge to be ever ready to offer one's service to the nation in any capacity.

The RSS is a self running machine powered by selfless citizens, and is a powerhouse for all the activities of nation building.

❑

10

Inculcating Values and Sense of Nationhood through Festivals

Doctor Hedgewar, the founder, had a different view about celebrating festivals. He chose festivals that carried some message for the activist and the society. The RSS celebrates six festivals through a Hindu calendar year. They are -

1. Varsh Pratipadaa
2. Hindu Saamraajya Din
3. Guru Poojan
4. Raksha Bandhan
5. Vijayaadashamee
6. Makar Sankraman

I will elaborate a little about all these celebrations and the thought behind each.

1. **Varsh Pratipadaa** - This is the first day of most widely accepted Hindu new year and based on 'Shaalivahan Shak'. It falls generally in the second week of April and called 'Gudi Padwaa' in Maharashtra. The festival is celebrated in most parts of the country in different names. It is now a well-established fact that the calculations of Hindu calendar based on astronomy are most scientific and accurate. Celebrating this day also connects it to your own ancient civilization which is one of the oldest living civilizations in the world.

   To the RSS volunteers this day has another emotional pull too. The founder of the RSS Dr Hedgewar was born on this day. The festival begins with a special salute in the memory of its founder.

   Since it is the beginning of the new year. new organizational set up, new postings and new responsibilities are declared on this day in the RSS. Handing over to the new team begins on this day.

This day is being slowly adopted by Hindu society in general all over India with large rallies and festivities greeting this day. An RSS inspired organization 'Sanskaar Bharat' has played a great role in popularizing this festival at social level all over India.

2. **Hindu Saamraajya Din** – This day commemorates the coronation of Shivaji, the most celebrated of Hindu kings who fought against all odds with limited resources at his command through direct and guerilla warfare. In the dark gloom of Mughal era when the Hindu society had gone into a shell believing that the only way to survive is to live a peaceful life, not bothering about the society and dharma. Power of Aurangzeb was at its peak and Hindus saw no hope of deliverance from his atrocities. At that time Shivaji rose to declare, "Hindavi swaraajya whaave – hee Shreenchi ichchaa", meaning , "Let there be a free Hindu empire, this is the will of Supreme God." In that atmosphere of gloom, he had the courage to break out of shackles of slavery. He was the first Hindu to declare a kingdom based on Hindu tenets. In terms of size it was not a very large kingdom. But, Shivaji was the one who rekindled the spirit of bravery in the hearts of Hindus and showed that it is possible to fight back and get back independence. Subsequent Maratha kings could reach the gates of Delhi. This is the greatness of Shivaji.

   It is the tragedy of our so-called secular polity that he has been reduced to a Maratha chieftain, thus pulling him down from the pedestal of a national hero, putting him in a smaller straitjacket of a cast-based hero and dwarfing his personality.

   The RSS chose this date to awaken the spirit of bravery and self-confidence. It may be underlined that RSS does not celebrate the birthday of any personality as its festival. Because it believes that the work done by an individual is greater than that individual. Thus, members of the RSS may celebrate Shivaji jayanti along with other citizens and participate in it, but the RSS considers his coronation as a more defining moment of his inspiring life and in the life of this nation.

3. **Guru Poojan** – I have already noted the philosophy behind this festival earlier on. It is important to note that the volunteer is not only supposed to sacrifice his money for the cause, but his other resources too. There is much used term in Hindi – "Tan, Man, Dhan" i.e. serve your motherland wholeheartedly with Body, Soul and Material resources. This festival is the day when a volunteer renews his pledge to serve the motherland and society with all means at his command. Status of a person in the organization is decided by the contribution he makes in all the

three aspects, and not by his monetary contribution. It is the most solemn festival of all. A volunteer may bunk daily shakha, may not attend other festivals, but he makes it a point to be present for this festival come what may, indicating the strong sense of dedication that this day invokes.

4. **Raksha Bandhan** - We all know that Hindu society is divided into as many parts as we can think of – be it caste, religion, social or class etc. The lack of unity and spirit of brotherhood is the bane of this society. Raksha Bandhan is a traditional festival in which a weaker person would tie the 'thread of brotherhood' or 'raksha bandhan' to the stronger person to seek his support or protection. So, a priest would tie it to his host, citizens to their soldiers, a sister to her brother etc. In fact, the first known story about Rakhi talks of Indraani, wife of mythical god of heavens – Indra, tying the thread on Indra's wrists. Though the festival has become more of a family function between brother and sister in recent times, the RSS has chosen this festival to send forth the message of universal brotherhood. On this day, volunteers not only tie this sacred thread of unity and brotherhood to each other but also go out to tie it to members of the society and reach out to under privileged sections of the society too. Thus, it becomes a social festival to spread the message of brotherhood and social amity at all levels.

5. **Vijayaadashamee** – We all recognize this festival as the day that celebrates the victory of good over evil. It is a festival that by its very name celebrates the spirit of triumph and bravery. It is the day when Hindus worship arms and workers worship their tools of production since centuries. The RSS has adopted this tradition and worships arms (shastra pooja) on this day. It is a day to rekindle the spirit of bravery and fortitude by remembering the fight that Lord Rama put up against Raavana with hardly any resources that could be compared with those of Raavana. We also remember that Rama was able to achieve this remarkable victory with the help of his tribal friends and unarmed forces of monkeys. It was a remarkable job of social organization.

   There is another significance of this day. This is the 'foundation day' of the RSS. The RSS was established on the Vijayaadashamee day in the year 1925. So, it is the festival when the RSS takes out a parade in public in full uniform all over India with its martial music band. On this day, the Sarsanghchaalak or the RSS chief is always present in the traditional parade in Nagpur, its headquarters and the place where this movement came into being. The RSS chief is not known for giving too many interviews or press statements, so this address to the volunteers all over

India at the end of the parade is supposed to give an indication about the RSS policies. Thus, his annual address is much awaited event for media and socio-political analysists too.

6. **Makar Sankraman -** This is a day celebrated throughout India under various names. It is the day when Sun enters North Solstice. It is the day, when the nature, and with her, the people throw off the inertia of winters to become active again with change in the season for the better. It is a festival that celebrates revival of activity in every aspect. Thus, it has a message for the whole society.

   In Maharashtra there is another custom linked with this day. People exchange sweets made of sesame seeds (til) and jaggery (gul/gud). At this time they greet each other with "til gul ghyaa aani gode gode bola", meaning, let us exchange this sweet and speak sweetly with each other. Thus, there is a message of social amity and sweet relations in this exchange.

   Since, it is the last festival of the calendar year, it is also the time within the RSS when stocktaking or peer review begins informally that would result in new responsibilities and postings, re-organization of certain activities etc. at the time of new Hindu year.

You will note that conventional Hindu festivals like Diwali and Holi do not appear in this official list of festivals. You will also find that all the six festivals have some social significance and some message. A few of the festivals are inward looking for the organization and the activist, while most others are outward looking and meant to reach out to the members of the society with some message.

It goes without saying that all the activists celebrate all other festivals as per their geographical and local norms and traditions with full gusto and local shakhas also take part in arrangements of many such festivities in their own areas. For example, our shakha used to look after the arrangements on the day of 'Mahaashivraatri' in the temple which was in the compound where our shakha used to be held. It used to be a day of very heavy rush and our job was to regulate crowds throughout the day. The reward we used to get was 'naashtaa' or snacks from the pujari at the end of the grueling day!

❑

11

Institution of Prachaarak

Prachaarak system is a unique institution within the RSS. A Prachaarak is a full time volunteer of the RSS. He receives no salary or honorarium. So, he is different from the full-time paid workers of other social or political organizations. He stays in the RSS offices (called kaaryaalay in the RSS terminology) or sometimes at sympathisers' homes where there is no office. He lives within very simple and bare necessities of life and leads the life of a celibate or brahmachaari. Though he lives amongst families and in society as a normal worldly being (grihasthi), he is a sanyasi or monk for all practical purposes. There are some exceptional cases where a person returned to normal family and professional life but, again, went on to work full-time for the Sangh like any prachaarak.

This system of offering oneself for some years or for entire life for the nation was initiated during the times of Dr Hedgewar, the founder of the RSS, and subsequently nurtured with care and love by Guruji who, more or less, created its institutional norms. The first batch of foot soldiers of Dr Hedgewar comprised students who had passed school and were about to join college. He asked each of his good students to go to different colleges in different states to study there and work for the Sangh there. Though they were not designated prachaaraks, officially. At that time, most of them became prachaaraks subsequently after completing their studies and created the foundation of this system. Credit of initiating the second RSS chief Guruji into shakha goes to one such student of Banaras Hindu University whom Guruji used to teach.

The RSS work is mostly carried out by members of society who carry out their normal duties of a student, a worker, a professional, an artisan or a farmer and a family man, called 'grihasthi' in Indian parlance. They give their time and dedicate their efforts voluntarily to strengthen the organization and spread its message. But, prachaarak is the soul of the organization. He is respected by every volunteer. He has a moral authority over and above the authority he is given officially within the organization. His sacrifice of the prime years of his life puts him up on a higher pedestal over and above the other normal volunteers and citizens. This is in keeping with hoary Indian tradition wherein a rishi or a sage commands more respect than a king or a businessman.

A prachaarak starts out with a commitment of minimum three to four years but many prachaaraks remain so till the end of their life. There is no compulsion to stay a prachaarak for life. But, once soul is enlightened with this sacrifice he, perhaps, feels more fulfilled in this role than any other. He may extend his commitment up to any period as he wishes. Thus, thousands of such noble souls surrender their lives for the upliftment of the society and motherland. There are a few stories of some prachaaraks who have actually turned sanyasis. Maybe, they become so spiritual through regular practice of yoga, meditation etc. that it leads them to this path. But, primarily a prachaarak is a karmayogi who firmly believes that serving motherland and the society is the best way to spiritual salvation. For example, there is an ordained sanyasi like Dr. Vigyananand of Vishwa Hindu Parishad (VHP), an IIT alumni, a Sanskrit scholar with multiple research degrees, who is a VHP prachaarak. Guruji had taken 'diksha' to become a sanyasi through Ramakrishna Mission under Swami Akhandaananand but the emotional call from Dr. Hedgewar to serve the society rather than look for his own 'nirvana' in Himalayas pulled him back into active social life. This aura of a spiritual personality may have rubbed off on other prachaaraks, and they too, generally, have a spiritual outlook in life. This is environment in which the first and subsequent generations of prachaaraks were moulded.

Tradition of a prachaarak being a brahmachaari is more rooted in practicality of working full time for the society without any bonds of family rather than any spiritual or organizational dogma. We see simple family people give so much of time and resources to the Sangh work that many times, families suffer and resent his focus on social work rather than family. This is true even for other dedicated people in social life outside the Sangh fold. Though, the passion for serving the motherland is fine, it is not practically possible for everybody to be as 'impractical' about his or her other duties to family. Thus, there is a need of a fully dedicated person without any family compulsions. This simple ascetic like celibate life also makes him immune to any kind of corruption.

There is a shorter period version of prachaarak called vistaarak. Here the commitment is for a shorter period of a few months to a year. The duties and style of work is same as that of a prachaarak, but duration is lesser with clear understanding that the person will return back to normal material life after that period. As the word vistaarak suggests, he is a person who takes up the task of expanding work of the organization. Generally, such a person is sent to a new area to help the organization grow there. There is an anecdote of a activist whose family was opposing his move to become a vistaarak. A senior prachaarak told him, "You should tell your family that you are going on probation as a trainee manager in a company called Hindusthan Construction Company. The company provides lodging, boarding, free travel and clothes but doesn't offer any remuneration. They will surely agree!" Though, said in a lighter vein, how true! We would happily allow our dear one to take up such a chance but recoil at the thought of giving away our dear family member for an abstract idea of nation building even for a short duration.

One of the outstanding traits of the RSS prachaarak is his utter simplicity and humility. An interaction with an evolved prachaarak is a humbling experience in itself. For me, meeting Late Chamanlal ji, a very senior prachaarak who used to stay in Delhi office of the RSS was a pleasure of meeting a fragrant, ever smiling pure personality with a spiritual aura. It also used to be a humbling experience. I will give an instructive illustration of his simplicity. He was very well known through his vast network and painstaking correspondence to keep in touch with hundreds of people when there was no internet. Post cards and inland letters were the way of life. But, as in the case of all prachaaraks, he was not a known 'public' face. Once, some industrialist with a reference letter from an RSS worker was to come to Delhi to meet Chamanlal ji and the message was received in Delhi. On reaching Delhi station, this gentleman found a thin pyjama kurta clad simple looking man waiting to receive him. He was greeted with a warm smile and folded hand, and this simple looking man picked up his bag to take him to kaaryaalay. This gentleman didn't talk on way, busy with his own thoughts. On reaching the office, he asked Chamanlal ji, "where is Mr. Chamanlal." Our humble man, said with a smile, "Shriman ji, I am Chamanlal!" This Chamanlal ji had come from a very well to do family in Punjab, was a person who could walk into Mr Vajpayee's or any other leader's home unannounced, whose call would be taken with respect by any VIP. He was a keen student of international affairs. He would never take anybody else's chair without permission, would stand up and offer water or tea to a visitor himself. He was an inspiration beyond words.

Generally, all the prachaaraks are good or excellent achievers in their field before they choose to give it up all. Many of the prachaaraks are gold medalists and university toppers. Many of the prachaaraks would have been great achievers in the field they chose because of their skills and academic qualifications. I am aware of a case where young activist wished to become a prachaarak but he was not given permission as he hadn't finished his graduation at that time.

I cannot name current generation of prachaaraks as they are supposed to avoid publicity of any kind about their own qualities or qualifications. The attempt to do so will become, literally, a roll call! But, I cannot resist giving a few examples to illustrate this point.

One of the earliest prachaaraks of the RSS, late Yadavrao Joshi was an accomplished classical singer. Ram Madhav narrated an interesting story about him. Dr Hedgewar heard him in a concert. He called him later and told him that he will teach him (Yadavrao) a patriotic song. Yadavrao used to say, "That song later became the song of my life", that is, he offered his whole life to the service of the nation. He was instrumental in establishing robust the RSS network in South India. Late Nana Palkar and Shivrai Telang were great writers. Nana Palkar wrote the popular autobiographies of the first and second RSS chiefs. Atal Behari Vajpayee was writing poetry since his prachaarak days and his name as a poet came to light only when he entered politics. He has written some of the most soul stirring patriotic poems. One of such poem is, "Hindu tan man, Hindu Jeevan, Shat shat Hindu meraa parichay" (Hindu body and soul, Hindu life, Cent per cent Hindu - this is my identity.) This is not the place to quote full poem, but it is the best exposition about what a Hindu and Hinduism is all about — an affirmative statement extolling the non-aggressive but enlightening role Hinduism has played in the world. Bachcharaj Vyas, ex-President of the then Jan Sangh was another great poet and many of his poems find place in the RSS songs. Shri HV Sheshadri is a Karnataka state literary award winner. Many prachaaraks, generally, become great linguists as a part of their job when they work in different states and regions. The prachaarak in my area in Mumbai, Anil Vartak, now posted in Delhi, is a Gold Medalist, M. Sc. (Tech) from IIT. Late Shri Rajendra Singh, erstwhile RSS chief was a great teacher of nuclear science and one of his mentors complained that RSS had taken away a promising nuclear physicist of India. He used to go straight from his RSS related tours to his classroom to take his lectures in dhoti-kurta with his trade mark the RSS prachaarak jhola.

A prachaarak cannot choose his place of work or field of work. He may be deputed to any area in India. He may even be assigned to another sister organization if that organization requests for help from the RSS. Many people are aware of Deendayal Upadhyay, Atal Behari Vajpayee and L K Advani being deputed to the then Jan Sangh on request of Dr Shyama Prasad Mukerjee, founder of Jan Sangh. Eknath

Ranade was relieved of his very important duties as Sarkaaryavaah (Secretary General) of the RSS to take up the work of Vivekanand Rock Memorial at Kanyakumari. We all know how successfully he carried it out. It is a national monument now. Dadasaheb Apte was released to organize the fledgling Vishwa Hindu Parishad. Shyam Gupt who pioneered the Ekal movement of one teacher one school is another example.

A prachaarak is supposed to adapt to the local environment and be one amongst the people with whom he works. There are incidents of pure vegetarian prachaaraks turning non-vegetarians when they started work in North East region of India as that's the way of life there. In early days, prachaaraks used to be sent to a totally new area with an introductory letter from Dr. Hedgewar to a friend or contact there. Doctor ji commanded such respect that this prachaarak would at least get a place to rest his back on reaching there. He had to adjust to whatever kind of support he could get, even sleep in the open sometimes. Prachaaraks would travel on foot or in better circumstances, by cycle for miles and could end up with sparse and irregular food, or no food at all. I suspect that the reason why many first generation prachaaraks have serious health problem is that many a time they had to live on raw grams, skip food and lead a very tough life till some sort of organization was raised in their area of operation. The travelling that this group does is beyond imagination. Guruji, the top leader of the RSS used to say, "Railway bogey is my second home". He had toured the entire country from East to West, from North to South 66 times in his 33 year tenure, including the last two years of his life when he was terminally ill with cancer.

Since a prachaarak is like a sanyasi, he is not supposed have any attachment to any organization or area. So, you find a prachaarak from deep South becoming almost a UP wala or a prachaarak from Maharashtra becoming more or less a Tamil over years. Since, the Sangh grew up in Maharashtra, all the initial prachaaraks and workers were Marathi speaking but some adopted Tamil, some Punjabi and some Gujarati as their preferred language. In early days, Dadarao Parmarth was sent to Madras Province, Tamilnadu of today. Later Datta ji Didolkar and Shivram Joglekar were sent there. These three laid foundation of the Sangh work there. They not only became one with the local population but also mastered the language and were proficient in writing books and essays, let alone reading and speaking. Similarly, Madhavrao Muley practically became a Punjabi and Laxmanrao Inamdar, the mentor of current Gujarat Chief Minister Narendra Modi settled down in Gujarat since his young days. This, again, is only an illustrative list.

Recently, some of the prachaaraks who were deputed to political field, have also become mass leaders and hold political power with elan. Shri Narendra Modi is a recent example. Shri Atal Behari reached pinnacle of power and used to simply say, "I am a swayamsevak."

This institution of prachaarak has also been adopted by other RSS related organizations like Akhil Bharatiya Vidyarthi Parishad, Vishwa Hindu Parishad and Bharatiya Mazdoor Sangh etc. The Sangh is generally requested to loan a prachaarak by any new the Sangh inspired organization that starts work in a new field. Later that organization is expected to create its own band of workers, volunteers and even prachaaraks. Thus, there are thousands of these quality people all over India spreading the good word about Hindu heritage, national unity, equality, social amity, dedication to society, its upliftment and citizen's duty in nation building. In general, helping India become a better place for all its citizens.

No wonder that in spite of virulent propaganda and campaigns of calumny against Sangh school of thought the critics can't stop its growth. The silent work by these virtual monks cannot be matched by hysteric outbursts of its critics. Positivity will always win over negativity.

❑

The Manifestation

Shalabh ban jalna saral hai sneh ki jalti shikha par,
Swayam ko til til jalaa kar deep bananaa hee kathin hai,
Sadhana ka path kathin hai.

It is easy to be a moth and burn oneself over the glowing flame of love, but it is very difficult to be a lamp which burns self, atom by atom to give light to others. Path to dedicated service is, indeed, tough.

-

—From a Sangh song

"All religions and sects are mine, all castes are mine, people living in hills and forests are mine. If they are unhappy then it is only because of our weaknesses. Our tribal society lying neglected because of a big section of Hindu society that considers itself clever; is my inalienable part. I will do whatever is necessary to correct the wrongs perpetrated over years, awakening within all this kind of strong resolve; Hindu society will rise in a unified way; a strong society that would stand in its place of birth, in its own land from Himalayas to Oceans with its head held high in the world."

—M S Golwalkar (Guruji), 1966

12

Offshoots : Sister and Associate Organizations

I have mentioned earlier about the gradual evolution of the Sangh in its working and its organization over years as the situations emerged that demanded something more from the RSS and its members. Interestingly, the term Sangh parivaar is a media invention. The Sangh leaders judiciously labelled the organizations working with inspiration of the Sangh as sister or associate organizations. They didn't deal with them in terms of parent child relationship, hence this term 'Sangh parivaar' was eschewed consciously. But, somehow with grace of media this term of the Sangh parivaar has struck roots. I will try to give a better idea of the major organizations of this family or 'parivaar' in this chapter.

Late D B Thengdi, one of the foremost ideologues of the RSS, described this evolution in the organization as 'gradual unfoldment' of the Sangh work. Beginning with the support Guruji gave to Dr Shyama Prasad Mukerjee by loaning him his best talents for Bharatiya Jan Sangh, today's all India level mass organizations like Akhil Bharatiya Vidyarthi Parishad (All India Students Conference) and later Bharatiya Mazdoor Sangh (Indian Labour Organization) were born. The Vanvasi Kalyan Ashram (Tribal Welfare Organization) was born in 1952 to serve tribal brethren; then came the Vishwa Hindu Parishad (World Hindu Conference) in 1964. The Saraswati Shishu Mandirs (schools) for providing high quality value based education were started much earlier in 1952, though a formal structure of working under a parent body of Vidya Bharati took form much later. All these organizations grew up to become number one organizations in their fields. These are massive people's organizations spread all over India with their own volunteer networks, autonomous organizational structure, constitution and even prachaaraks, full timer volunteers.

The **Bharatiya Jan Sangh** (Indian People's Organization) was born in 1951. I don't consider it as the first offshoot of the RSS in the sense that it was not initiated by it or its members. However, it was the first experiment for the RSS to send out its tried and tested people into another organization to help them organize their activities outside its scope so far, in another sphere of social life. The Senior RSS leaders did toy with the idea of floating their own political party as a strategy when ban on the RSS was not lifted in spite of being given clean chit by CID and commission of enquiry about Mahatma Gandhi's assassination, presentation of written constitution and a peaceful satyagrah by its members. A background paper for it was circulated among senior members and also 'leaked' to mediators and police to give an idea how they could hit the Congress where it hurt most—decimation of the Congress monopoly in politics. They had also noted that during fierce political onslaught on the RSS after Gandhi's murder there was hardly any support from any politician when the RSS was banned and falsely implicated in assassination of Gandhiji. In this backdrop other senior members persuaded Guruji to help organize the proposed political party that Dr Shyama Prasad Mukerjee wished to organize. Thus, when Dr Mukerjee approached Guruji to help him nurture his proposed political party the Jan Sangh, Guruji agreed to support him in his endeavour, though rather reluctant. He firmly believed that politics or government is not the answer to the developmental needs of this country, and this required social action and dedication of the society itself.

Dr Mukerjee was a fierce nationalist and had resigned from Nehru cabinet as the Railway minister on the issue of the 1949 Delhi Pact with Pakistani Prime Minister Liaqat Ali Khan. Mukerjee was firmly against Nehru's invitation to the Pakistani PM, and their joint pact to establish minority commissions and guarantee minority rights in both the countries. He wanted to hold Pakistan directly responsible for the terrible influx of millions of Hindu refugees from East Pakistan, who had left the state fearing religious suppression and violence aided and abetted by the state. He opposed Nehru's decision to allow Kashmir to be a special state and have its own flag and prime minister. According to this decision, no one, including the President could enter Kashmir without Kashmir's prime minister's permission. In order to oppose this decision, he announced, *"Ek desh mein do Vidhan, do Pradhan and Do Nishan nahin chalenge"* (A single country can't have two constitutions, two prime ministers, and two national emblems.) He was incensed by Nehru's virtual abdication of responsibility on integration of Kashmir with India even as he took over Kashmir issue from Sardar Patel, stopping the march of Indian troops to trounce the first attack through infiltrators by Pakistan and then taking the issue to UN in spite of opposition from leaders like Sardar Patel. Later, after formation of the Jan Sangh, he organized a protest march to Kashmir in 1953. He died an unnatural death due to lack of treatment, rather due to mistreatment of the state government run by Sheikh Abdullah, the then chief minister and grandfather of the current Chief Minister Omar Abdullah. Nehru had no grace to even set up an inquiry to find out exactly what happened to his former cabinet colleague. It is also indicative of his lack of vision that he had to arrest same Sheikh Abdullah soon and keep him behind the bars for years, before Indira Gandhi brought him out of the woodwork to sign a new accord on Jammu and Kashmir.

The involvement of young prachaaraks led by Pandit Deendayal Upadhyay led to steady consolidation and growth of the Jan Sangh over years till it was merged in newly formed entity, the Janata Party in 1977 following emergency and advice of Jai Prakash Narayan. With more and more involvement of the RSS prachaaraks like Jagannathrao Joshi in Karnataka, Bachcharaj Vyas in Maharashtra and others in all the states etc. and workers at all levels, it had become a full-fledged sister organization of the RSS. Its new avatar Bharatiya Janata Party came into being in 1980 as the erstwhile members of the Jan Sangh had to leave party due to shenanigans of Socialist group within the then Janata Party. Many non-Jan Sangh members of the party also left the Janata Party and joined the BJP as they felt that the Janata Party had not stood by its principles.

It is worth noting that the Jan Sangh was not founded to establish 'Hindu Rashtra' or Hindu nation. For that, there was a hardcore Hindu party like the Hindu Mahasabha with illustrious leaders like Veer Savarkar. The Hindu Mahasabha and Savarkar were not exactly fascinated by the RSS style of working and thought that it was too soft, not militant enough to convey and force the concept of Hindu Rashtra. Savarkar had rather critical opinion of the RSS and believed that it was not effective. This opinion changed only in later stages of his life, probably after he appreciated the impact of its work in different areas of social life vis-à-vis the condition of his own Hindu Mahasabha. Dr S P Mukerjee himself was a member of the Hindu Mahasabha before he charted his own course. He laid strong stress on nationalism and non-partisan politics where policies were not based on religion and all citizens got an equal opportunity of progress.

Pandit Deendayal Upadhyay gave the Jan Sangh a truly Indian economic theory of Integral Humanism based on his years of study of Hindu ethos and working at the ground level as a Sangh prachaarak. If I were to summarize the theory, Integral Humanism sees the individual as the centre of an outgoing spiral where the individual is a part of family, society and the nation in an integral manner. All these units are interlinked and don't form concentric circles, disjointed with each other. It says that all economic policies should take into account not just physical needs of the individual, but also his all-round progress and spiritual and emotional fulfillment. They should reach out to the last individual standing in social hierarchy. It talks of total development of human beings of the society on the basis of 'chaturvidh purushartha' - fourfold fulfillment of an individual - on the basis of fulfilling 'dharm' (spiritual needs and ethical practices) 'arth' (economic needs), 'kaam' (physical and material needs), and 'moksha' (nirvana or liberation from the cycle of birth and death). Before this philosophy could be turned into a practical theory of development, he was murdered and the case was never properly investigated by the government. In spite of the efforts to create a viable economic model by various scholars and research on the subject with the help of Deendayal Research Institute it has not taken a concrete shape though DRI has used it to create its own applied model of development with various successful experiments in rural transformation, under the leadership of Nanaji Deshmukh.

Deendayal Upadhyay talked of 'chiti' (an equivalent term in English would be a mix of inherent spirit, intellect and soul) of the nation. He proposed that every nation must have an economic and political system which is close to its 'chiti', only then will that model succeed. You cannot impose a system which is alien to its 'chiti'. We can understand now, why the half baked socialist system failed in India and why Communism has not been able to grow beyond two states. It also explains why unbridled capitalism will not succeed in India. Marx gave a theory of historic evolution of economic model but even in his case, there was no practical model. Many a models were developed but no successful model has come up so far. In case of the Sangh school of thought, the application of this theory was in the domain of the Jan Sangh and then the BJP, which has kept it aside quietly or at the most, paid it lip service.

The Akhil Bharatiya Vidyarthi Parishad (ABVP) has a distinct personality in student movement of India and is known for its nationalistic approach and agitations in support of issue related to national security and education. A charismatic professor, Yashwantrao Kelkar, an ex-prachaarak, founded ABVP in 1948 along with some other colleagues, including Dattopant Thengdi. In a way, this was also an offshoot of ban on the RSS when many senior activists decided to create new organizations for national renaissance rather than sit idle. Within years it became a dominant student organization, winning over young students with its agitational but positive approach to student problems, national problems and due to its nationalistic orientation. It went on to win most of the student council elections.

Incidentally, ABVP was the first organization to start the trend of beginning a function with 'jyoti prajwalan' or lighting of the lamp. Till that time, ribbon cutting was the norm. Among many agitations it conducted one was against infiltrators from Bangladesh much before it had taken alarming proportions. I could mention many more of their agitations but there is no space in this size of the book. After the initial help it took from the RSS with full time organizers or prachaaraks, it was successful in creating its own methodology to influence young students to become full time volunteers for the organization. Many of who became prachaaraks of ABVP later on. At a time when there is a unifocal approach of most students on careers, to be able to persuade them to give precious years for the nation is quite an achievement. ABVP was one of the rare the RSS related organizations not banned during emergency and all of us used this platform to carry on the struggle for democracy. Arun Jaitley was one of the star ABVP student leaders at that time and toured India extensively. Prof. Bal Apte, currently vice president of BJP was one of the key activists during emergency.

ABVP's most important contribution to national integration is its trail blazing programme 'Students' Experience in Interstate Living' or SEIL. Under this scheme, young students from North East Indian states were escorted to places like Mumbai and Pune etc. They stayed with ordinary middle class families who hosted them and put them to schools along with their own children. They would finish the schooling and return to their native land, taking with them lovely memory of India as their motherland and affection of other citizens of the country for them. They carried with them the message of national integration. We are aware that many of our friends talk of North East and its citizens as if they are from another country and refer to them in a derogatory manner. This movement attempted to reverse the trend and succeeded to a large extent. Many politicians of these North Eastern states have gone through this experience and their approach to local problems is more nationalistic, to whichever party they may belong. Bringing plight of Arunachal Pradesh and Chinese policies to dominate the region to light was possible due to such elements in the North East. There are hostels now in Maharashtra catering to North East students. Thus, today we have a large contingent of such youth who fight with separatists and terrorists in their regions and keep the flag of national integration flying.

Bharatiya Mazdoor Sangh (BMS) was established in 1955 by Dattopant Thengdi, a rare combination of an organizer who was also a hands-on leader with feet firmly on ground and a theoretician. He came up with a dynamically different philosophy in trade union field. Its basic philosophy is, 'Industrialize the Nation, Labourize the

Industry and Nationalize the Labour'. Incidentally, Dattopant Thengdi worked in INTUC on invitation from its President Mr P Y Deshpande first to gain experience in working of trade unions before he launched the BMS. From day one it was visualized as a trade union whose base sheet-anchors would be: Nationalism, working as a genuine trade union, keeping itself scrupulously away from party politics. We know that all the national trade unions were linked to one or the other political party, overtly or otherwise till that time. Another differentiator of the BMS was that they considered themselves as stake holders in the organization so, as a policy, they would not damage any machines or premises where they worked even if they went on strike. It struggled its way up slowly in an arena highly dominated and infiltrated by the Communists and the Congress party. It speaks volumes about its staying power, long term vision and depth of its work that it held its first national convention only in 1967 after 12 years of hard work on the field. At the time the number of affiliated unions had reached 541 and total membership was 2,46,000. The BMS insignia symbolizes the rhythm between human controlled industrial development and agricultural prosperity. This is clearly depicted by impression of strong, confident and erect thumb of fist in between moving wheel and sheaf of corn. Incidentally, BMS is the first one in the trade union field to use human organ as a part of its logo. It promoted a dynamic and daring economic stance that the income-ratio in India should be one and ten.

Over the years it became number one trade union in India rising against the labour unions entrenched in the field for decades. It has its presence in all sectors of economy. Bharatiya Kisaan Sangh (Indian Farmer's Organization) was borne out of BMS with specific focus on farmers' issues. It has major presence in many of the states of India. 'Bharatiya Shram-Shodh Mandal' (Indian Labour Research Group) formed by BMS is a research based institution, established in 1980, to promote objective studies based on impartial examination of facts and developments in the industrial field.

An important practice initiated by the BMS is to observe traditional Vishwakarmaa day, celebrated traditionally by artisans of India, as the Labour Day for Indian labour. According to the BMS, Vishwakarmaa had more significance for Indian labour than May Day.

It would be interesting to note that D B Thengdi had written an epitaph of Communism way back in sixties when it was at its peak. He predicted the breakdown of Russian system somewhere in late 1960s or early '70s. I heard him in a RSS training camp in 1973 giving a detailed analysis about his thesis. I believe that the monograph on the subject is still available. He had firm belief, based on his in-depth theoretical analysis and available data, that Communism will fail and so will capitalism in its present form. The second part of the prophecy has also turned out to be correct as the events of last few months show. He gave theoretical underpinning to the RSS view that only Hindu philosophy has the right answer to civilizational problems of coming times as it is the most scientific and integral thinking on temporal issues that govern human behaviour. This is the only philosophy which talks of material needs as well as spiritual needs for all-round happiness of a human being. As famous Russian author Dudintsev said, man does not live by bread alone. Other economic theories of the left and the right treat a human being only as a consumer with physical needs. This is the prime reason they fail to give a complete solution for happiness. His enunciation of 'Integral Humanism' espoused by Pandit Deendayal Upadhyay used to be the high point of any camp or workshop.

Media has for years been talking of the ABVP and the BMS as student and labour wings of the BJP, either out of ignorance or bias. I had been active in the ABVP also during emergency period and had been attending its meetings, known many of the members and teachers associated with it for years. Similarly, I have been meeting BMS leaders during some joint meetings of associate organizations, where all these organizations make presentations and discussions are held. Never can anybody doubt that these are autonomous organizations and the BJP has no influence over them in matter of policies or programmes. It is possible in highly politicized cities like Delhi etc. that some the BJP members, specially ex-ABVP people, may be helping the ABVP members in student body elections. But, to imagine these big organizations as wings of the BJP is baseless and laughable. It is true that many ABVP activists who leave the ABVP and wish to have a political career end up in BJP because, for them, the BJP is a natural party to enter politics. They couldn't possibly go to Socialist groups that have more parties than members; or to the Congress as they had fought its erratic and pro-Communist and communal education policies for years. The intellectual training that they had during student days would naturally lead them to the BJP. Many of them have gone on to occupy powerful positions in the BJP. The fact remains that ABVP, as an autonomous organization, doesn't listen to the BJP on its policy and programme matters at organizational level and is in no way its subsidiary. There has been lot of cross traffic between the RSS, the ABVP and the BJP. Many ABVP prachaaraks have joined the RSS after their age took them out of student politics and taken up responsibilities in the RSS.

The BMS is a fiercely independent body and it resisted all attempts to merge it with other trade unions as suggested by Janata Party constituents after election win of 1977. It is a known fact that it opposes BJP on many policy issues. One will also note that there is hardly any exchange of volunteers between the BMS and the BJP, so the talk of it being wing of the BJP is just critics' imaginations running wild.

Another media created myth is that **Rashtra Sevika Samiti** (Indian Women Volunteers' Association) is a subsidiary organization of the RSS. In fact, I read an article by a so called progressive lady accusing the RSS of being anti-feminist and subordinating women by calling its women wing volunteers as 'Sevika' as against calling its male members as 'Swayamsevaks'! I can only pity these overtly hair splitting dialectics that Marxists simply love to employ and confuse people. All such critics have missed the dynamics of the RSS. If they took care to read the history of Sevika Samiti, they would realize that it was started by a self-motivated lady Smt. Laxmibai Kelkar, popularly called 'Mausee ji' in 1936. A lady with a modern outlook, who had lost her husband in young age, she was highly appreciative of the work of the RSS. She wished to start a similar organization for women in times when tradition bound a woman to her home and hearth and she had no independent identity. Smt Kelkar wished to fight this status quo and bring her out of her home and contribute to the social well-being of Hindu society. She was convinced that the woman of the house was the one who initiated and nurtured value system or Sanskaar in the society and she need to be made aware of her responsibility. A woman is more than only a wife, mother or sister. With this background she met Dr Hedgewar and argued for an organization on lines of the RSS. Doctor ji conveyed his inability to organize such an organization for women as it was beyond his knowledge and talent. But, he assured full co-operation to her if she were to start a parallel organization for women. Thus, Rashtra Sevika Samiti was born.

Rashtra Sevika Samiti has its own intellectual training material and methodology which is quite different from the RSS, though it borrows the physical training part and support from the RSS. Samiti is totally focused on women's' issues. It has presence in all parts of India, though not in such a big way as RSS. It is a cadre based organization and doing great service by giving women an early orientation in life about their important role in the society. It runs a large number of social service projects running in hundreds, focused on women welfare. It has its own prachaarikas who take the bold step of dedicating ripe years of their youth for social cause. In Indian society it is not easy for a bachelor or single woman to leave home and work for the society. When we consider Samiti's work and the sacrifice of its activists, it is foolish to accuse the members of this organization as backward looking, to say the least. It is unfortunate that in the name of progressive thoughts any organization or people who preserve great traditions of Hinduism and give a modern angle to these values to motivate young women, can be abused or tarred with any brush very imperiously by the so called progressive feminist organizations and glamour struck media.

It may be the right place to give a very straight answer to the accusation that the RSS is anti-woman and male chauvinist since it doesn't take women into its fold. First of all, apart from the RSS all other organizations in the RSS fold actively encourage women to participate in their activities. The number of women activists working through the Sangh inspired organizations would be much larger than all other social and political organizations put together. Since many years, apart from regular shakha, women are invited to its festivals, workshops, seminars and lectures. It has offered full support to Rashtra Sevika Samiti to grow and offered it advice on any matter that the organization requires.

The RSS sees women as playing a very pivotal role in imparting the right value systems in the family and providing moral and physical support to social development of the society in every sense of word. The RSS volunteers show highest respect to womanhood and no programme of the RSS has ever seen any misbehaviour of any kind with any lady, as volunteer is moulded by the noble thoughts and sees mother and sister in the families he visits or works with. I saw a very straight and simple reason behind it as I grew from a child to a senior worker in the RSS. The intense physical activities and games played in shakha cannot be done together. On a practical level, presence of opposite sex creates distraction for the volunteer who is supposed to work unwaveringly towards his mission. We have seen how Rashtra Seva Dal which considered itself as a competitor to the RSS slowly lost its relevance and when most of the leaders marrying and settled down to domestic life. This group used to be referred as virtual marriage bureau in lighter vein in social circles. Nothing more should be seen behind the decision of Dr Hedgewar to organize the RSS as a male organization. As the scenario changes, as noted above, apart from daily shakha and its related activities, women are invited in all the RSS programmes. Monthly or festive get-together see families come together and celebrate them together. Late Prahladrao Abhyankar, a very senior Sangh functionary, is quoted as saying, "Shakhas don't have women members but the Sangh has." We should note that the RSS related organizations had more powerful women at the top much earlier than the self-proclaimed most progressive organization like the CPM. Its politburo got its first woman member only after decades of its existence. It is amusing subtext that the lady happens to be the wife of the General Secretary of the party. I have underlined this strange paradox not to deride anybody, but to underline the fact that this is a social phenomenon because of the late start Indian women got in the social and political life of the nation.

I may use this place to bring out another paradox of Indian socio-political scene. That is, all, yes, all political parties for years had been dominated by Brahmins, without exception. Whether it was the Congress (starting from Nehru to most of their powerful regional heads like GB Pant etc.), or Communists (recall late Dange, Namboodaripad), or Socialists (Madhu Dandavate, Limaye et al) etc. etc. You would be surprised how long the list can be. We are proud that none of these great people played casteist politics and fought for an equitable society all through their lives. So, to keep painting the RSS as an organization dominated by Brahmins is nothing but an inverse play of casteist policies and refusal to accept that this was a result of the educational advantage that Brahmins had during the earlier century for various historical reasons, rather than a devious plan by Brahmins to dominate national political life. Now, we can see that there has been a vast change in socio-political scenario after decades of democratic polity. Within the RSS and its associate organizations, vast number of leaders come from the so called OBC or SC/ST groups. The BJP is derided as 'Bania' party by left-secular lobby, but the fact is that most of the times it has one of the largest number of members in all the elected bodies from SC/ST categories.

Vanvasi Kalyan Ashram (VKA) is the largest Hindu organization working for tribal welfare, serving around 8 crore tribal people in its areas of operation. It was founded in 1952 by Ramakant Keshav Deshpande, popularly called Balasaheb Deshpande, who left his legal practice under inspiration from Guruji, with a small hostel in a dilapidated building donated by Raja Vijaybhushan Singh. Before that he had worked in Jashpur on government deputation on request of Thakkar Bappa, a renowned Gandhian, who headed this mission devised by the then Chief Minister Ravi Shankar Shukla for tribal welfare. He was able to open 110 schools in a short time and ran many innovative welfare measures. He went back to Nagpur after the death of Thakkar Bappa but was persuaded by Guruji to return to Jashpur and dedicate his life for tribal upliftment.

The effort of VKA like all other social service projects of the RSS is not to provide charity but to make local populace self-reliant and generate self-confidence at individual and societal level. Effort is also to help them gain confidence about their ancient traditions and practices and bring them closer to the mainstream national thinking. This means work in all segments of social life – education, health and rural development. It faces lot of opposition from Church which feels threatened by this inroad into what it perceives as its monopoly area and ideal ground for doing God's own work i.e. evangelism. It is unfortunate that media plays into the hands of this lobby and portrays work of the VKA only as a counter to Church activities. People like Mathew S J, accuse and criticize the RSS and its associates for not taking care of their less privileged brethren and strengthening the forces of status quo in the Hindu society. But, in the same breath, they show alarm and throw fits that now these organizations are working in this area. Instead of appreciating the fact that Hindu society has woken to woes of its less fortunate brethren, it portrays it as a divisive work, as if only the Church has a birthright to 'serve' this segment of the population! So, a conversion is freedom to choose but a reconversion back to original faith is communalism and divisive. There is enough evidence available about the hate campaign run by evangelists, getting money from all over the world for their 'noble' cause of saving the souls of non-believers, against Hindu gods and all its cherished beliefs done not just orally but through booklets. Actually shoe is on the other foot!

Saraswati Shishu Mandir, one of the largest chain of schools in India with nearly 27,000 schools was founded in 1952 in Uttar Pradesh with initiative of Rajendra Singh, Nanaji Deshmukh, and Deendayal Upadhyay; young RSS prachaaraks at that time. These are all unaided schools with very reasonable fee who provide board level education and with traditional Indian ethical value system. The teachers of these schools are known for their passion for education and national service.

Vidya Bharati, an umbrella organization of many educational trusts was established in 1977. Saraswati Shishu Mandirs have been brought under the umbrella of Vidya Bharati recently. Vidya Bharati takes care of these schools and also other institutions right from primary schools to postgraduate institutes. It offers quality education at low cost that too without any government grant. The schools follow NCERT syllabus, but apart from this, they also provide education on moral and nationalist values to turn them into duty conscious citizens. *Indian Express,* in a recent story on great results of these schools in Orissa as compared to other schools noted that, consistently better than average results from these schools prove that teachers and students with high emotional quotient and commitment inspire better results.

Vishwa Hindu Parishad (VHP) the most maligned organization from the Sangh fold has, actually initiated many far-reaching actions for reforming Hindu society and these should have been recognized as its signature tune. However, the Ram Janmabhoomi agitation changed its focus and also the image of VHP totally. Vishwa Hindu Parishad was founded to bring together all sects and faiths that traditionally fall under Hindu fold, and persuade various heads of mutts and temples, trusts etc. to come on a common platform to address serious problems of Hindu society. It was probably the only the Sangh associated organization to which the head of the RSS, Shri Guruji paid personal attention and devoted lot of time and efforts. He delayed even his last phase of critical radiation therapy for cancer to attend state level conference of the VHP in Gujarat.

Its agenda also included improving the working of temples and making them a vehicle of social change by taking more active role in temporal affairs that affected their followers' live or affected Hindu unity rather than only rituals. Till then, trust members generally did not look beyond the temple and its maintenance, that too poorly. Many such trusts would become personal fiefdoms. Effort was required to bring in some social angle and dynamism in religious affairs of the Hindus, so that the saints would not just give sermons from their maths or trusts but come to the common people and inspire them to reform their faith and make it inclusive by taking in all sections of the society, regardless of caste and creed.

The Sangh felt that the work of the VHP was very critical for the Hindu society; hence Guruji took upon himself to meet various gurus, saints and holy men. HH Swami Chinmayananda of Chinmay Mission played a major role in this initiative. A Sangh prachaarak Dadasaheb Apte was deputed for this work. He was a scholar in his own right and could reach out to the Hindu saints and gurus with his sincere work and humble approach. The VHP was officially established in 1964 at Sandeepani Ashram, the headquarters of Chinmay Mission in Mumbai and Swamy Chinmayananda presided over the first meeting of the VHP in which many other great saints of various Hindu faiths and sects were also present. Its theme is "Dharmo Rakshati Rakshitah", i.e. Dharma protects, when protected.

The first plenary session of the VHP was slated during the Maha Kumbh of 1966 at Prayag (Allahabad) that came up immediately after its formation. VHP organizing committee had an enviable task of bringing together the leaders of all sects and faiths that shared umbilical relationship with Hinduism. It was not an easy task. Never had the Hindu saints and leaders and gurus of other sects had come on a single stage. Many of them had huge ego issues, some of them based on age old customs. There were many such other complexities. But, such was Guruji's saintly persona and so hard he worked on them in his own inimitable gentle style that slowly, nearly all the saints agreed to attend this session. I have mentioned earlier that Guruji was an ordained sanyasi under tutelage of Swami Akhandaanand, a guru-bhai (with common guru) of Swami Vivekanand. Such was the power of passion in Doctorji's simple speech that it is said that it went straight to heart. No doubt, Guruji couldn't say no to him. He sought permission from his Guru who gave his permission to return to Nagpur and work for the RSS. He was a sanyasi in normal worldly clothing all through life. He had a spiritual aura. It is said that he literally lay prostrate before many saints to persuade them to come on a single platform.

This first grand conference saw, for the first time, the Shankaracharyas of all the four maths set up by Adi Shankaracharya and heads of almost all the well-known maths (religious centres of spiritual gurus), temples and sects etc. attending the session. It was also attended by Jain munis, Sikh saints and Buddhist monks. It was a veritable Kumbh Mela of great evolved souls. The biggest and the historic achievement of this session was a resolution negating the division of society on lines of castes and the practice of untouchability. It was passed with great persuasive power of Guruji who worked behind the scenes with Swami Chinmayananda and venerable head of Pejawar Peeth to make the holy men to agree to break free of age old taboos and rigid mindset. It was nothing less than a revolutionary moment for Hindu society.

Subsequently, many reformist programmes were taken up by VHP. This included helping non-Brahmin people to learn rituals and work as priests. The VHP also supported initiation of women priests against generally established norms. It was able to mobilize masses for improving conditions of temples in various cities and towns. Thus, VHP has been a highly progressive organization.

The biggest and defining event in its organizational life came with Ram Janmabhoomi agitation. The subject had such passionate appeal that it subsumed all other works and agenda of the VHP at that time. The movement was about constructing a temple that befitted the status of Ram as the most popular and venerable God for Hindus among its pantheon. There are historical facts that prove that the site where the disputed Babri structure stood, was the site of an ancient Ram temple. There were enough local and historical accounts of various battles fought for its restoration. As is the practice of victors of Semitic or Abrahamic religions who destroyed all centres of faith of local population, this temple too had been destroyed. It is not a coincidence that even Krishna Janmabhoomi and the most venerable Shiva temple at Kashi faced the same fate. It was natural for Hindus to feel the need to have the temple which they believed was the birthplace of their dear lord Ram. Unfortunately, the secular cabal with strong lobby of Marxist historians who control all academia in India would simply dismiss the proofs submitted by scholars who presented the Hindu side simply as myths. They have arrogated the task of giving certificates of authenticity upon themselves. Like true cultural fascists, for them truth is that which suits their world view. Rest is 'mithya'!

It is indeed tragic that this politics of vote bank and noisy posturing backed by ever obliging fifth columnists of Marxist school in media, forced Indian Muslims to identify with a marauder like Babar and not with their cultural hero Ram. Their culture and traditions even today are more close to Hindus, naturally so, as they also belong to the same stock. Most of the Indian Muslims have, afterall, been converted to Islam by sword of attackers like Babar. For Hindus importance of Ayodhya is similar to that of Jerusalem for Jews, Muslims and Christians.

The movement was able to convey the message that Hindus do not get justice even in their own land without resorting to extreme forms of agitation. The unfortunate events like destruction of Babri structure that followed were not expected by anybody. Since, this subject is subjudice I cannot make comments on it in detail. But, it seems improbable that if the destruction was pre-planned then 'kar sevaks' would not arrange for some good tools but perform this superhuman task in a few hours using things like uprooted steel rods of barricades etc. that worked for them as tools. The speed with which the structure came down speaks of the extreme passion that these kar sevaks carried in their hearts. Debris of that size would take days if not weeks to clear even with some implements. They were cleared overnight without any such mechanical help. It must have been made possible only by dedicated and passionate volunteers who were there in thousands, not by some conspiracy of a few hundred people. And, there is no way a conspiracy hatched by hundreds and thousands of people can remain a secret. The continuous stonewalling of various proposals for a peaceful resolution led to such militant exception. There is a whole series of events which show why tempers reached that pitch. One needs to remember that this was the second time a large gathering had come together for the Ram Temple. The first event saw brutal police action which left hundreds injured and scores of people killed. People had braved all kinds of persecution and oppression to reach Ayodhya that time and went back after pressing for their agenda. It was natural that the tempers ran very high the second time around.

During this period of high pitched agitation, the more militant wing of the VHP, Bajarang Dal was formed. Durga Vahini for young women was also launched who were trained in the Hindu ethos and also martial arts to generate self-confidence. Many youths who found the inclusive and reformist style of the RSS too mild, joined Bajrang Dal. I am not much enamoured by its style and ways of working. Once in a while they go overboard with some half baked notions of

Hindu culture and the way to protect it; and end up alienating more people than bringing Hindus together. They are borne out of circumstances created by secular extremists. I also believe that the VHP has not been able to control this energetic young wing. If only their energies could be channelized to constructive reforms agenda of the VHP, they have a huge potential energy.

It is interesting that Naxalites and Maoists are not called members of Marxist parivaar, while Bajrang Dal is called a part of the Sangh parivaar. By a common yardstick, if Bajrang Dal is a member of the Sangh parivaar or even totally disowned group like Ram Sena is also its member, Naxals and Maoists too are by all means, members of Marxist parivaar. The ambivalent approach of CPM government of West Bengal towards Maoists and protection to Naxalites through various so-called human rights lobbies is more eloquent testimony than anything else. It is only now that they are on the receiving end that their language is changing.

It is a sad fact that negative actions of Bajrang Dal attract more media attention than the positive, constructive and peaceful work done by other organizations like the RSS, the ABVP, the Vishwa Hindu Parishad and the Vanvasi Kalyan Ashram etc. I have never seen any decent coverage of wonderfully organized reformist conferences of the VHP, highly disciplined protest march or camp of the ABVP, nor have I seen coverage of a grand and flawlessly organized camps or parades of the RSS. Such coverage is a rarity.

In this massive disturbance over nearly a decade, the more positive agenda of the VHP took a back seat for many years. But, gradually these issues are coming back on the action plan of the VHP. The VHP has thousands of social service projects in cities and tribal belts for economically and socially disadvantaged section of the society.

The VHP too has its own systems of inducting full-time volunteers or prachaaraks and has a strong organization. I am very sure that the VHP will remain a major catalyst in reforming the Hindu society and make various institutions more society oriented with service to the society, removal of inequity and promotion of social amity, promoting learning of ancient scriptures, getting rid of archaic customs etc. as their primary goal.

Swadeshi Jaagaran Manch (SJM - National Awakening Forum) that burst upon the scene suddenly in 1992-93 with the advent of globalization era in India, had clear economic agenda of opposing unbridled globalization before strengthening of Indian industry and commerce with internal liberalization; did not work systematically for creating a practical economic model. Though, it was meant to spell out a strong nationalist economic agenda, it came out as a defensive organization fighting the aggressive western capitalist imperialism and not confident about success of India in that environment. As the scenario unfolded, we find that the lack of confidence was unfounded. The Indian industry, including the much neglected SME segment came out of the rough patch with flying colours, barring those who did not move with times and did not focus on upgrading skills and quality.

According to a recent article by Prof. Vaidyanathan of IIMB, Our economy can be broadly summarized as 20 per cent agriculture – mainly small and medium farmers; 20 per cent government – central, state, municipal, PSUs, etc; 15 per cent corporate (companies governed by the 1956 Companies Act, of which some 8,000 are listed and 200 or so are traded and five or so are influencing the entire market); and 45 per cent non-corporate sector, consisting of partnership and proprietorship firms. Even in manufacturing, these firms have more than 40 per cent of the value addition. The non-corporate sector is the dominant player in all the service sectors apart from IT which is a small part of this total service sector. SME segment has clocked a compounded annual growth rate of more than 8 per cent in the last decade.

The SJM could have given ideological strength and a new model to the government and this segment of the Indian industry. It is sad that the SJM ended up frittering away its energies in sloganeering and agitational approach to economic issues. Thus, a golden chance to define an economic policy based on Indian ethos was lost.

During this period, for once, the Left and the Right (by conventional idiom) were on the same side! Importance of the SJM lay in raising a note of caution against unbridled liberalization for external MNC giants without corresponding support to Indian industry that hobbled on a three-legged race of self created red tape and licence raaj.

As history unravelled in free India, newer organizations were born, supported by the RSS with generous help of organizers and prachaaraks. All these are cadre based mass organizations and extension of the RSS vision in action in different social spheres. Nearly all of these have been number one organizations in their fields as independent and audited surveys show.

Other organizations

Many other organizations were born in different social sectors in subsequent years. There are also organizations working in different social sectors like cooperative movement, teachers etc.

In fact, the situation today is that even regular activists, sometimes, don't know which new organizations have come up and what they are doing in different sectors! There is hardly any segment of social action where people trained in the RSS or influenced by the RSS philosophy are not present.

Kushtha Nivaarak Sangh is a lesser known organization but doing sterling work in its field was established in 1962 by Sadashiv Katre in tribal area of Champa, Madhya Pradesh. He was a simple common swayamsevak who was cured of leprosy but suffered hugely due to this disease. He used to volunteer at a local missionary charity that worked for leprosy patients, but did not like the fact that missionaries converted those who came for cure and support there. Guruji asked him to put this resentment to good use and rather than fighting missionaries, start an organization with a positive approach of 'seva' or service. That is how this organization was born. He was supported by local swayamsevaks and state prachaarak in this work. Today, swayamsevaks of Uttaranchal, Karnataka, Maharashtra and Punjab are working in this neglected field with compassion. Many noble souls and good people are supporting this organization.

Ekal Vidyalay movement is one of the most dynamic fast growing organization that has come up in recent times. This movement is supported by many associate organizations like Friends of Tribals (FTS), Van Bandhu Parishad etc. A senior RSS prachaarak Shyam Gupt heads this initiative. Within 10-12 years of its working, it has already established 30,000 schools, predominantly in eastern part of India. It is poised to move into other regions also. These are single teacher schools. These teachers set up the school in a single room or under trees or in a room provided by some Samaritan or the panchayat; and teach underprivileged children. Now, they are also being trained to provide primary preventive healthcare support and simple medicines with primary health kits.

Sanskrit (Samskrita) Bhaarati under the guidance of Chimu Krishna Shastri, an RSS prachaarak, has done a great service to promotion of Sanskrit language by simplifying its learning. It has created thousands of Sanskrit speaking Indians with its scientific and simple technique of learning Sanskrit. Sanskrit Sambhashan Shibirs run by Sanskrit Bharati and other associate organizations which train you in conversational Sanskrit have been hugely popular. Sanskrit is the mother language of all Indian languages and many a European languages also. There are scholars working outside India who have found thousands of Sanskrit words in their own languages.

It is a known fact that the most important biotech research in MNC laboratories is happening on the basis of Ayurveda knowledge.

It is more or less mandatory that anybody doing research in biotech or Ayurveda (nowadays obfuscated under the term herbal medicine) needs to know Sanskrit. That it is the most scientific language and most suitable for computer programming due to its perfect syntax is old hat now. It is unfortunate that we Indians still believe that it is a language for priests. Parents and schools nearly force children to take French etc. as it is more 'scoring'! In this scenario an organization like Sanskrit Bharati has trained thousands of people in a few days to get preliminary grasp on the language, even helped villagers to speak Sanskrit. It has published 40 books and cassettes for easy Sanskrit learning. Around 1985, Mathur, a village in Karnataka State became a Samskrita village when a large number of families, irrespective of their caste and creed and profession, started to speak Samskritam in their homes. An effort is underway to develop another village, Mohad in Madhya Pradesh as Samskrita village. Recently Jhiri village was in the news for becoming the next Samskrita graamam. Sanskrit Bharati is also active in many cities in US now.

Itihas Sankalan Samiti is another smaller and relatively less known entity floated in 1972 by people who view Indian history differently and don't wish to colour their views by what has been put up as gospel truth by British historians and lapped up by our secular and Marxist historians. It is possible that intellectual inertia doesn't permit these well entrenched intellectuals to do some original research at this age. This organization was responsible for giving much required support to people who wish to do research on various non-researched and undiscovered aspects of Indian history.

A research work began under eminent archeologist Dr. Wakankar that has used latest scientific tools including satellite imagery to establish the existence of river Saraswati, based on Vedic descriptions and verses, and which British historians claimed was a myth. This thesis has claimed on the basis of scientific proof and evidence from Vedic verses that Saraswati was indeed the lifeline of Vedic civilization identified earlier with Mohenjo Daro and Harappa civilizations, later extended to hundreds of sites in the same riverine area. It was identified with a dried up river bed which seems to be that of river Saraswati. This discovery would also challenge the theory of Aryan invasion and large scale violence to send Dravidians packing to south. Truth would be established that the people living on the banks of Indus and Saraswati shifted to other areas on Ganges river and further south for reasons other than aggression by Aryans. Thus, effectively burying the pet theory of British school of historians and their followers putting all 'outsiders' from Aryans, to Chengiz Khan to Shaka and Huns, and progressive historians' darlings, Mughals at par.

The prevalent theory wishes to submit that India is a veritable highway stopover or settlement where all other travellers, hunters and aggressors came and settled, so there is no difference between Aryans or Hindus and Mughals. This theory is being challenged by historians with researches like the one about river Saraswati and discovery of scores of other archeological sites along the Indus and Saraswati river courses to the utter dislike of left lobby, hence, Arjun Singh in his blind opposition to whatever the RSS did, with active abetment from Marxist lobby, stopped grant to this research. Incidentally, the UPA government in its recent answer to a question in Lok Sabha in December 2009, has confirmed that recent research proves the existence this ancient river. Now, what should we call this attempt at falsifying the history in a bid to prevent its saffronization?

Interestingly, Babasaheb (Umakant Keshav) Apte, the inspiration behind Itihas Sankalan Samiti wrote a monograph on possible history of ancient India, *'Hamaare Rashtra Jeevan kee Pramparaa'* (Traditions in our national history) juxtaposing the Puranic stories of Dashaavataar (stories of ten incarnations of Lord Vishnu) onto archeological and geographical evidence. It is quite a riveting view based on his analysis. I don't think that it purports to be the RSS line. It is a theory that seems to have led to a fresh line of thinking about history of India since antiquity and gave Itihas Sankalan Samiti a sense of direction. This theory goes against the established wisdom perpetrated by the British historians and the alternative view that Aryan and Dravidians are from same racial stock with difference being limited to colour of the skin that may be a result of geographical and environmental factors.

This organization has local district level committees that are working on documenting historical facts of that particular area, thus compiling a comprehensible district level documentation of possible historical facts on a micro-level that may lead to some interesting macro-level historical model not evident so far.

Sanskaar Bharati is an organization which promotes Bharatiya (Indian) art form and culture through various activities and events. Dr V S Wakankar was the moving spirit behind this movement. Its two main objectives are – promoting originality, creativity and social and educative content of art and second to realize in Man – Nature's greatest piece of art – the fulfilment of "Satyam, Shivam, Sundaram". It promotes folk arts in all its facets and conducts various training classes to expose people, particularly young children to rich cultural heritage of India.

The most notable of its activities is its promotion of the Hindu new year which is spreading all over India and is being celebrated very enthusiastically by all the sections of Indian society. Humungous, record breaking rangolies in Thane city in Maharashtra, early morning cultural programmes including dance and music recitals on banks of holy Ganga river in Kashi, huge colourful processions in Mumbai and many other places in India are the manifestations of this event. Another innovative and inspiring programme which attracts thousands of school children all over India is its national competition of patriotic songs.

Vivekanand Rock Memorial in Kanyakumari run by Vivekanand Kendra is an associate organization of the RSS. It is an autonomous and large organization by itself now. Its initial set up as Vivekanand Rock Memorial was supported and nurtured by a senior prachaarak Eknath Ranade. It has developed and trained its own missionaries. The memorial at Kanyakumari was built with great difficulty and against strong protests from Christian clergy of the area which abetted local fishermen against this memorial. But, the RSS volunteers of the area fought all this off with resilience and inner strength. Finally, the grand and solemn memorial that we see today, was born under the able leadership of Ranade. It is now a national monument and major tourist attraction. It runs its own relief works, schools, yoga training schools etc. all over India with special focus on North East. Scientific study and research on Yoga is another of its forte.

There are thousands of organizations that operate at local level all over India in fields like education, health, rural development and environment. I have tried only to give an idea about all India organizations. The list can go on and on. But, this itself is a subject or has within it possibility of a number of subjects for doctoral thesis. I have only tried to give a fleeting view of the spread of the RSS work in different social and geographical segments of India. One would be surprised to note that research on the RSS and its allied organizations as a doctoral thesis is not only discouraged but actually disallowed by concerned heads of major universities due to entrenched leftist lobby. I know of only of one such thesis done by Dr Sadhana Modh whom I have quoted earlier. There may be a couple of other exceptions. But, there are hundreds of doctoral theses on the RSS done by people outside India.

It may be the right place to point out that major organizations listed above like BJP, ABVP, VHP, BMS, VKA etc. have grown big over the years and have their own cadre, sympathizers and supporters. They can no more be seen through the prism of parent-child organizational relationship. I feel that the RSS can no longer guide them as much as advise them or collaborate with them. It is like a son growing big enough that his feet now fit into father's shoes. In Indian tradition it is said that once child's feet fit into father's shoes, he should be treated like a friend. This is what is happening which the outside world has not yet begun to appreciate. I have reasons to believe that RSS does feel that it should not play a guiding or dominant role in such organizations. In corporate terms, the RSS equity in these subsidiaries has diluted and they have become independent corporate entities themselves with the RSS having only a critical holding but not controlling stakes.

❑

13

RSS, Nation and Society

Second Line of Command

Many people of the present generation are aware of the social service work of the RSS or seva, as the RSS defines it, though not the spread and depth of this work. But, not many are aware of the sterling role RSS volunteers have played in the defence of the country and fought the fissiparous and centrifugal forces right through pre-partition days to the present. It has acted like a strong second line of defence. It has been around even when the state apparatus hasn't worked in time or failed; so we might say it works virtually like a second line of command.

I will try to provide only a 'fast forward' view of many of the stirring tales of struggle and sacrifice. *RSS – Vision in Action* provides a vivid account of such fight backs in the interest of national integration by dedicated unsung national heroes. Most of the information and incidents have been taken from this book as it is an authentic account narrated by the erstwhile Sarkaaryavaah of RSS, HV Sheshadri.

When the partition became a real possibility, people thought only RSS could avert the tragedy and there was a huge groundswell in its base. The RSS volunteers prepared themselves for the worst, to fight this idea of partition and also be ready for any eventuality. The declaration of independence was, in fact, brought ahead by 10 months by British to avoid a situation where this popular tide may turn heavily against partition and lead to difficult situation. The original date declared for declaration of freedom of India was June 1948, but it was brought ahead to Aug 15, 1947, fearing strong backlash and popular support against partition in which the RSS was playing the role of catalyst.

There was a grand conspiracy by Muslim League supporters to assassinate all members of the government and all Hindu officials and thousands of citizens on 10 September 1947 and hoist Pakistani flag on Red Fort. This horrible incident was averted due to timely information to the government of India by young volunteers of RSS. This incident is recorded in the chronicles of Dr Bhagwandass, a freedom fighter and a Bharat Ratna recipient.

At the time of partition, hundreds of swayamsevaks lost their lives defending their Hindu brethren, stuck in areas that were to go under Pakistan, from Muslim plunderers. Many volunteers lost their own families and family fortunes left behind in Pakistan but they went ahead mindless of their own safety. A very moving account about the painful plight of volunteers and prachaaraks of the time has been captured by a Marathi writer, Neelkanth Deshmukh in his small novel, *Naahee Chira Naahee Panati* – neither ray of light nor the lamp. A N Bali has written a moving account of these sacrifices in his book *Now it can be Told*. Says he, "not a single survivor of partition can, but pay his respect to the RSS volunteers for saving their lives and safe passage to India as well as taking their care when they landed up in refugee camps."

Infiltration of Pakistani tribals into Kashmir was stoutly resisted by the Sangh members during July-October 1947. There were major riots in Jammu city when around 20,000 Muslims of that region decided to take control of Jammu as a part of annexing J&K with the help of tribal Pakistanis supported by Pakistani army. Right from holding onto their villages, providing intelligence to army, supporting army movement, strengthening and rebuilding of Srinagar airstrip for air force planes to land, they worked relentlessly, oblivious of their own safety or of their family members. Many lost their lives and members of their family. This was the period when the Maharaja of Kashmir was still not sure about the accession of J&K to India. Guruji met him on 17 October 1947 to persuade him to sign the treaty to save J&K from takeover by force by Pakistan. By the time situation had already become very grim. Finally, he signed the treaty. During all this chaos, the RSS volunteers held fort for Indian army at the risk of their lives till it could take over.

Supporters of the RSS formed a new political party – Praja Parishad to fight separatists in J&K and struggle for full integration with India. The struggle saw major phases in 1948, 1950-51, 52-53. The oppression was unimaginable with Delhi government being deaf to the calls of patriotic Indians in the fond hope that Sheikh Abdullah would get it out of the mess, not realizing that his National Conference was playing this game of separatism through various moves. Leaders of Praja Parishad like Dr Balraj Madhok toured all over India to bring this threat to the attention of the nation. There was heavy censorship and no news was allowed to pass to and fro J&K about the agitation and various human rights violations against volunteers of Praja Parishad. Senior leaders were put behind bars and beaten up. The agitation reached its peak when Dr. Shyama Prasad Mukerjee led a march in June 1953, ending in his medical murder on 9 August 1953 by the hand of J&K government. Another spate of atrocities on agitators was let loose. Suddenly, on 9 August 1953, GOI saw the light and dismissed J&K government, arrested Sheikh Abdullah and agreed to make many changes to the constitutional status of J&K which finally led to a feeling of one country, one people, one flag and diluting the status of autonomous J&K. Having succeeded in its mission of stopping National Conference designs, Praja Parishad merged with Jan Sangh.

Many of us are not aware that territories under Dadra Nagar Haveli were 'liberated' in a satyagrah led by 100 RSS swayamsevaks who raised the tricolour on the government buildings on 2 August 1955. They were feted years later and recognized as freedom fighters. The RSS swayamsevaks were involved in the freedom struggle for Goa in every phase. They were part of satyagrahi teams, including their prominent leader like Jagannathrao Joshi. They arranged for the food and shelters of satyagrahis who came in thousands during this struggle. In 1955, a swayamsevak Mohan Ranade raised the Tricolour in Panaji and was in prison for 15 years even after Goa was freed from Portuguese in 1961.

During 1962, Communists had supported Chinese aggression. Their leaders like Basavaponaiah went to the extent of saying that India was the aggressor, while a section of the party claimed that Chinese forces were liberating India from capitalist exploitation. Some of them were arrested for anti-national activities. There were major fissures in party on this issue which ultimately led to its break-up. As an abetment to Chinese, Communist trade union controlling water transportation services in north eastern region went on strike to create hurdles in supply of materials to Indian army. BMS (Bharatiya Mazdoor Sangh) fought this tooth and nail. It took a decision to have very strong unions in all defence establishments to stop any such blackmail in future.

A massive movement was organized to oppose transfer of 9000 sq. km. of Kutch to buy peace with Pakistan. The RSS fully supported an agitation of Jan Sangh to fight it tooth and nail. One of the biggest rally was witnessed in front of Parliament in August 1965. Similar transfer of land of Tin Bigha signed in 1974 was also fought tooth and nail on border of Bangladesh in which the ABVP (Akhil Bharatiya Vidyarthi Parishad) played a key role. Hundreds of agitators were beaten up, put behind bars. This went on for years. A senior swayamsevak was killed in police firing in 1980. Finally, the government understood the strong sentiments of people who would have been isolated in Bangladesh due to giving up of this strip of land and the agreement was modified in 1992.

During subsequent wars against India, from 1962, 1965 to 1971, the Sangh volunteers were there - running free canteens for army men, supporting the army by holding on to the supply lines. There are soul stirring stories from different wars against Pakistan about how swayamsevaks led by their local leader in places like Rajouri, Fazilka and Ferozepur refused to vacate a village or a town inspite of Pakistani shelling and raised the morale of local populace, the local administration and supported the army in every possible way. This support of the RSS has been provided right from Kutch to Rajasthan, Punjab borders to Jammu & Kashmir and to Bangladesh border.

Recognising the role the RSS played in all such national emergencies, Pandit Nehru invited them for Republic Day parade inspite of opposition from die-hard Sangh opponents. 3000 strong RSS contingent in full uniform participated in the march with just three days' notice.

From early days of Bangladeshi infiltration, the RSS has been agitating, petitioning, raising concern about this dangerous infiltration. It would surprise the reader that this infiltration by design started way back in 1906 under directions of the then Nawab of Dhaka. ABVP and the then Jan Sangh were in the forefront of such agitations. In 1950-51, Jan Sangh formed a committee of highly influential citizens which finally forced the government to push back nearly 2.20 lac infiltrators which were traced by the Sangh and Jan Sangh workers. ABVP was in the forefront of the agitation to stop Bangladeshi infiltration in Aug-October of 1983. It is sad to note that Communist government has covertly supported this Bangladeshi infiltration to augment its vote bank. Similar agitations were conducted by ABVP in Bihar, which was also a hotbed of this active infiltration. The conversion of the border districts in Bihar and West Bengal into near Muslim majority areas is not a result of growth in local Muslim population, but a part of plans of maulvis under the thumb of extremist elements of Pakistan and Bangladesh to control these border districts.

During the building of Rajasthan canal, years back, local people saw a sudden spurt in Muslim claims in Barmer and Jaisalmer areas. The Sangh and ABVP got into action and it was found that a large number of Pakistanis had crossed over to Indian side to file false complaints and grab land. Even local Muslims supported the Sangh in this work to identify these people and thousand of them were thrown back.

We are too well aware of the recent agitation conducted by local people in Jammu who had been fed up with their continuous marginalization in government and step-motherly treatment to Jammu and Ladakh region. All the talks of political settlement are centred around Kashmir valley and its separatist elements as if Jammu and Ladakh and their Hindu and Buddhist citizens don't exist! It is strange that Jammu has less number of seats in the J&K Assembly though it has more area and more population. Their revenue contribution is more but more resources are used for Kashmir. It is a set convention that J&K will never have a chief minister from Jammu region, whatever the result of an election. All this sense of being exploited and treated as second class citizens exploded in fury when the land given for temporary use for Amarnath yatra was taken back under threat from extremists and terrorists. It was an agitation which had entered each and every home of Jammu and people fought at every street corner. Women, children and men – all came on streets. The RSS provided organizational backbone to the agitation to provide organizational and logistic support which was totally run by citizens of Jammu. The markets were shut closed for weeks. People lived with great difficulty but refused to surrender to the whims of the government that professed to be that of J&K but worked only for Kashmir. Finally, the state and central government buckled and an agreement was signed. It is tragic that these patriotic agitators who waved Tricolour were often compared with extremists who waved Pakistani flags in Kashmir.

ABVP volunteers, the RSS workers, VHP and many Hindu missionaries have paid heavy price with their lives working in Naxalite infested areas of Jharkhand, Chhattisgarh, Orissa and North East. The RSS volunteers have been murdered and maimed in broad daylight, in front of students in class, in markets by Communist goondas in Kerala for years. Finding no support from the government hostile to it, sometimes the RSS volunteers have also retaliated in self-defence as newspaper reports tell us. Even teachers of the schools run by such organizations are not spared. Murder of Swami Laxmanaanand in Orissa became a news because of the popular backlash it created in that area. There are heart breaking instances of the RSS volunteers like one in which they were picked up in Tripura by extremists and taken to Bangladesh border never to be seen again.

This fight for national integration continues even today. Local village defence committees in Jammu region are fully supported by the RSS members at real risk to their lives. This is the reason why PDP and NC are unhappy with the RSS and labele it communal. Associate organizations of the RSS have set up special schools for displaced Kashmiris and people affected by terrorism. These schools have members of all communities including Muslim children, and there have been no attempts to convert them.

It has been rightly said, price for liberty is eternal vigilance. And the RSS, as an organization has been the vigilant arm of the nation all these years.

This would be the right place to recall that Dr. Hedgewar suffered two jail sentences during the satyagrahas in 1920 and 1930. He was in the organizing committee of the Congress session held in Nagpur during this period in the year 1920. He had proposed a draft resolution in the Nagpur session of the Congress in 1920 stating that the party's aim was "to liberate the countries of the world from the vicious circle of exploitation by the capitalist countries." This resolution shows that his priorities were very clear at that time too. The vision was not religious but nationalist and economic. In 1930s, the RSS members were also part of his contingent. In keeping with his philosophy, he gave up the post of the RSS chief and gave it to another senior worker before he went on satyagrah.

The SS volunteers supported 1942 agitation by whatever means they could. Many agitators were given protection in homes of the RSS swayamsevaks and supporters including that of Lala Hansraj Gupta, who headed the RSS in Delhi during those times. Since, stand of Doctor ji was clear that volunteers should participate as citizens and not as the RSS, there is no record of the RSS people who participated in such agitation. Another factor to be understood is that the RSS was a very young organization and its members joined it in their early age - around 10-12 years. Most of them were minors during the 1942 Quit India movement. I quote here from a mail I received from an elder citizen who was a young swayamsevak at that time, "I was around 19 year old at that time. At that time there were two choices either to join the movement for freedom or unite the Hindu Samaaj. I thought the masses had no discipline. I strongly felt that if the society is well-disciplined and well-united, it can achieve the goals faster. I felt that youth should work on this side and middle-aged people, matured adults should join directly to the freedom movement." I have given more information about 1942 movement and the RSS view about it in the annexure.

Doctor Hedgewar was clear from the beginning that the RSS was a man making mission and part of the society. Any action outside its scope should be done by the volunteers themselves either individually or with another organization. The RSS thought was that unless there is a strong and disciplined organization with substantial number of self-motivated people that could influence the society to act in a united manner, the struggle may not result in desired results. He had sensed that a weakened Britain due to World War II in 1940s provided an opportunity to free India with an organized, disciplined and patriotic force. He worked very hard to bring the RSS to that strength. It is said that even in sleep he would murmur, "Time is fast running out and yet we have not reached our goal."

Positive Force of Social Harmony

The RSS swaymsevak is trained from the day of his induction in such a way that caste and sects etc. have no meaning for him. He sees all members of the society as his brethren. He has a much larger identity of a Hindu. As he gets more involved in this work, his world view becomes more compassionate and all enveloping, inclusive. No person is small or big by his profession or riches, nor by caste. All his actions are in tune with this mental makeup. He doesn't need preaching about equality and social harmony. The initiative taken by VHP to declare untouchability unacceptable by various saints of Hindu community, open criticism of casteism and untouchability by the RSS heads is to be seen in this context.

The RSS has undertaken conscious organizational level steps to break the caste based divide and reform people's thinking to rise about caste and religious divide. Organizations like Saamaajik Samarasataa Manch have worked hard to remove this sense of discrimination and bias among communities. But, most touching is the way individual activists have brought about a sense of social harmony effortlessly through their individual behaviour and actions. Ramesh Patange, a noted Marathi writer, in his book *Malaa Umagalele Doctorji* (Doctor ji, as I understood him) is a poignant account of a so-called Dalit's rise from being a tailor's son living in slums to becoming a respected literary authority through the portals of the Sangh. It explains how a person from low rungs of the society can realize his potential without any outward act of charity to reach his true potential.

I recall the heated atmosphere in the society when VP Singh injected Mandal poison in Indian polity that managed to drive caste based wedge afresh in the Hindu society. The slowly disappearing walls of mutual distrust and caste based consolidation since independence were suddenly given new strength with his most cynical ploy of implementing Mandal Commission recommendations which were lying in the cold for decades. There was no public debate, there was no attempt at creating a consensus or sensitizing people about the problems that scheduled castes, tribes and backward caste people face. The issue of reservations suddenly became a burning topic with much more bitterness.

In this highly surcharged atmosphere, senior leaders of the Sangh decided that the volunteers must be sensitized to the plight of their less fortunate brethren and make them understand the issue of reservations from their perspective. Swayamsevaks being a part of this society, were also upset with these developments. Special three to four hour long workshops were conducted at various places, addressed by senior RSS workers and prachaaraks, some of them belonging to dalit groups or backward castes and some from higher castes. The lectures were followed by heated discussions. Dr Balasaheb Ambedkar's life and works and the tribulations he faced were explained all over again and swayamsevaks asked to be compassionate and understand what other less fortunate brethren were going through. It changed my perspective too. Whenever the subject of reservations comes up, I put forward the view of less fortunate members of the society even at the risk of being shouted at angrily by family members or others in the group. I can only say that it was not easy, but the Sangh leaders managed to calm the turbulence to a great extent at the risk of even losing some members.

I recall similar sacrifice that the RSS members did to keep the Sikh-Hindu unity intact during height of separatist movement and terrorism in Punjab. Since, the RSS was the biggest obstacle in the militant designs of creating a wedge between Sikhs and Hindus, its members were targeted by the terrorists. The mindless firing on swayamsevaks in a shakha in Moga was the biggest massacre of the RSS people during this time. Individuals were also targeted. But, activists were asked not to lose their calm and fight for the organic unity that marked relationship between Sikhs and Hindus. The RSS formed special relief committees and offered help to widows and other members of the families affected by terrorism in terms of financial help, occupational training etc. Of course, this feeling of brotherhood was equally nurtured by Sikh community and they too paid with blood for this effort of not letting anything break centuries of kinship. Incidentally, alternative terms for Sikhs and Hindus in Punjab used to be 'keshdhari' and 'sahajdhari' people. Many families since the times of Guru Gobind Singh would offer their eldest son to the 'panth' i.e. Sikh faith as it was considered the sword arm of Hinduism since the earliest days of the birth of Sikhism. Many Gurus sacrificed their lives to protect dharma which is Hindu dharma. Who can forget the martyrdom of Guru Tegh Bahadur or sons of Guru Gobind Singh who were buried alive in the walls of the fort at Sirhind by Mughals? It is said in Punjab that relationship between Hindus and Sikhs is like nail and the skin. It is not easy to separate them. Finally, the forces of nationalism and national integration won and peace returned to Punjab.

1984 anti-Sikh pogrom was an acid test for the Indian citizens and the Hindu society. Contrary to the short public memory which only conjures up Delhi, post-Indira Gandhi assassination, the violence against Sikhs was abetted by the Congressmen across India wherever possible. We cannot call these riots as it was highly one-sided affair. Just to give an instance, while during Gujarat riots of 2002, one- third of the dead were Hindus, in case of this anti-Sikh violence there was hardly any casualty apart from that of thousands of unfortunate Sikh brethren. The RSS swayamsevaks not only hide Sikh families in their homes but also challenged rioters to go back and spare Sikhs. These attempts at mass homicide were made in nearly all the cities of North India. Balasaheb Deoras, the then chief of the RSS came out strongly against this carnage. The RSS chief of Punjab cautioned Hindus not to fall prey to anti-Sikh reactions. In places like Patna, Bharatpur, Ranchi and Kanpur, swayamsevaks and their seniors played key role in defusing the tension. In Deoband, the local RSS sanghchaalak, stood in front of local Gurudwara challenging people to stop and calm down. In Kanpur, the RSS volunteers actually fought with ruffians to stave off their attack on Sikh families. In South, in Coimbatore, VHP worker gave shelter to several Sikh families whose shops had been attacked and burnt down.

I would like to digress a little here and remind you that it was not the first time that the Congress hooligans went on a rampage. In the aftermath of Gandhi's murder, the Congress supported hooligans had taken to streets and spit venom of hatred against the Sangh volunteers for no fault of theirs. This violence was more severe in Maharashtra which was home to the RSS movement. They burnt and looted homes and shops of the RSS workers recklessly. Famous Marathi producer Bhalji Pendharkar's studio in Kolhapur was reduced to ashes in this mindless vendetta. Guruji urged his followers not to get provoked as any retaliation could lead to serious consequences for Hindu society. So, they suffered silently with forbearance.

The recent celebrations in 2008 commemorating 300 years of Guruta Gaddi, that is the declaration of Guru Gobind Singh ji that Holy Guru Granth Sahib would be the Guru of Sikh faith and there won't be any other Guru after him, were supported wholeheartedly by the Sangh parivaar with active participation in it. This participation included a grand langar in Nanded Sahib and festive programmes all over country etc. It took initiative to explain to the society at large that Guru Granth Sahib is one of the most egalitarian holy book with collection of words of wisdom of not only the Sikh gurus but also from all over India from saints, sufis who belonged to Hinduism and Islam and from all levels of social hierarchy.

Proactive action of the BJP Chief Minister Yediyurappa of inviting Karunanidhi to unveil the statue of great Tamil poet philosopher Thiruvallur in Bangalore was a landmark event in the post-independence history of India that scotched an unseemly controversy hanging fire of 18 years. It heralded a new era of mutual respect through this effort to bridge the politically created and nurtured political and cultural divide between Kannadigas and Tamils. This resulted in Karunanidhi reciprocating and inviting his counterpart to unveil the statue of the great Kannada savant Sarvajna. One can always expect such positive action for social harmony from the Sangh members.

The RSS volunteers have arranged for all sections of society to attend social festivals like Ram Navami, Gita Jayanti and Ambedkar Jayanti etc. Examples abound in places as diverse as Gadegaon and Akola in Vidarbha, Mallapally in Tamil Nadu, Udupi in Karnataka and many more places. Many swayamsevaks have taken personal initiative to educate or guide less fortunate and neglected brethren toward better life. The RSS took lead in celebrating Dr Babasaheb Ambedkar birth anniversary all over the country. The centenary celebrations were organized with all organizations of the Sangh parivaar taking part in them enthusiastically. Other similar functions are regularly held by organizations like ABVP and Saamaajik Samarasataa Manch etc.

As a part of celebration of Golden Jubilee of satyagrah in October 1982 to allow 'harijan' entry into Guruvayoor temple in Kerala, VHP organized a public reception of 27 surviving satyagrahis. At the same time, one hundred harijans decided to start a 200 mile march to end century old custom of not allowing harijans to have food in main meal hall of Krishna temple. Contrary to expectations of Communists and their cohorts, The RSS decided to give full support to the move. The marchers were accorded warm welcome all along the way. The RSS leaders also were able to persuade the temple authorities to break from the past and allow this common food partaking. They agreed. It was a soul stirring scene to witness all the society together with its Harijan brethren having food together in the main meal hall of the temple. Many such events have taken place all over the country with many saints taking lead in breaking century old shackles.

Provincial conference of VHP in Udupi, Karnataka in 1969 was attended by thousands of people and dharmaachaaryas from all shades of Hindu faith. They declared in the conference – "In pursuance of the objective that the entire Hindu society should be consolidated with the spirit of indivisible oneness and that there should be no disintegration in it because of tendencies and sentiments like 'untouchability', the Hindus all over the world should maintain the spirit of unity and equality in their mutual intercourse." The conference gave a stirring call, "Hindavah Sodaraah Sarve" (All Hindus are brothers).

Guruji's silent persuasion to all saints and math heads and swayamsevaks' background work led to this transformation. Saints like Swamiji of Pejawar Math went into backward colonies to bless them and the movement slowly picked pace with many other math heads joining the movement.

Sanskrit teaching was taken to 'harijan' locality in Mysore. A one month long Veda Shikshana Shibir was taken in Hariharapura near Shringeri where boys from all sects and casts learned together and stayed together. And opponents of the RSS call it 'manuvadi'!

Similar initiatives have been taken in Andhra Pradesh. People from so-called low castes were trained with the help of Tirupati Tirumala Dewaswom Board in Hindu rituals.

In Ernakulam, under auspices of VHP, a massive conference was conducted in which training was given to socially backward sections at Adwaita Ashram in Alwaye in the presence of chief priest from Ezhava community, assisted by a Namboodiri. This programme was personally blessed by His Holiness Swami Jayendra Saraswati, Shankaracharya of Kanchi Kamakoti Peetham.

There are instances of happy inter-caste marriages between a swayamsevak's sister or daughter and a dalit or low caste colleague, adoption of children of slums by senior swayamsevaks to look after all their needs from food to studies, going out of way to invite such basti members for marriage etc. Though there are many examples in this regard, the most people would recall the marriage of Pramod Mahajan's sister (a 'brahmin') to Gopinath Munde (a member of 'Scheduled Tribe'). Even in rigid caste based society like Haryana, swayamsevaks have gone out of way to attend wedding of their so-called low caste colleagues and helped in every way as if they were part of the family. I know of an ABVP prachaarak who married a Muslim girl about 25 years back and he was blessed by his senior leaders. All his friends from the RSS and ABVP attended the marriage in full force. Such examples also illustrate that the Sangh people are as humane as you and me, and they too fall in love and have love marriages. But, they believe this to be sacred and profound emotion that should not be commercialized and trivialized.

To promote social brotherhood and sense of equality and self respect for all sections of Hindu society, the RSS volunteers in Delhi organized 'devi poojan' of nearly 10,000 girls of which 5000 were from slums. Bimal Kedia in Mumbai has been celebrating Diwali continuously for nearly 15 years with the young boys of a local orphanage by offering them dinner at home with his family and friends. Such examples of individuals could be in thousands.

2500 years ago, Lord Gautam Buddha was denied entry into Kashi. To this day, there was an atmosphere of confrontation. However during the VHP World Conference in January 1979, His Holiness Dalai Lama was invited for the conference and accorded welcome by the mantra chanting Vedic scholars. It was a moving experience for the Dalai Lama and a historic movement for Hindus and Buddhists.

In Tamil Nadu, swayamsevaks celebrated Raksha Bandhan festival in a Christian school. The principal was, herself, present for it and said emotionally, "I too am a Hindu — a Christian Hindu." Christian scholars have been called to be part of some RSS festivals and programmes in Kerala.

Seva Bharati runs sanksaar kendras in many slums all over India to impart good values to children who don't get a chance to have such an education. The effect on them and their family is electrifying and gives them an entirely new dimension in life. There are cases where fathers have given up drinking because their sons or daughters would come and touch their feet in the evening while they were drunk. It sparked an emotional upheaval in them.

Bhatke Vimukta Samaaj Parishad is an organization which works with the lowliest of low, people condemned to lead worst life with a stamp of criminals put on them since the time of British. Known as Pardhis and similar other communities, they are social outcasts eking out a living somehow in the dark periphery of this supposedly civilized society - unseen, unheard, picked up first in case of any robbery or theft. They are scared of so-called normal society people and, generally, keep away from them. Girish Prabhune, a prachaarak, started work amongst them in a village near Solapur. Members of these communities have broken families, run away members, some in jail for some crime, or others only on suspicion, being easy prey to police. Children in these communities are forced to do odd jobs and not encouraged to study. Breaking all such internalized habits, this organization has persuaded them to look forward to a better tomorrow. Today, a number of facilities have been raised for their schooling including a school where they can study with flexi timings because of their odd jobs. After years of effort, the first batch of S.S.C. passed students came out of the school run by this organization last year.

In Tamil Nadu, Dravid Kazhagam (DK) had picked up the now largely discredited theory of Aryan-Dravidian/North South divide and racial disharmony floated by British and ran campaigns in the name of reforms to run down Hinduism under the guise of anti-Brahminism. The RSS did not have much a base till late in Tamil Nadu, so DMK cadre (political arm of DK) didn't have any real exposure to the RSS and its swayamsevaks. However, when they were thrown behind prisons during emergency, they got to know the RSS closely and it changed the view of their cadres. DMK followers were surprised with the warmth with which they were met by the RSS volunteers in jail and the way they maintained ties with their families boosting up their morale while they were in jail.

Hindu Munnani and others have been organizing various programmes and marches to bring out harmony between various caste groups within Hindu society. Soon it had to join battle with DMK and DK for revival of Hindu religion and fight against divisive and hate politics of these groups. Nearly all Hindu saints and missionaries organizations, temple committees joined in these efforts. There was a time DK would take out a procession of Lord Rama, Sita and Laxman with chappals and shoes around their necks in Tamil Nadu. But, with challenge thrown by Hindu Munnani by announcing that people should not vote for those who insult Hindu gods, DMK had to eat a humble pie. Now, the time has come when the biggest processions are seen at the time of Ganpati visarjan in Chennai. With rise of the RSS through its spread of shakhas, many disillusioned DK and DMK members have also joined the RSS. Their efforts to drive a wedge between supposedly high caste Hindus and low castes failed to cut ice, when they saw the equally loving treatment that the Sangh members give to all children irrespective of their caste or faith.

A senior colleague of EV Ramaswami Naicker, founder of DK left DMK disillusioned and also attended functions of the RSS. He disclosed that EVR had, in fact, written to Dr Ambedkar when he was thinking of leaving Hindu fold, and impressed upon him not to leave Hindu fold and fight for dignity and rights within it.

Thus, the RSS has been striving silently and selflessly for social harmony in a political atmosphere where people try to divide society with hatred to create their separate vote banks.

Duty Towards Society (Seva)

Doctor Hedgewar, the founder of the RSS had responded to a question, "What will the RSS do in future just by building up its organization?" by saying, "The Sangh will not do anything, but swaymsevak will do everything." When he said this, people did not understand what exactly he meant. But, as the Sangh work spread and grew beyond the mandatory shakhas, the nature of work and methodology of such work also changed or began emerging. New organizations inspired by the Sangh philosophy of unity, discipline, nation building and service to the society came into being. Activists branched out into new areas and activities.

The founder's instructions were clear. The RSS was to work as a part of the society, taking society along, and not stand out as a separate organization, while taking up any task. Therefore, as far as possible, the RSS does not take up any work outside its own day-to-day activities in its name. Nor is a volunteer or swayamsevak supposed to publicize his name for any work he has done. So, though many volunteers were working in many fields, they did so as general citizens or as a part of some other organization. In today's language, they were already social activists, but not permitted to publicise themselves by the RSS code of conduct. Many activists in social service arena had started work before the Sangh officially made 'seva' as one of the activities even at the level of shakha.

These social service activities are called 'Seva karya'. Definition of Seva in the Sangh philosophy is different from charity. Seva is giving back to society, in whatever little way, something in return for what society gave you. It is not a favour you do to others, but a return of the favour the society has done unto you by giving you all that made you what you are. To quote Swami Vivekanand, "Look upon every man, woman, and everyone as God. You cannot help anyone, you can only serve: serve the children of the Lord, serve the Lord Himself, if you have the privilege." A volunteer may take up any activity of social utility and his colleagues and the Sangh will help him in that work.

During subsequent years, many inspired activists started work in various segments of the society for social upliftment. They multiplied in hundreds and thousands. All these people were inspired by Swami Vivekanand's exhortation to serve the poor downtrodden brethren as the image of God himself. Soon a need was felt to organize these social service activities in a better framework.

HV Sheshadri was the Sarkaaryaavah (General Secretary) when this activity was given a formal structure. Central leadership exhorted each shakha, specially the shakhas which are attended by adults or senior people to adopt at least one social service project in its area. This focus on social service became a source of social reforms that the RSS envisaged. The seriousness with which this subject is taken is shown by the fact that a member of the central committee, a senior prachaarak is given charge of the 'seva karya' for monitoring and supporting the activities in this field.

The Centenary celebrations of Dr Keshav Baliram Hedgewar were conducted with great enthusiasm in 1989. This occasion was used to create funds for seva karya and projects were initiated all over India in thousands.

Today over one hundred fifty thousand social work projects are going on across India - from low profile ones like libraries, cheap rented medical equipment to poor and needy, to path-breaking ones like Ekal Vidyalay and Arogya Rakshak in remote areas of India; to hospitals, blood banks, orphanages, schools, hostels, environment, projects for fishermen, rural development projects as also local level projects.

There is no segment where people inspired by the RSS are not serving the society. Seva projects cover education, health care in all its aspects, medical, child welfare, social harmony, tribal welfare, environment, rural development and disaster management. In terms of geographical spread, these activities are operational in all corners of Bharat, from Kutch to Arunachal Pradesh, Jammu to Kanyakumari, with hardly any district untouched by them. Urban population in slums (or seva bastis - as RSS calls them) to people in rural areas and tribal in deep forests, all sections of society are covered under some project or the other.

It would surprise many to know that except for a few rare exceptions, these seva projects do not draw any government grant. They are entirely supported by the society at large. It strengthens one's belief that that if the work is genuine, society is always willing to lend its helping hand to it.

It is a telling commentary on the state of affairs of our country that inspite of so much of work being done by thousands of NGOs apart from the work done by the RSS affiliated organizations, the effect on ground seems to be minimal, a mere drop of elixir in the ocean of despair. I feel the major reason for this is that the governments run by petty politicians have abdicated their responsibilities and have been playing only politics for short-term gains. Thus, these activities which should have been a supplementary service to the society have come to take up responsibility abdicated by the governments.

The numbers of seva projects run by tbe RSS and the RSS inspired organizations are huge. It is difficult to cover even some of them with justice. So, I will just mention a few of the projects in a very brief and hope that readers will go ahead and read more literature on the subject on their own. There are a few books that have tried to do some justice to the vastness of the subject. H. V. Sheshadri's book *'RSS- Vision in Action'* has tried to give a bird's eye view by covering some projects from different segments while another book, *Seva – Amrit Kumbh* in Hindi has covered more projects, for which the writer Dr Shantaram Hari Ketkar has moved all over India and covered a large number of projects in a structured manner. In recent years has the RSS started compiling data of various activities now and releases a summary of it in its annual conference (Pratinidhi Sabha). There is a dedicated website of Seva Bharati as also a magazine providing detailed account of seva work.

The RSS, like Hindu society itself, carries the cross of poor documentation. As a genetic shortcoming, even the organizations run by its people face the same problem. Thus, collecting data or finding enough material is not easy. Only recently have these organizations understood the importance of documentation and started work on it. I recall the comments of a young volunteer in Gujarat where I had gone with a team to study disaster management work done after the Gujarat earthquakes of year 2002. As the group showed us some photographs of clearing debris, carrying the dead bodies out of it, providing relief in relief camps etc, this young teenager, smiling ironically, commented, "we have learnt some lessons. Now we take photographs to record our work, because we know press will not give coverage to work done by the Sangh." It pains my heart that even in such noble causes, press plays a partisan role.

Given below is a summary of various social service projects going as on Feb 2009. For ease of compilation, they have been set into mega verticals. Within them there are number of sub-segments. As you read some representative accounts after this table, you will be able to grasp the vast spread and depth of these activities.

Sewa Karya as on Feb 2008								
State (Kshetra is region) (States as per RSS structure)	No.of Places	No.of activities	Types of Activities					
			Edu.	Health	Social	Self-Reliance	Uday Gram	Prabhat Gram
2	3	4	5	6	7	8	9	10
Kerala	1477	4617	785	1006	1964	852	33	-
South Tamil Nadu	3167	8714	922	380	7323	89	15	6
North Tamil Nadu	237	1346	520	310	206	-	-	-
Dakshin (South) Kshetra	**4881**	**14677**	**2227**	**1706**	**9493**	**941**	**48**	**6**
South Karnataka	2050	7431	2217	389	2350	2275	42	18
North Karnataka	485	1218	151	97	286	684	-	-
West Andhra	403	731	452	53	204	22	4	3
East Andhra	426	470	181	205	72	12	-	-
Dakshina Madhya (South Central) Kshetra	**3564**	**9850**	**3001**	**944**	**2912**	**2993**	**46**	**21**

Konkan	954	1307	442	642	74	149	4	1
West Maharashtra	361	679	218	353	44	164	7	-
Devgiri	544	1262	331	312	124	495	-	-
Gujarat	429	722	275	318	49	80	9	4
Vidarbha	304	510	171	145	138	56	-	-
Paschima (West) Kshetra	**2596**	**4480**	**1437**	**1770**	**429**	**844**	**20**	**5**
Central Bharat	2200	3595	2059	361	1028	147	19	3
Maha Koshal	1051	1233	1109	25	54	45	18	7
Chhattisgarh	2788	2882	2528	13	68	273	8	4
Madhya (Central) Kshetra	**6039**	**7710**	**5696**	**399**	**1150**	**465**	**45**	**14**
Chittor	89	304	122	65	80	37	-	-
Jaipur	91	253	119	38	79	17	10	3
Jodhpur	112	197	86	29	27	55	12	3
Uttar Paschima (North west) Kshetra	**292**	**754**	**327**	**132**	**186**	**109**	**22**	**4**
Delhi	104	2006	598 134	534	740	-	-	
Haryana	91	427	125 37	99	166	3	-	
Punjab	127	570	290 74	91	115	-	-	
Jammu & Kashmir	288	328	263 11	14	40	-	-	
Himachal Pradesh	46	91	64	11	4	12	-	-

Uttar (North) Kshetra	**656**	**3422**	**1340**	**267**	**742**	**1073**	**3**	**-**
Uttarakhand	180	254	192	32	8	22	4	2
Meerut	202	321	70	116	75	60	26	2
Brij	310	625	142	205	219	59	10	4
Paschima (West) U.P.Kshetra	**9692**	**1200**	**404**	**353**	**302**	**141**	**40**	**8**
Kanpur	191	495	192	84	169	50	15	-
Avadh	159	413	103	205	77	28	22	-
Kashi	113	558	124	200	200	34	21	2
Goraksha	331	364	83	97	133	51	29	-
Poorva (East) Uttar Kshetra	**794**	**1830**	**502**	**586**	**579**	**163**	**87**	**2**
Uttar Bihar	48	72	24	15	8	25	20	-
Dakshina Bihar	148	250	108	44	49	49	9	1
Jharkhand	1272	1616	262	18	28	1308	4	1
Uttar Madhya (North Central) Kshetra	**1468**	**1938**	**394**	**77**	**85**	**1382**	**33**	**2**
Utkal (Orissa)	998	1539	459	516	184	380	10	1
South Bengal	183	273	134	78	12	49	17	3
North Bengal	154	258	24	205	1	28	9	-

Poorva (East) Kshetra	1335	2070	617	799	197	457	36	4
North Assam	4246	4843	231	4190	223	199	18	-
South Assam	432	437	26	397	-	14	10	-
Assam Kshetra	**4678**	**5280**	**157**	**4587**	**223**	**213**	**28**	-
Total Sewa Projects by Sewa Bharati	**26778**	**53279**	**16208**	**11665**	**16412**	**8994**	**408**	**66**
Vishwa Hindu Parishad	25922	72370	25922	23204	22394	850	-	-
Vidya Bharati	729	9682			1000			
Deendayal Research Institute	10238	1000	3147	2741	6795			
Vanvasi Kalyan Ashram	-	13969		1050		1286	-	-
Bharat Vikas Parishad	**48**	461	149	41	60	-	-	-
Rashtriya Sevika Samiti	-	168	98	57	13	211	-	-
ABVP	-	68	6	45	10	7	-	-
Total Anya Sanstha	**46619**	**98768**	**39004**	**27138**	**30272**	**2354**	-	-
Grand total	**73397**	**151979**	**55206**	**38758**	**46674**	**11331**	**408**	**66**

A Few Illustrative Examples

The above compilation does not cover disaster management and relief work as it is done on adhoc basis, as and when a situation demands. However, it contains long term resettlement projects taken up for the disaster affected people. I will touch upon a few of the disasters that were so mammoth and terrifying that people still remember them. Needless to say the RSS swayamsevaks reach every place where they can, even before the government agencies or other NGOs reach. Thus, there are countless disasters that have seen the RSS workers risk their life and limbs to save people and give them immediate relief.

The mega disasters like the tidal waves in Andhra Pradesh, dam break and subsequent flooding in Morbi, Cyclone in Kandla port in Kutch, Gujarat, followed by the most devastating earthquake in Gujarat in year 2002, famines of Bihar and Maharashtra, earthquake of Maharashtra, recent Tsunami in South India and floods in Bihar are some of the incidents that people recall. The RSS volunteers even take up the task that others avoid or don't have stomach to do, like picking up decaying and deformed dead bodies from debris with high risk of contacting some infection apart from stench and the sheer guts it needs to do such a job. They set up relief camps in shortest possible time with least resources, all contributed by local Sangh volunteers and other people of society in that region to begin with. A young volunteer shared his experience rather morbidly, "We had experience of picking up decaying bloated bodies after Kandla cyclone, job during earthquake was a little easy as the bodies were dry and light."

These boys are not some disaster experts nor are they paid workers, but the love for society and its members drives out any fear or feeling of inadequacy as they rush out to help fellow members. I have heard some super human feats from totally normal human beings with inspiration they draw from their daily shakha work. People who would never jump from a single floor, went up in 3 or 4 storied buildings with tied up sarees and brought back people stuck in badly damaged buildings after the earthquake. It is just one example. If you listen to other countless stories you would get goose pimples. If you were present there in those days, you might have collapsed out of sheer emotional exhaustion.

All the relief camps are run without any religious bias. There are examples of Muslim families being given special space to perform namaaz. During one such disaster efforts were made for them to perform their Ramzan fasts properly. On an earlier occasion Guruji had said, "Let our workers work in the right spirit of Dharma making no distinction in doing service to whoever he may be, a Christian or a Muslim or any other persuasion. For, calamities, distress and misfortunes make no such distinction. They afflict all alike."

Many senior the RSS workers realized that disasters are part of life and the swayamsevaks have worked in these situations for years. Every time there is a re-learning process. So, it was decided recently to have some structure for disaster management work. With this in mind and the learnings over year, a disaster management module has been introduced in the annual Sangh Shiksha Vargs of one month duration that select the RSS activists attend once a year.

I have already talked of thousands of schools running in cities, towns, villages, tribal areas from South to North and West to East. Of the educational projects, Ekal Vidyalay is a unique project which I have covered in another chapter describing associate or sister organizations of the RSS. There are organizations that run mobile laboratories for schools in remote villages as also vans that educate children and expose them to science education in an innovative way. In most of the places, the RSS offices double up as study centres for poor students in the area as also unofficial hostels or sleeping arrangements for students who come from villages to study in towns. Gopinath Munde, a prominent leader of BJP stayed in the RSS office in Pune for a few years while he was studying for his graduation.

A new initiative by **Sewa Bharati**, called 'Swasthya Mitra' is a kind of 'bare foot doctor' primary health project. Within a span of two years, there are around 2500 health volunteers who are recruited from the village itself, trained in primary healthcare - both preventive and curative, recognition of some critical diseases of those areas and assisting the affected people in reaching the right place for medical attention. Currently, the major focus is in North East. The volunteers are paid a nominal amount per month. As and when they get time, they also run small 'bal wadis' for the children and inculcate value education to them as well as assist them in their schooling. The results are outstanding. This could be a major movement in coming years.

Deendayal Research Institute and a few other organizations are focused entirely on self-reliance through rural development, afforestation, horticulture, farming using of traditional systems with innovations in new environment for better returns, indigenous technologies etc. Its Gonda project in UP is considered a must visit project for people who wish to work for rural development. It empowers people to utilize various facilities floated by government and banks instead of giving out doles or funds itself. It encourages initiatives taken by local people in farming activity, seed development, irrigation etc.

Seva Sagar project by swayamsevaks of Sagar tehsil in Shimoga district of Karnataka state has carried out many a movement of social transformation. But, most interesting to me is their project of afforestation which started with a resistance movement against felling of trees in a 90 acre area, followed by a 'Vriskha Laksha Andolan' (movement for lakhs of trees) under this, each village is encouraged to have its own forest land with gifting of saplings on auspicious occasions. They have fought off destructive planting of eucalyptus for plywood industry as they are harmful to the nature. Such projects are coming up in different states now. Dr Babasaheb Ambedkar Trust, Aurangabad has also adopted this idea.

RSS is carrying out a number of I**ntegrated Rural Development** projects across India.

The villages under rural development projects are divided in two categories - the Uday gram is where the movement has just begun and Prabhat grams are those which can be considered model villages. Rural development is one of the focus development area in the RSS seva scheme of things. Late Rajju Bhaiyya, the then Sarsanghchaalak of the RSS outlined three priorities for this initiative. The villages should be 'kshudha mukta' (hunger free), 'rog mukta' (disease free) and 'shikshayukta' (literate).

Dr Hedgewar Seva Samiti began work in Nandurbar, identified by Government of India as one of the most backward 50 districts about 7–8 year back. Today, this trust is running 270 flexible timing schools for tribal boys and girls that are being manned by full-time workers who have come out of these schools. Tribals here move to Gujarat for livelihood after Kharif season is over. To take care that children do not miss their education, a residential school has been started. The Samiti has done tremendous work in agriculture including new agricultural practices in collaboration with scientists who come on site to guide farmers, research in agriculture, seed bank, environment protection that improves land productivity, farmer clubs for exchanging technology and other information with each other, community production centres for oil and 'aamchur' (dried mango powder) that will reduce workload on womenfolk, micro-banking groups etc. This project is taking support from various government and non-government bodies including Sir Ratan Tata Memorial Trust in its endeavour.

Gau Vigyan Sansthan, near Nagpur has been doing lot of research on utilizing various products made out of cow produce. It is fashionable to laugh out and ridicule at this kind of research. It would be foolish to write off medicinal cures defined clearly in Ayurveda treatise available. When the world is accepting the Vedic wisdom, it would be a tragedy to laugh it off who westerners actually copyright these cures. The organization has already got two patents for two such products. It is now well-established that organic farming is best for man and land. People are paying more to get organically grown food. Various organizations working on these principles have proven that cow is productive and even economically viable animal from its birth to death. It is not just milk and ghee producer but also organic manure, medicines etc. But as usual, we shall accept this only when it comes from the West. Gaushala at Keshav Srishti near Mumbai runs a self-sufficient project selling various kinds of products made of cow produce. It doesn't depend on donations to take care of non-milk producing cows.

Some organizations are working on urban renewal. **Janaadhaar Sewaabhavi Sansthaa** in Latur takes contract for garbage collection and disposal. It employs educated boys and girls as supervisors and uneducated ones as workers. Employees are also taken from amongst the cured leprosy affected patients coming from Mahatma Gandhi Kushtdhaam in an adjoining hamlet. It has spun off women's savings schemes under micro-finance banking as also self-help groups. The glow on the faces of these unfortunate brethren is seen to be believed after they have become productive assets to the society and become self-sufficient with due respect given to their job. The project is led by a young engineer swayamsevak who gave up his profession for this programme. The vision of this organization states - Self Employment, Co-operation, Education, Security leading to Dignity.

There are some outstanding examples of institutions working in public health. I would just talk of one - **Dr Hedgewar Hospital** run by a trust called **Dr Babasaheb Ambedkar Trust** in Aurangabad. Started 17 years ago by a team of dedicated doctors with the RSS background with personal loans and pawning their wives' jewellery in a house given to them by a local RSS leader, today this organization has a 160 bed hospital to be upgraded to 300 beds soon, arguably the best in the region and has treated 2.5 million patients in 15 years at nearly 1/3rd of the cost of private hospitals. Its blood bank has been adjudged one of the best in Asia. The most important part of the narrative is that it runs 50 other projects under its wings in slums and nearby villages ranging from education, computer training, water harvesting, women's self help groups, micro-financing, HIV/Aids, afforestation, plantation of fruit bearing trees etc. etc. - leaving out hardly any section of the society in the region. Inspired by it, another group of doctors fresh from colleges have decided to start a similar project in Nashik. It took six to seven years of sustained visits by the doctors of Dr Hedgewar hospital to motivate this young band of aspiring doctors through their exposure to social projects and other activities that led them to this new direction in life.

Vivekanand Yoga Anusandhana Samsthanam (Svyasa, in short) University, Bangalore headed by Dr HR Nagendra is a well-known name that carries out basic research on Yoga and various facets of Indian knowledge as applicable to human well-being at physical as well as mental level. Svyasa University has full-time bachelors and masters courses on Yoga. This project was initiated much before Yoga became fashionable and a money making business.

There are more than 5000 women's' self help groups and micro-finance groups in southern Tamil Nadu alone supported by Sewa Bharati. Such self-help groups and micro-finance schemes are being run totally by women very successfully in thousands of villages and poor colonies all over India, giving them new hope in life.

Then, there are local level organizations all over India running schools and other social projects. I can think of 'Asmita' in Jogeshwari, Mumbai which came into being during Emergency in an economically backward area. Today, it is housed in a well-designed building, running schools, vocational guidance centre and various other projects, run very efficiently by the people from the locality itself.

With nearly 1.50 lac projects all over India, you can well imagine how much work is being done in various sectors. The narrative above is not even a representative list. It is now up to you to know more about them.

Defending and Nurturing Hindu Faith

Insidious attempts to convert Hindus to Christianity and Islam by force or lure have been going on for centuries now. Revered Swami Dayanand Saraswati stresses again and again that conversion is an act of violence against spirit. It is the worst way of disturbing a person's peace of soul when he or she is also forced to change behaviour, customs and belief that he or she carried since birth and collective memory which goes back to centuries. Thus, conversion is not just change in mode of worship, to which nobody would have any problem. The harmful impact is felt when major section of society is forced to cut itself off from its roots with forced new behaviour right from dress to social conduct, thus dividing the society on sectarian lines.

Conversion by force is recorded in history, especially during Mughal period. Unless we digest this bitter truth and accept it; also explain to our Muslim brethren that nearly all of them are Muslims by sword and they had no choice, there is bound to be some unease. A few, like zamindars or jagirdars may have changed religion due to thirst of lucre but they were very few. Thus, a change in last 8-9 generations shouldn't mean their being forced away from their cultural legacy of thousands of years. They would be much comfortable and happy with acceptance of their ancient legacy. Even Pakistan is trying to appropriate the culture of Harappa and Mohenjo-Daro and Taxila University to legitimize its nationhood. Then, why should we give up on our rich and great heritage? Indonesia, inspite of being one of the largest Islamic country today, hasn't disowned its ancestors. They proudly display it through their names and their arts in public life. Thailand is a predominantly Buddhist country, but proudly displays its Hindu heritage through display of Puranic tales like 'Samudra Manthan' as the centre piece in its new airport, significantly called Swarnabhumi Airport. It also has statues of Rama and other displays about Mahabharata in and around its capital city.

Similarly, forced conversions by Church, specially backed by Portuguese colonialists in places like Goa, Daman and Diu are too new to be recounted all over again. There has been lot of attempts to wipe away the memories of torturous inquisitions, but only records can be wiped off not the memories. Church forces under British patronage used all kinds of guile and subtle force to convert majority of tribals in North East by the time India was independent. Special laws were made to suit missionaries in North East while stopping other Indians from visiting these areas. Special permits are required even now for Indians to visit many parts of this region.

Nothing can be done about that which is history. The RSS resolved that conversions - forced or by allurement or fraud would not be allowed anymore in independent India and it worked along with its associate organizations with vigour to stop these practices wherever it could. This resolve is not against Christians, Muslims or any other community, but against the attempts at changing the demographic structure of India and also putting seeds of unrest in the society. It has helped thousands of people to return to their original beliefs.

Following is a small account of work done by various Hindu organizations with the help of the RSS to fight a tough battle against the agencies that are fuelled by billions of dollars for evangelization from countries from west and by Saudi petro-dollars. If you were to pick up the RBI reports on donations coming from abroad, you shouldn't be surprised to find that huge majority of these are being funneled to these evangelist bodies. *Tehelka* magazine ran a story on funds being funneled into India through FCRA donations. In the story it says, "According to MHA figures, the funding for Christian mission agencies have shown a regular increase. Also, over 80 per cent of the voluntary organisations receiving foreign funds are Christian Mission agencies."

Though the RSS has been working silently in this direction for decades, the nation as such woke up rudely to these harsh realities in 1981 when 800 Hindu families converted en-masse into Islam in Meenakshipuram. Isha-ud-ul-Islam, the body spearheading this drive boasted that they expected around 1,00,000 'harijans' to come to the liberating religions, Islam. Whole of South Tamil Nadu was targeted. Every week, newspapers talked of some mass conversion ceremony or the other in one village after another. RSS swung into action and formed Hindu Ottraumai Maiyam (Centre for Hindu Unity) which was a forum for various Hindu organizations like Hindu Munnani, VHP and others. The leaders of the organization moved around and persuaded the heads of various mutts in this region to come out and help secure justice for 'harijans'. Hindu religious leaders of various sects understood the gravity of the situation and also the injustice done to their own brethren. The movement gathered force and any further damage the Hindu society was stopped. Kerala saw the efforts for conversion both from Islamic organizations as also by Church. With sustained growth of the RSS and support of society, these efforts were thwarted over time to some extents.

North East, for decades, has been a major centre for conversion especially by Christian missionaries, earlier supported by British and later by non-action of 'secular' government. Since, the times of British, there were efforts to separate them from Hindu mainstream by labeling them 'animists'. Guruji challenged this notion and pointed out that the root of animist is animus which means principle of life. Not only that, Hindus too worship nature and animals. 'Naag' worshipped by Nagas is also worshipped all over India. For example, in Tamil Nadu it is worshipped along with Lord Subramanya. Naag panchami is celebrated all over India. Animals and birds form the background of pantheon of Hindu gods and goddesses as their vehicles. Though, the Sangh was little late in reaching out to North East due to limitations of manpower and resources, it picked up the gauntlet by 1970s.

Naga freedom fighter Rani Ma Gaidinliu was invited to World Hindu Conference in 1979 in Prayag (Allahabad). She was overwhelmed and pointed out how Naga leaders had fought British. She formed an apex body 'Harake Conference' that represented three major tribes of Nagas. Harake means Pure Faith. Bharatiya Janjaati Samskriti Manch (Indian Tribal Cultural Forum - ITC) was soon formed which worked hard to enlighten the tribal brothers about their ancient heritage and their own methods of worship. Saraswati Shishu Mandirs were set up in 1981 in Nagaland and Manipur. Till then, the only education they were getting was from Christian missionaries where Bible was taught in local language or in government schools which offered 'secular' education. They were not aware of their own traditions and practices. Medical centres by Vanvasi Kalyan Ashram too were started.

Translations of Ramayan, Geeta, Buddha and Chaitanya Mahaprabhu's lives were released by the ITC forum in Khasi dialect in Meghalaya. Adi Research Centre was started in Arunachal Pradesh. Karbi tribals rediscovered their Vaishnav roots and traditional poojas, yagyas etc. have been restarted. Karbis now trace their ancestry to Bali and Sugriv, Tiwas trace theirs to Sita and Mishmis of Arunachal Pradesh to Rukmini, hence Krishna. In year 1988, a Christian principal of Aizwal College talked about Ram Katha in tribal customs. Vidya Bharati encouraged studies in local tribal languages. Today, there are nearly 200 schools in this region. Apart from this, Ram Krishna Mission has been doing exemplary work as also many other Hindu organizations. All this has halted the tide of Christian conversions and also strengthened nationalist feelings amongst various tribes and local population.

Years ago, the RSS and VHP fought to remove Muslim encroachers on the tribal lands in Cachar ranges of Assam and fought against Church designs on cremation grounds of Karbi and Anglong tribes. All this also went a long way in strengthening the morale of local people and fight back attempts to browbeat them into accepting other religions. ABVP campaigned hard to declare Sardar Tirot Singh as a Khasi freedom fighter and finally Meghalay government gave him recognition and declared his birthday as a holiday.

During all these activities, Hindu activists and missionaries have faced immense hardships and hurdles from leaders of the Church, including threats of murder. Even the locals who give shelter to these workers are threatened directly or through extremists, some have even lost lives. So strong is the persecution that a friend of mine from Mumbai, who had gone as a prachaarak to North East, had to return as he could not face tough conditions created against him by the Christian missionaries there. But, movement carries on with grim determination.

In Madhya Pradesh, the game of missionaries was first exposed by Niyogi Commission set up by the MP's Congress government in 1951. Vanvasi Kalyan Ashram was established in 1952 and has grown from strength to strength with genuine social support system for tribals through various programmes. It has also reversed the conversion game of missionaries. In Jashpur, the fight began with struggle to return grabbed land of tribals by Church authorities with the help of the ex Raja Kumar Singh Judev. VAK and VHP have led the movement of 'ghar vapasi' (return back to faith) very successfully. Tremendous amount of work has been done in form of Bhajan mandlis, yuvak kendras, satsang samitis, schools etc.

M L Kaul in *Kashmir – Past & Present, Unraveling the Mystique,* writes in the chapter eight, "The Hindus not given to the campaigns for proselytisation outright rejected the suggestion of Maharaja Ranbir Singh, a scion of the Dogra dynasty, to reconvert the Muslims to the fold of Hinduism as they were forcibly converted to the faith of Islam and were willing to hark back to their original faith and creed. Even the influential elements among the Hindus of Kashi are said to have turned down the suggestion of the Maharaja." This supposed act of tolerance can be seen as one of the crucial factors behind current disastrous state of affairs in J&K. Learning lessons from history, the Sangh took proactive action in following the footsteps of Swami Dayanand, founder of Arya Samaaj movement, Swami Shraddhanand and Veer Savarkar who had worked hard through 'shuddhi movement' for people who vished to return to Hindu fold. Guruji, Chief of the RSS called for a fresh 'shuddhi' movement while responding to his reception on completion of his 51 years. He called for converts to come back to their original faith.

Vishwa Hindu Parishad, in its first plenary session in 1966 in Karnataka witnessed an unforgettable moment in history when revered head of Pejawar Peeth declared "Na Hindu Patito Bhavet" i.e. no Hindu is ever fallen. With one stroke the stigma of caste based discrimination and reconversion was removed. Then on "paraavartan" and "ghar waapasi" became a watchword for Hindu organizations working in various parts of Bharat.

VHP took out Jagannath Rath Yatra across tribal areas of Orissa which covered around 1000 places from March 1986 to May 1988 in which around 3–4 million people participated. Dilip Singh Judeo led hundreds of converts back into Hindu fold by washing their feet in the presence of various religious heads.

There are thousands of Chauhan Rajput Muslims in Rajasthan who got converted to Islam after defeat of Prithviraj Chauhan. Though they are Muslims by faith, they follow all the customs of Hindus. They were being pressurized by local maulvis to drop all Hindu practices and become staunch Muslims. They got so fed up that they went to the head priest of Pushkar temple who happened to the chief of the RSS there. He organized their return to faith with full honour. Same kind of customs are also seen in Jammu where Muslims recognize their Hindu antecedents with love and pride. Reconversions have also happened in north east in places like North Cachar and other places with support from VHP. In Valsad, in Gujarat, there is an annual Maaval Mata Yatra in which all citizens irrespective of their religious practices participate. Some of them have come back to their original faith now. A few years ago a massive congregation of tribals from all over India participated in a religious festival named 'Shabri Kumbh' at a place in South Gujarat which is believed to be the place where mother Shabri lived when Lord Ram visited her during the search of his wife Sita. It was attended by around 60,000 tribals and other Hindus with full support from Hindus from all over India. It was a sight for sore eyes and a great emotional pilgrimage for tribal brethren.

I regret to repeat myself like a cliché, yet again, that this is just a glimpse of great amount of work that the RSS and its associate organizations have done to beat back the curse of conversions. People on the ground, where these organizations work, often complain "you came nearly 30 years too late." But, historical compulsions, shortage of resources, active opposition and persecution by 'secular' lobbies exploited by Church and Islamic organizations still leaves lot to be done.

❑

14

Current Scenario

From a small beginning in Nagpur as a group of young boys playing in playgrounds, the RSS grew into a protector of Hindu community before and after partition, a sword arm of India during various attacks and a saviour in various calamities. With its expansion into nearly all the fields and segments of society after 1948 its presence is all pervading. As seen earlier, social service activities inspired by the RSS cover nearly the whole gamut of social activities. From a cultural organization it has grown into a movement of Hindu renaissance and nation building. It is no more restricted to the RSS shakhas, but new grounds for accretion to strength and its ideological spread have emerged.

Inspite of this steady but strongly rooted growth, question marks have been raised about its achievements during all these years of existence. Any person in social domain in today's fast moving life gets impatient and despondent when he or she cannot see changes happening fast enough. It is like a parent looking at his or her child everyday and not sensing any real change, till he looks at some earlier photographs or some neighbour or relative exclaims, "Oh, how has she grown and changed!" The activists who have dedicated their lives, or best years and moments of their lives to this cause would surely be going over their lives once in a while and thinking, "was it worth it?" In the ebb and rise of history, such questions do arise. The initial chapter about landmark events in the life of the RSS has given alert reader an overview of its growth, evolution and contribution to national life of Bharat.

Critics as also well-wishers talk about the decline in the RSS these days as reflected through its shakhas on open grounds and its presence in the middle class areas, its natural recruiting ground in its earlier phases. Thus, even as recruitment to its ideological school of thought is taking place through different associate and sister organization, visible presence through shakhas on playgrounds is not as impressive as it was once. I view it as a consequence of the change in the whole social dynamics in last few decades. The social atmosphere that followed independence and the preceding generation laid stress on commitment to nation and social causes, moral values etc. That generation worried less about material gains and did not mind foregoing material growth for social good. Middle class of the time represented this approach. One could find even elitist members sacrificing their comfortable life to do something for the society. But, in the intervening period, with high influence of consumerist culture, success has come to be measured in terms of money and political power, resulting in a near amoral society. The middle class of present has become so enamoured by career of the child and earning money that there is no time or inclination for social work at a larger social level. There will always be exceptions and there still are. But, it doesn't detract from this basic submission. Children are put into coaching classes right from 9th standard, and they don't get out of this vicious circle of coaching, entrance exams, hunting for best colleges and courses till they get settled and married. Thus, the best productive years of youth who contributed to major social movements earlier on are today buried in various coaching classes and institutions. This alarming lack of interest in the country and its affairs is also reflected in large number of vacancies in officers' cadre in armed forces. A recent news story informs us that Boy Scouts numbers in US have dwindled by 43 per cent during the last decade.

Let me share a simple fact. Each year around 16,000 new volunteers go for the Sangh Shiksha Varg (approx. one month training for workers) across the country. They are always fresh faces as there is no provision of repeat course in this. Generally, one out of five volunteers who undergo one week primary training workshops ultimately go for the first year training. This means that nearly 80,000 new volunteers qualify each year to take up some responsibility or the other in the organization. These are young people who have decided consciously to dedicate their time and energy for the society. I am not sure if there is any other organization in the world, let alone India, which can boast of such a large number of dedicated fresh joinees each year.

Having submitted one simple measure of sustained growth of the RSS, I may confess that one more factor contributing to falling number of youth joining social movements and fields of activity like armed forces or less lucrative fields like teaching is the kind of education that our 'secular' lobby has thrust upon this nation. It is totally amoral, bereft of any ethical, moral and patriotic content. Media, in line with same thinking, is more interested in projecting negative images -whether in politics or social fields or glamour. It is not interested in positive stories of people who are working silently for social upliftment and growth of the nation. Thus, a young boy and girl grows up in a negative atmosphere, without any moral values or attachment to motherland, enamoured by glamour and consumerism, worried only about personal self satisfaction.

On the other hand, the lesser privileged sections of the society have become more conscious of their surroundings and want to be a part of democratic process, improvement in their individual life as well as their society. So, these youth are more active in various social movements of any hue. This has happened with the RSS too. Its visibility on yester years' playgrounds has reduced but its presence in lower strata of society, in lesser privileged localities has increased tremendously. That is why the number of shakhas has kept growing though not where we are used to see them. Similarly, the growth has continued in rural areas where there is a huge social churning. Thus, this talk of decline in the RSS ranks stems from a comparison with its own earlier image and not backed by facts.

The RSS can and shall take corrective measures to keep engaging the youth from middle and upper income group through other alternative means. But, even if the leadership has grasped this problem, it has been slow in taking corrective action to keep this segment involved with its work and philosophy. However, as noted above, recruitment through other associate organizations has grown tremendously during the years. Social service projects have got large number of educated youth from all segments of the society involved with social causes.

If we look back, the RSS and its organizational set-up in the form of shakhas was a novel and innovative concept. All through its decades of existence, the RSS has not shied away from experimenting with different methods of social mobilization, organization and opinion building. There have been innovative attempts in the form of new concept like IT-shakhas which touch and organize young people through the web. These are shakhas where people meet on the net and discuss various issues. The members meet periodically and also take part in camps. There are more than 50 IT-shakhas currently in Bangalore alone, with their own weekly get-togethers, training camps and other social service activities. Many activists have taken to social service in a big way and they have attracted surprisingly large number of young boys and girls in thousands who volunteer to work for different social service projects not only in their own areas but also in other parts of the country. Many sympathizers and volunteers have taken to creating blogs and websites that espouse cause of Hinduism, Hindutva and present alternative views on Indian history etc.

An effort has been made recently to reach out youth through the net and through campaigns in colleges and public places to come out to serve society by contributing their weekend time or one week in a year during vacations. Message is 'One week for the nation'. This experiment recently taken up in Vidarbha region has evoked highly encouraging response. These new experiments and their success show that there are large number of youth who, given the right motivation, are still ready to get involved in social service and nation building. the Sangh will, surely, search for more innovative ideas to involve today's youth in nation building in a bigger way.

The RSS has networked with various other organizations working in the public domain, religious, voluntary and reforms movements. It believes that it doesn't have a monopoly on nation building or man building. So, it cooperates with various organizations with positive approach to nation building and social awakening wherever possible. It believes that all well-meaning positive forces of national re-construction must work together, because there is so much to do and speed at which this is happening is too slow. The response from other organizations in various social fields has been encouraging. We can look forward to more velocity and momentum in its work in coming years.

❑

Epilogue

Shuddh sattvik prem apane karya kaa adhaar hai

i.e. Pure spiritual love is the foundation of our work.

– From a Sangh song

15

The Ultimate Secret

I must confess that, so far, I was only giving you information in a dry mechanist way by talking about form and structure of the RSS. Yes, I talked about its reach, its organization, philosophy, its work in different dimensions of national life, some live examples of people who make up this organization. But, I feel that it may not have adequately brought out the essence what makes it all possible. I have given strong hints about what keeps it going and growing through various real life anecdotes. But, I have not clearly stated the ultimate secret of the RSS which has more to do with spirit and heart, than with intellectual understanding of this phenomenon.

The RSS, like most successful social or cultural movements, is ignited purely with fire emanating straight from the heart — heartfelt pain and compassion for the society and a burning desire to do something to improve it. The aura of patriotism and burning desire for nation building is all enveloping through its various activities and programmes.

Unalloyed love for the motherland and readiness to do anything for it is passed on by the seniors to the juniors through their conduct. This passing on is purely through example. Only last week a colleague of mine shared a story about his mentor in his shakha, who had unfortunately died falling prey to cancer at a relatively young age. This gentleman Yashwant Prabhudesai had come from Ratnagiri with a bank job and joined the same shakha that I used to attend as a boy. Like any ambitious married young man, he managed to purchase a house with some loans. Just as he was about to shift to his own home, he came to know that a few of his junior wards in shakha were appearing for engineering exams and they did not have place for studies as their houses were too small. Without a second thought he decided to postpone his house-warming and pooja till after their exams. He gave the house over to those four young boys for three months. Not only that, but he would come personally on many nights to look after their well-being and never failed to make tea for them before going back!

The spirit of sacrifice that the RSS invokes in its members translates in such simple acts that one doesn't even note it. What value would you attach to an RSS worker Bhaurao Belvalkar's sacrifice who went as a teacher to the annual month long Sangh Shiksha Varg without a single break for 36 years, foregoing his summer holidays and simple pleasures of family life?

As I mentioned in the initial chapters of the book, I don't know of many people who became members of the RSS after understanding its goals and objectives. It is a more recent phenomenon with the advent of Net based social networking. An overwhelming majority of people came to the Sangh shakhas attracted with its games, songs, disciplined and a very cultured environment. But, they graduated to more serious business influenced by unselfish love of their seniors, their conduct in personal life and their honest dealings with others. Simply a case of leading by example. It is an irony that people talk of the need of towering icons who could influence us positively, but overlook examples around us that could transform the way we look at our own lives and society around us.

The sense of brotherhood in the RSS is infectious. In this era of purely career driven, self centred life, you do not easily believe that such people, with only unselfish love to give, exist. The sense of being part of a very big family is all pervading. This is what keeps a person going in worst of times. Pure selfless love that the RSS members radiate for each other and society, sense of joy with which they sacrifice for the society and nation brings more people into its fold than anything else.

Nearly all the people who have kept working through life for long years in the RSS, those who went on to become prachaaraks have generally been influenced and mentored by their teacher (or shikshak as the RSS members call him), a senior activist or a prachaarak. I have recounted many stories in preceding pages that illustrate this point. It reminds me of a light hearted Sangh geet (song) in Marathi village dialect which says, "We have been moulded, you too should get moulded. A touch of paaras has turned us into gold, and gold has become one with paaras." (Paaras is a mythical elixir or magic stone that is supposed to convert a base metal into gold with its touch.)

The total faith that this brotherhood generates is seen to be believed. This faith pervades all relationships within the Sangh ecology. A good swayamsevak is supposed to have excellent relations not only with his fellow member but also with his whole family. So, all his family members become his family members and they too adopt him as one of them. Volunteers are told that if they wish to be a good kaaryakartaa or worker, they should be able to enter the kitchen of the other person as a son, as a brother.

The spotless character developed in the Sangh shakhas is a cause of envy for all other social organizations. While some appreciate it, for others it takes the form of visceral hatred. People of any ideological leanings are much more comfortable contributing to various social causes when approached by the RSS swayamsevaks. This character building is through live role models and the motivation one gets from setting up higher selfless goals for one's life.

Swayamsevaks are told by their seniors during lectures that any ideology and organization passes through three stages - ignorance, ridicule and acceptance. The RSS has passed through all these phases successfully. Its members are told not to react to irritants, nor to sap energy by responding to pointless criticism and keep working silently. Ultimately the positive results if its work would result in acceptance of its philosophy and its approach to national re-construction. They understand that today's critic can turn into a supporter once he sees the RSS closely.

While people and organizations, supposedly equipped with much better intellectual armoury who ridiculed the RSS have fallen by the sides in the march of history, the RSS has kept pace and grown with each stride. This, in no way, means that intellectual rigour is not required by a social organization like the RSS; it only underlines the fact that intellectual knowledge by itself does not guarantee the success of a movement. Any movement must appeal to the heart to grow and succeed; and its participants must be motivated with live icons from amongst ordinary people around us to drive them to give off their best.

❑

16

Secretiveness of the RSS and the Media

I had noted in the beginning of the book that the exercise of writing this book began with a news story that talked of secretiveness of the RSS. I am sure, by now, any unbiased reader would have realized that there is nothing secret about the RSS' working and its organization. It is more a problem of lack of familiarity with the idiom and language that the RSS uses, which is different from the ones established by the dominant intellectual elite and media. It is also a problem to understand an organization which doesn't work on established norms of a typical Indian social organization, its non-interest in publicizing itself or its work.

I quote below an interesting passage from Guruji's biography written by the veteran prachaarak Ranga Hari, published recently. To a certain extent it provides an insight into the mindset of an average the Sangh worker and why it reacts to publicity and media the way it does, specially the previous generation of the RSS workers. Guruji had nursed the RSS for 33 years with his strong spiritual and intellectual personality. No doubt, he dominated the thinking of two generations comprehensively.

In the first year after his appointment, a well-known scholar asked Guruji during his Bombay tour in 1941, "Are you opposed to publishing literature about the Sangh? Why don't you create various kinds of literature to spread Sangh's ideology?" Guruji's response was, "I hope that a great scholar like you would be well-aware of the tradition of this country. We give more importance to spoken word - 'shruti'. As long as one can manage with the spoken word, one should work through this system only. The Sangh swayamsevaks make contacts by visiting homes and meeting people face to face; and move forward on the basis of 'shruti', that is sharing what they have experienced in their own life. While doing this, based on our experience about the growth of organization, if we feel that it is no more possible to work without 'smriti' i.e. written word, we shall not hesitate to create 'smriti' or put our thoughts and philosophy in writing. Is it not correct to say that in our own country, code of conduct – 'aachaar samhitaa' – was written only after 'shruti' had been established?" Bouddhik (intellectual training) in the Sangh falls under this classification of 'shruti'. This is not an exhibition of one's intellect, but a radiation of emotions of the heart.

There is another example in Guruji's life which indicates his abhorence to any kind of publicity for service done to the society by the Sangh volunteers. An illustrated book about the RSS volunteers' role in Indo-Pak war of 1965 had been published. When it was gifted to Guruji, he returned it, saying when a son serves his mother he does it as his dharma and doesn't go to newspapers broadcasting his services. What swayamsevaks did was their duty to the motherland and there is no need to publicize it.

Younger generation of the RSS volunteers is more open to the idea of going to the media and telling its story, but is either ill-equipped due to lack of such a culture in the RSS or media itself isn't much interested in publishing stories that may project the RSS and its associate organizations in a positive light. While this is true of a major section of media which is dominated by secular-Marxist parivaar, there is also a sizable section in media which simply doesn't know about the RSS and is carried away by the impressions created by this dominant section. The sheer inertia and disinterest in doing some legwork and research to understand the spirit of the RSS work and its positive social impact leads to absence of information about the RSS in general media. I have mentioned in earlier parts how established groups hound out pro-RSS people from their media houses, universities and institutions. It is a fact that can be the subject of research by itself that could tell us the extent to which this intellectual subversion and persecution goes on.

During my innings as media in charge for Mumbai for the RSS, I found that very few journalists turned up for briefings and discussions with the RSS leaders. They were interested only in the RSS chief as they never understood the collective nature of its leadership. It hardly took invitations to visit camps or special programmes seriously. Reports would not be found in media even in cases where a journalist had visited the programme. Either it would have been blacked out or the person may have found it rather boring with no negative story line. Since my young days, it has saddened my heart that none of the massive RSS gatherings, marches, camps were reported in the so-called national press, though regional press would generally cover them. It never seemed to amaze a press person that an organization could organize a camp of 10,000 or 20,000 volunteers for three days immaculately without any chaos with the help of amateur volunteers working part-time. I recall seeing a photograph of a group of nine-ten hapless RSS volunteers taking bath under common taps in a camp in UP that had 20,000 attendees, but not an image of such a grand and disciplined gathering! It didn't matter to them that a student organization could hold a disciplined convention with delegates paying out of their pocket even for travel without a single instance of misbehaviour on station or with members of opposite sex. Stories of such blackouts or at best presenting a ridiculous report has been a regular feature for RSS.

Though, most of enlightened readers would be aware of such distortions or blackouts, let me just narrate a few recent examples. But, before that I would cite the episode which has led to this anti-RSS stance influenced as it is by Nehruvian-Marxist nexus. I have given a brief idea about the envy RSS aroused in the Congress which led the leftist Congress leaders to push for cornering the RSS even before Gandhi's murder. I have covered it in a little detail in the annexure. Now, media knows about the truth completely with kind of information available easily about the truth of non-involvement of the RSS in any way from the CID report cited in Chapter II and Kapur Commission report. Still falsehood of the RSS being instrumental if not being directly responsible for Gandhi's murder is repeated ad-nauseam by press as and when anybody indulges in this sheer character assassination. It is also repeated routinely by reporters to embellish their report whenever they talk of the RSS. Some of us would recall that the RSS finally decided enough was enough and hauled Arjun Singh to the courts. This case was reported in the press, but it did not follow the case well enough to show how Arjun Singh has shied away from courts with one excuse or the other and tried to wriggle out of a difficult situation.

This RSS phobia and anti-Hindu sentiment has gone to such ridiculous length that Arjun Singh's friend Digvijay Singh, the humanist member of the Congress who still supports theory of false police encounter in Batla House case in Delhi, or commiserates with terrorists' families, is alarmed that students educated in the RSS run schools are entering portals of Indian Administrative Services. He is worried about incursion of nationalist philosophy but not about amoral education being imparted by our schools that throw up rootless educated youth with no idea about ancient Indian culture and spiritual wealth! And press laps all this up happily without questioning his honesty towards his own party, government and police force. It is not at all embarrassed at such phobic and intellectually corrupt politicians corrupting Indian social arena totally. The same press which has gone to town today, when Arjun Singh is down and out, about Union Carbide story was totally asleep when the incident actually happened. It didn't follow such a shameful story. Probably, Arjun Singh could gain their 'empathy' and persuade them to kill such stories with his well-known tricks of the trade at that time. The fact that a person like Anderson could not have escaped without complicity of the Centre is being handled very 'sensitively' by media so that 'fair name' of Rajiv Gandhi is not besmirched. The Union Carbide tragedy has been reduced to Anderson's escape and all other worst aspects of government's apathy, negotiating most pitiable and embarrassing settlement in financial terms, misuse of funds etc. have all been forgotten in this most shameful episode in post-independence history.

The most recent example of ostrich-like behaviour of the press is coverage of Deganga riots in West Bengal, where Muslim hordes tried to stop Durga pooja there and turned riotous as they couldn't succeed as Hindus resisted their moves. Temples were desecrated, idols broken, shops looted and burnt. The incident happened on 6 September 2010. It first came into print media on around 8 September after Army had been called in to restore confidence of common people. 200 army personnel had to be posted there. Police was a mute spectator to the outrage even as their officer received serious injuries. The leader of rioters was allegedly, TMC MP from the area! Only *Pioneer* and *Times of India,* Kolkata edition covered the news, while TV world was totally blind and deaf to it. Significantly, this small town is only 35 km from Kolkata and near the Bangladesh-India border. Similarly, Bareilly riots were also hidden from public view for more than a week last year. Imagine something even fraction of this happening in Gujarat! Thus, it seems allergy to RSS is borne more out of inveterate dislike of fundamentalist seculars for anything to do with Hindus or Hindutva and under the impression that any love for 'minorities' (read Muslims) is true sign of secularism.

I have cited example of media's negative role in the second part of the book that played ostrich to the truth uncovered during Ram Janmabhoomi movement during the excavation of the land there. It went on repeating that nothing conclusive was found, though reports were quite emphatic about there being a 'temple-like structure' below the mound called Ram Janmabhoomi etc. Now that the court decision is out, one can see how only the aspect of 'faith' in court's ruling is being highlighted while the 'proof' aspect has been sidestepped. None of the so-called 'national newspapers' has cared to study and present detailed study of Archeologycal Survey of India that was the basis of court's conclusions that the Babri structure was built over ruins of a temple. Same media has gone on to present views of so-called experts from secular lobby junking the report with selective excerpts as if they present gospel truth. I have noted censure of these so-called experts by High Court judges in Chapter IV already that nails their untruths. Most of the media has let off rabble rouser Shahabuddin off the hook who had boasted years back that Muslims would surrender the land voluntarily if it was proven that Babri structure was built on the ruins of a temple.

Case of Jhabua nuns' rape is still not very old. The whole media went berserk indulging in accusations against RSS/VHP for this horrible deed. But, when police inquiry and court cases proved this to be a case of rape by their own religious brethren, press forgot to publish it prominently, nor did any editor or so-called senior journalists thought it fit to apologise for causing harm to the RSS image. In the same vein, we know the different parameters adopted for covering the murder of Graham Steins and Swami Laxmananand Sarswati. While murder of Graham Steines was a 'heinous crime against humanity by the Hindu extremists', murder of Swami Laxmanaanand Saraswati was a 'routine inside page news' till there was violence. Violence immediately became the main news by 'horrible communal killings by the RSS/VHP goons'. Not only that, almost entire debate in this issue was covered by media without a capable VHP person on panels in nearly all discussions on the topic. Narendra Modi and his government have been pilloried for Gujarat riots with worst kind of adjectives even after a few reports have exonerated him and cases are still on. Even though one-third of unfortunate dead people are Hindus it is a 'pogrom'. But, even after it was proved that Teesta Setalvad had used immoral stratagems like tutored witnesses, false evidence, false stories she was not brought to book on TV or print media and made to face the fire.

Ram Sene violence in Mangalore was linked to RSS and then to Hindutva parivar and RSS castigated without getting its side of story heard. Ram Madhav had given a statement criticizing Ram Sene and refuting any links to it but the statement was buried in one para handout in inside pages of newspapers, and media went on merrily shredding the image of the RSS to pieces. Fact that a Congress corporator's husband was part of Ram Sene was swept away in this tsunami of adverse propaganda. In the same vein, there is no sympathy from the left-secular lobby for the poor Muslim teacher who has been issued a virtual fatwa disallowing her to teach without burqa, not a word from these 'liberals'. There is no howl of indignant protest when a teacher's hands are chopped off for allegedly insulting the Prophet and he is relieved of his duty by self-professed Mujahids.

We had given time to a very senior journalist from *Times of India,* whom we thought was a good friend to interview Ram Madhav when he had come to Mumbai as a keynote speaker for one of our programmes. He had a good serious sitting with Ram Madhav, and remember, it was an exclusive interview which had covered many subjects. And what do we get the next day as an anchor story on the front page of the newspaper? "The RSS considering replacing its khaki half pants in uniform with full length trousers!" There was not a mention of any other subject covered in that Q&A! I am sure, Ram Madhav is not a person who would put in one hour on a raging 'ideological' issue of half pants *vs.* full pants!

After the recent Tsunami disaster in Tamilnadu coast and other parts of South India RSS volunteers, as usual, were amongst the first to reach the disaster and start relief work. I have this from personal account of a friend of mine who is not a member of the RSS and had gone with his own small group immediately. How many newspapers thought it fit to laud this selfless service?

This year, RSS Chief Mohanrao Bhagwat took a countrywide tour of 50 cities over one year (one public programme every Sunday). All the programmes were in full uniform for the RSS volunteers apart from general public. Total attendance may have gone into million plus This should have been a news in itself. However, in the last leg of the programme, Kerala saw an unprecedented get-together of nearly one hundred thousand volunteers in full uniform from across Kerala in grounds near Kochi. It was a spectacle worth watching when these people did physical drills in sitting posture and collective singing of an RSS song. The whole lecture was given in Hindi by Bhagwat and translated in Malayalam by a senior RSS functionary. I am sure, hardly any reader of this book would have read this news at all, let alone in the next day newspapers, probably apart from local dailies of Kerala. So much for the so-called 'national' press. When the RSS supporters use Youtube for disseminating such news, Sagarika Ghosh calls for censorship on net!

The most laughably sad spectacle of media bias has been exposed yet again when it was found that new Rajya Sabha members Tarun Vijay and Arun Dave, one ex and one current prachaarak, had no assets! Media has not celebrated the story of value based and moral life of these anti-thesis of modern politicians, on the contrary it is trying hard to find loopholes in this story. There was a debate on CNBC where Karan Thapar, Vinod Mehta and their ilk refused to believe that it is possible. I can understand media kings disbelieving that a much appreciated journalist like Tarun Vijay can lead his life committed to his mission without amassing any wealth in spite of being in media for decades, it is probably embarrassing for them!

A simple Anil Dave in the thick of Madhya Pradesh politics without assets is an anachronism hard to digest! Then, these media czars harangue people on lack of morality and values in politics and tar all the politicians with black brush of corruption, greed to come out as sole shining champions of morality in public life.

I have come to the conclusion that the veil of secrecy is not drawn by the RSS, but it is a veil pulled over it by media itself. It thinks that by closing its eyes to the biggest voluntary organization in the world and not letting people know about its contributions to the society, he or she is doing a service to the society. But, actually it is doing a disservice to it. May be in its own judgmental wisdom it has decided to be the prosecutor and the jury; and decided that the RSS work must be kept a secret from the society so the harm can be kept to the minimum.

However, inspite of the examples I have cited above, I feel that for this state of affairs, the RSS has to blame itself to some extent. Since it is an abiding part of mental makeup of the RSS workers based on the founder's directive to keep away from publicity and propaganda and work silently, it is difficult to break away from this method of working. I think, this idea has been stretched too far, for too long. There is a sense of negativity about media in the RSS establishment for the reasons noted above. On the other hand, media is more responsible for such a negativity and lack of interest in it, not the RSS. For the RSS, media is unnecessary waste of time, or at the best, a necessary evil. It has, not so far, looked at it as a crucial tool to disseminate its views and ideology; as something that is a muthe st in today's battle for the minds. I hope the positive nationwide impact that Mohanrao Bhagwat's statement immediately after Allahabad High Court judgment created and the way media carried it for days will convince the RSS media managers (if there are any) that media can respond positively if handled well and given due weightage in its public relations exercise inspite of carrying a secular chip on its shoulders.

I fervently hope that this book will to convey the essence of the RSS to the readers and lifts the veil of secrecy a little. There is a list of references and recommended readings in the annexure which is, by no means, exhaustive. Some of these books and many others are available on the internet. It is a short list, just enough for you to start your journey of rediscovering political and social side of Hinduism, real history of this great land Bharat, its heritage and contribution to the world in almost every field about which you can be really proud; in the process, understand the RSS philosophy better and move into future with a positive frame of mind.

❑

17

Saffron Terror

Last few months have been vitiated by secular lobby ably supported by the Congress-UPA government to implicate Hindus and the RSS as terrorists to please its vote bank. The duplicity of this lobby vis a vis Sangh and Hindus is exposed very well by the coverage of a news of manhandling of Mirwaiz Farooq in Chandigarh by Kashmiri Hindus and supposedly VHP workers on 25th November. TV news channels, especially *Headlines Today* went overboard in describing this incident as growing intolerance of Indians (read Hindus) that is 'hallmark' of Indian society. Now, imagine a Hindu missionary espousing some Hindu cause against some alleged Muslim atrocities and Muslim youth had attacked him, what would be the reaction? I am sure, it would be - Hindu seer (or whosoever) had provoked Muslim youth who felt aggrieved about 'xyz' cause, it could be any 'cause'.

Thus, a Kashmir stone-pelter is 'aggrieved Kashmiri youth, but a Hindu Kashmiri youth persecuted and left to fend for himself living in hellish conditions is 'intolerant'! Will any of these media guys have the guts to go to Srinagar and talk to these Muslim Kashmiris trying to convince them to offer protection to the Kashmiri Pandits who have been hounded out by them? The obvious answer to this rhetorical question is they will not as they are well aware that they will not get this soft treatment of being manhandled like Mirwaiz got but they would be executed by a bullet in their head there and then. So much for sermons on tolerance to Hindus.

Worthy commentators forgot that nearly 4 lac Hindus have been thrown out of Kashmir by 'tolerant' Muslim leaders in the name of 'liberal' Kashmiriyat as they were inimical to their goal of separatists. And after more than two decades, if a few Kashmiri youth feel anger at about their fate - being refugees in their own country, of living in pitiable conditions for years with no promise of return to their homeland, without any rights or privileges that any Indian enjoys and more so a Kashmiri (read Muslim) citizen; our intellectual leadership is horrified. They are not surprised that not a single Hindu Kashmiri has really turned terrorist inspite of years of persecution. Do they wish in their hearts that they should also turn terrorist so both sides look evenly balanced and 'poor Kashmiris' who threw out their own flesh and blood are not shown in poor light?

Coverage or lack of it about blockade in Manipur for weeks leading to untold hardships can be attributed simply to the fact that sufferers are local tribes while perpetrators are extremists and terrorists belonging to Christian groups supported in most of the cases by local Church. There is no outrage in chatteratti and self appointed opinion leaders, or in media.

I have quoted elsewhere from Francois Gautier and Koenrad Elst that Hindu community on the receiving end for centuries having lost millions of its members to hordes of violent marauders culminating in partition of its mother country has not reacted with any extreme actions except when provoked through riots. They have not tried to set the wrongs right through extremist terror whether it is North East, or Kashmir or any other part of India facing terror attacks for more than a decade now (Infact, much longer in North East). We remember 26/11 but our memories are short; more horrendous acts have taken place for years. If after so much of provocation, only a handful of Hindus have been allegedly found to have taken to the path of violence, it only underlines the non-violent nature of Hindus due to their cultural ethos. Instead of appreciating this tolerance, Hindus are being labeled 'saffron terrorists' with only a few shreds of evidence. They are exceptions who are sought to be made an example of Saffron terror.

My strongest objection is the use of word 'Saffron' itself. Saffron represents the highest values of our civilization, a civilization flowing uninterrupted for thousands of years, one the oldest and the grandest. It is a shade of divinity and sacrifice that is revered by Hindus of every shade. One cannot toss it around just to sound dramatic.

The RSS, as an organization has stood upto all kinds of persecution through democratic means since its first brush with government persecution with the murder of Mahatma Gandhi to current times. It is again being targeted and efforts are being made to somehow link it to terrorism. Look at the simple facts, 85 years of a highly disciplined and well networked organization, millions of members across India. An organization that is under microscopic gaze of secular and Marxist lobby all these years ably supported by police and intelligence agencies. But, they have not been able to stick any dirt on it about terrorism or serious violence all these years. Recall that it could wage an underground fight against emergency in a totalitarian police state with its vast network of volunteers and sympathizers for nearly 18 months. Imagine what the RSS can do if it takes up extremist path earnestly.

The RSS has never responded to such mud slinging. But, this conspiracy has reached a new nadir in its attempt to implicate a highly respected and very senior prachaarak like Indresh ji. Ruling class tried to implicate the then Chief of RSS M S Golwalkar (Guruji) in 1948 and failed miserably. This is the first time in its history that the highly respected institution of prachaarak is being targeted this time.

Let me give a brief idea about Indresh Kumar. He is a prachaarak for over 40 years. He has served in J&K and other part of North India. He has worked in J&K through worst of terror days and was threatened with death a number of times due to his work amongst people to raise their confidence and fight back against terrorists. He escaped a few attempts on his life by separatists. He was instrumental in setting up village defence committees with co-operation of local armed forces in areas where Hindus and anti-separatist Muslims were thinking of abandoning their homes. It was an effort which turned the tide against terrorists in border areas of Jammu & Kashmir.

Indresh Kumar is patron of Forum for Integrated National Security (FINS) that was founded a few years back. Through FINS he has helped activate thousands of ex-service men, policemen, defence experts to contribute to the national well being with their services by working out systems for national security and aid government in its efforts to fight internal and external threats. Today, FINS may have the largest database of security experts in India who are giving new ideas and strategies to fight threats to internal and external Indian security. Last year a huge convention was arranged in Haridwar during Kumbh Mela that was attended by thousands of experts. The reason for arranging it during Kumbh in Haridwar was to make common people aware about the security environment of the country so they can contribute their efforts at local level to improve national security.

Since last couple of years, Indresh ji has initiated dialogue with Muslim leadership - both social and religious - in a free and frank manner that has been highly appreciated by patriotic Muslims Indians. He does not hide behind rhetoric when he addresses Muslim leaders and commoners but is frank and forthright, and talks heart to heart. Thus creating an atmosphere of trust. He is instrumental in launching a new forum for Muslim Indians who oppose outdated extremist ideology of theocratic Islamist ideologues who create issues that are not of any relevance for their society today. The idea is to help Muslims come out of their ghetto mentality nurtured by successive secular outfits to garner bulk votes of a community that has not yet come out of post-partition trauma and is further pushed into dark corners of Indian polity by raising superfluous agenda that keeps harping on religious identity, outdated religious issues and a falsely created fear psychosis. Is this what made the ruling class push the buttons against this senior prachaarak?

Hints of such an approach are clear from other ruling party leaders like Rahul Gandhi and Digvijay Singh. Comparison of RSS with extremist and Islamist supremacists like SIMI is not born out of ignorance. Though, it may be true of Rahul Gandhi, but one can't say the same about his key political trainer cum advisor, Digvijay Singh. Can supposed national leaders be so ignorant that they cannot differentiate between a law abiding pro-democratic nationalist organization and organizations wedded to pan-Islamic supremacy who do not have faith in Indian constitution that wish to overthrow in favour of Shariah and Islamic ideology that treats non-believers in Islam and other minorities as second class citizens?

One just has to read Koran to understand the Muslim psyche. The Muslim apologists will always say that the Koran is being misinterpreted by the likes of Taliban. But any one who reads Koran, chapter after chapter and verse after verse will understand that it does nothing but propagates violence and intolerance against the disbelievers - 'kafirs' or infidels read non-Muslims. If I were to reproduce even a few verses from Koran on this subject, this book may be banned and I may be booked for spreading hatred and disaffection between communities. Nor is this book is not about Islam. But, I would surely invite you to read Koran in its entirety rather than be taken in by either of extreme view on either side.

One just has to view the status of the countries that are being ruled by Muslim majority communities around us. These are the politicians who happily wink their eyes when a criminal violent leader Asad Madani is allowed to come on bail with honourable mention in assembly of Kerala and given protection to run his nefarious activities. These are the leaders who talk of democratic right of dissent against nation state for separatists of Kashmir and their cohorts, but crack down on people who fight such anti-national forces.

Let us remember that RSS has fought many bans in its 85 years of life which it fought successfully within democratic limits and came out victorious. Had it really decided to take up guns against the state with its millions of disciplined supporters and workers, imagine what havoc it could have wrought. Years of anti-Hindu stance of the successive state governments and central governments, their inaction against predominantly Muslim terrorists who have had a free run for years killing thousands of innocent has definitely created resentment among Hindu community. But, it has not spawned terrorism. Or else there would be hundreds if not thousands of Hindu Kashmiri terrorist by now. All they have to show as a form of 'violent' behaviour is their dharnas, protest marches. Even that has alarmed the government and media. All that Hindu society could throw up to show this resentment was half a dozen alleged terrorists. One can detect a sense of relief amongst secular lobby and ruling class that finally they can show off their secular zeal by making an example of this motley group of extremists. By raising suspicions against RSS and its respected prachaaraks, does it secretly wish to see a backlash from RSS volunteers and prove a point to their vote banks?

This mentality shows that the Congress has not changed its spots even after decades. It showed the same mentality when it used Gandhi murder excuse to ban the RSS and persecute its supporters. That, the Congress leadership can go to any extent is proven by the fact that Gandhiji was not provided right security in spite of a misfired plan by people like Madandas Pahwa against Gandhiji just a few days prior to murder of Gandhiji by Godse. This, in spite of Pahwa's confessions about the plans to kill Gandhiji. Does it not implicate the then government of Nehru in allowing this tragedy to take place by providing him security of only one hawaldar with a lathi? Argument that Gandhiji refused protection is specious to say the least. The state has many ways to provide unobtrusive security. And who was made the whipping boy? The RSS of course! The RSS is also at the receiving end of extremist Hindus since long. As noted elsewhere, Saavarkar had a poor opinion about the RSS and also envied its progress.

An old swayamsevak from Gwalior, where the murderers of Gandhiji actually trained told me that a group of Hindu Mahasabhaites requested him to let them hear to All India Radio on the day Gandhiji was murdered assuring him that there would be a big news in the afternoon news bulletin. He was one of the fortunate few who had a radio at that time. They showed him sweet boxes they had arranged for greeting the news. He, a young boy could not understand the significance of their eagerness till the actual news assassination broke out on the radio. He as a young staunch and active RSS volunteer felt, like many others of his time that Godse was deliberately trained to recite Sangh prayer when he went to the gallows to implicate the Sangh somehow. The habit of the Congress to 'settle scores' runs since those days and was witnessed in all its splendour again after Indira Gandhi's unfortunate murder with anti-Sikh pogrom.

The under-current of fear of the RSS' organizational strength and its ability to use democratic institutions to awaken people against faulty policies of Indian rulers and their policies, inculcate character, discipline and national awareness has passed on through generations of the Congress like a congenital defect. They are also aware that the RSS will never actually take up the path of violence and will behave in an ethical manner inspite of all the provocations. This decency of the RSS goes against it just like decency of the Hindu kings worked against as they fought wars within framework of dharma of the times and even let an enemy go scot free after defeating him. Prithviraj Chauhan is a well known example of this misplaced sense of dharma and big heartedness when he let go Mohammad Ghori not once, not twice but seventeen times! And he was not alone in this show of gentlemanly behaviour, history is replete with such examples. Hence, I suspect that the provocation to Hindus and the RSS is a deliberate ploy to generate a backlash and help them consolidate their vote banks.

Maybe it is time the RSS changed its policies that follow the tradition of Lord Rama who always worked within the bounds of dharma, thus called 'Maryaada Purushottam'. It is time it starts following strategies of Krishna who stretched the rules of dharma sometimes to confront the enemy that was not following dharma and taking undue advantage of decency of Pandavas.

❑

Annexure

Author's Note

When I set out to write this book, I had meant it to be a kind of primer about the RSS for lay people who wished to know about the RSS, its philosophy, its method of working and manifestation of its philosophy. Then, when I showed it to some friends, it went through some revisions. People giving their critical inputs, both within and outside the RSS, felt that the RSS has been targeted for decades by media and vested political interests on some unfounded information. The untruths and partial truths have been circulated and repeated so many times that people have stopped questioning them. It was felt that it was necessary to set record straight specially about the RSS and Gandhi's murder, the RSS and its participation or non-participation in freedom movement and the background to the antagonism that the RSS faces from the Congress and its leftist friends since 1947–48. Since, the RSS side of story is not easily available on bookshelves for various reasons, I decided to add an annexure covering these aspects from some authentic source.

I chose latest well-referenced and researched biography of Shri MS Golwalkar, better known as Guruji, the second and longest serving Sarsanghchaalak as the basis of this annexure. It has been written by a very senior RSS prachaarak Shri Ranga Hari in Hindi and was released a few months earlier. Considering the importance of references in this section, I have listed the original references used by Shri Ranga Hari in this part of the book.

Annexure I is a small essay about all the Sarsanghchaalaks or Chiefs of the RSS since its inception. Since, Sarsanghchaalak of the RSS is supposed to give direction to the RSS movement, but is hardly seen or heard by common people, it was felt that a little information about them and their impact on the RSS would be a good idea. *Annexure II to V* cover the recent historic period of 1942 to 1948.

Though this section is a little longer than an annexure should be, I think, it will be highly appreciated by serious students who sincerely wish to know about the other side of the story.

I take this opportunity to thank Shri Ranga Hari for allowing me to quote freely from his book.

Annexure I

Sarsanghchaalaks of RSS and their Contribution to RSS Growth

I was a young boy when I saw and heard Guruji, the second Sarsanghchaalak. I was too young to understand or analyze him as a leader of the movement. I could sense a feeling hushed awe when he entered any meeting place. However, I have worked in various capacities from third Sarsanghchaalak onward. As a common worker of the RSS, I have looked upto them, attended their meetings, their discussions and Q&A sessions. I thought it would be a good idea to look at their work as a witness to their times.

I may add that Sarsanghchaalak is a guide and philosopher of the RSS and is not supposed to be hands on policy implementer. The decision making and policy making in the RSS is a collective team activity, thus, to give full credit of work during his tenure to Sarsanghchaalak would not be correct. But, it is equally true that each Sarsanghchaalak, by virtue of his primacy and respect he commands, creates an impact on the Sangh work which is reflected in organization's working and growth due to his leadership, even as he takes along his team that may have people even senior to him. This is typical of the Sangh that the importance of a person is not defined by his age or the place he comes from. May I caution that these views are not based on serious study of their biographies or other sources, they are based purely on my live experience during their times or working with them of course impressions about Dr Hedgewar and Guruji are based on their study.

1. Founder Dr KB Hedgewar alias Doctorji (1925-1940)

I have mentioned about Dr Hedgewar extensively in the book. He did his study in medicine from Kolkota where he was consumed more with an urge to do something to free the motherland. He was an active member of Anusheelan Samiti, underground movement of revolutionaries. He was also senior office bearer at state level in pre-independence Congress before he launched the RSS. It is but natural that his name crops up routinely in any discussion about the RSS. His contribution to Indian social organizations' creation, management and growth is incomparable. That is more important even than the fact that he was founder of the RSS. He created an entirely new model of a social and cultural organization.

Some of the firsts to his credit are – the idea of daily get together for a minimum one hour period to instil a sense of moral values and patriotism, discipline, inculcating non-monetized value system and spirit of sacrifice and working as a team not as individual right from young age. This seemingly simple idea of devoting at least one hour daily for the society and nation finally motivates simple ordinary individuals to devote not just an hour but even their lives; idea of paying out of pocket for all your activities, not expecting anything from the society but giving it back, confidentiality while contributing to the cause of society and organization as per one's capacity, thus no chance of money influencing decision making at any level, choosing a symbol and not an individual as the 'Guru' or 'master', thus giving a clear signal of avoiding personality worship or personality oriented activities; shedding personal ego, setting example by highest possible sacrifices himself thus leading by example, a truly indigenous training methodology for workers, transforming a common citizen swayamsevak into a committed social worker. All this led to creation of an organization based on structure of 'shakhas' that has grown and consolidated since 85 years with no splits or bitter power struggle – the bane of Indian social organizations.

Apart from these signal contributions, he set ground rules of keeping the Sangh and its work separate from political environment by creating as much insulation between the two as possible. If a person were to take up any political activities, he was to do that as an individual and not as the Sangh representative or the Sangh. He stuck throughout to his basic philosophy that the 'Sangh will do nothing, swayamsevaks will do everything'. As an example he resigned from the post of Sarsanghchaalak (Chief) and handed over reins of organization to another leader when he participated in satyagrah during struggle for independence.

Without any show or publicity, he strengthened movement against untouchability, women's empowerment and took Hinduism out of ritualism and reignite its cultural spirit.

2. Shri MS Golwalkar alias Guruji (1940–73)

Shri MS Golwalkar alias Guruji was recruited by one of his students into the Sangh quite late in life when he was teaching at Benaras Hindu University (BHU). He was a postgraduate in Zoology and Bachelor of Law. He was lovingly called 'Guruji' by his students among whom he was very popular due to his huge treasure of knowledge and ever willing nature to help them, whether they belonged to his class or subjects or not. Thus, this popular way of addressing him as Guruji has nothing to do with his being head of the RSS. The Saffron flag is the only guru in the Sangh.

He would have become a 'Sadhu' in the Ramakrishna Mission order of Swami Akhandaananda but for this interlude in Benaras and subsequent incidents in his life. He had taken 'diksha' from Swamiji i.e. he was an ordained 'sanyasi'. He was simply bowled over by Dr Hedgewar's fierce patriotism and selfless hard work. His elevation to the highest post at a young age of 34 years was a big surprise for everybody outside the Sangh. But, it reinforced the philosophy of promoting talent rather than work on the principle of seniority in the organization. Subsequent history attested to the wisdom of Doctor Hedgewar's choice.

Guruji held the reins of the RSS for the longest period of 33 years in its history. A period that saw tumultuous events of independence movement, climaxing in a blood soaked partition, the first and the toughest ban on the RSS and its removal, restoring the young organization back to health and putting it on path of phenomenal growth. He was instrumental in seeing the growth of the small plant that had blossomed under Doctor Hedgewar's guidance into massive banyan tree of the RSS that stuck roots all cross India in every nook and corner. Like a Banyan tree many sub-root systems and branches of allied organizations sprouted in nearly all the social segments both horizontally and vertically. He systematized the organizational methodology given by Doctorji into a mature science of organization and human building.

He was probably one of the most well-read persons of India at that time with wide ranging interests from Arts to Science, from technology to spiritualism etc. He could talk with any person from a child to an intellectual with enough interesting knowledge sharing with ease. This, coupled with his divine spirituality created an impact on the organization far beyond just physical growth and consolidation of the organization. His spirituality and asceticism seeped through Sangh in nearly all its aspects. The institution of prachaarak system - the backbone of organizational growth - has a spiritual halo with ascetic and celibate lifestyle probably due to lifestyle and personality of Guruji. The resulting near spiritual way of working in the Sangh carries an indelible stamp of Guruji's spiritual practices. It is interesting that not many RSS people are ritualistic, though. In one of his speeches he was resoundingly critical of people who thought that following rituals makes one religious and spiritual. In another place he says, "Worship is not business. This is pure surrender, a one sided affair. We only give. Only people, who surrender their all, can pull a nation out of the ruins of destruction and take it to the pinnacle of glory."

To me, the most long lasting contribution of Guruji to consolidation and unification of Hindu society, apart from expansion of Sangh work, was bringing together of heads of various Hindu sects, religions and traditions on one common platform of Vishwa Hindu Parishad, attempted never before in Hinduism's thousands of years' of history. To make these leaders to declare untouchability as 'un-Hindu' was something only he could achieve due to his humility and charming equation he had with nearly all spiritual leaders of the time at spiritual level.

His role as the rock solid and aggressive supporter for Hindu refugees abandoned by the then Congress leaders and later Indian government led by them is unforgettable. The price that swayamsevaks paid for their valour is recorded in the Sangh history, though neglected by Indian historians for the fear of glorifying 'communal' patriots. He and his band of thousands of dedicated workers not only saw to their safe passage to India as far as possible but also their rehabilitation.

Of course, it was under his sagacious and patient leadership that young RSS as an organization survived highly pernicious and oppressive ban in its life. No other organization could have probably survived the ruthless state force under the misplaced urge of Nehru to 'crush' the RSS. It is to his credit that in spite of this ruinous ban, subsequent satyagrah resulting in nearly 77,000 supporters spending 5–6 months behind bars, losing their jobs, businesses, the Sangh revived and grew in following years. One of the reasons may have been that he carried no rancour against anybody and was ready to extend his hand and go an extra mile for harmony of society. For example, he was an admirer of Sardar Patel for his sterling role in unifying India and became his good friend though he had succumbed to Nehru's partisan politics and supported and continued ban on the RSS till circumstances forced him to rescind it. Pandit Nehru probably realized his folly later in life after shameful 1962 debacle and invited the RSS to join the Republic day parade in 1963. Guruji agreed readily and a contingent of 3000 volunteers in full uniform participated in the parade that year.

3. Shri Madhukar alias Balasaheb Deoras (1973–94)

Balasaheb Deoras was a quintessential product of the organizational process set up by Dr Hedgewar. He was an ordinary swayamsevak who grew up into a social worker and leader. He was one of the first recruits of the first shakha started by Dr Hedgewar. He was trained as a lawyer but dedicated his life to the RSS work after this.

He was one of the top 3-4 key leaders of struggle to lift ban on the RSS in 1948. Guruji was behind bars during most of the time and his young band of volunteers had to carry on with this struggle with periodic guidance from him. He was an organizer par excellence, a down to earth person. Guruji used to say that if you wish to know about Doctorji, look at Balasaheb. He was a totally hands-on person with great rapport with swayamsevaks. He was approachable and open to any question and patient with his answers, howsoever trivial they may seem to others.

He had a clear and scientific perspective of Indian society and its ills. Though fight against untouchability and support for reforms in Hindu society had been a silent work of the Sangh for long time, he spoke resoundingly "if untouchability is not a sin then there is no sin in this world" and asked Hindu society to "throw it out lock, stock and barrel".

The doomsayers in newspapers had raised the bogey of 'After Guruji who?' and began writing virtual obituary of the Sangh. But, his own silent and strong working, coupled with a personality neutral system developed by the Sangh as an organization saw sustained growth of the organization.

Balasaheb Deoras' lasting contribution was the structured approach he helped create in social service arena where the RSS was present for a long time but it was not given a formal structure till then. What started as a plan to set up 1000 social service projects during Dr Hedgewar's birth centenary in 1989 has grown to over 1.50 lac social service projects now His solid backing for equitable harmonious society (samaajik samarasataa) led to a movement that has seen coming together of people with differing views on the problem of discriminative caste system but a common goal of resolving it with social harmony, with a sense of equality, not political haranguing.

His decision to align with democratic anti-corruption movement symbolized by 'navnirman andolan', persuading Jai Prakash Narain to lead the agitation through his colleagues like Nanaji Deshmukh and others was a courageous move that his opponents had not imagined. His subsequent leadership in the fight for democracy during emergency showed the Sangh's and its cadres' commitment to democratic ideals. His support for dissolution of Bharatiya Jan Sangh to merge in Janata Party must have been one of the toughest decisions of his life. But, it altered the political geography and history of India forever.

Though he himself stayed away from the media like his predecessors, he made the RSS more media friendly and open to interaction with the media.

He was at the helm of affairs during historic 'Ekaatmataa Yatra' and 'Ram Janmabhoomi Andolan', movements that changed the perspective of Hindus about their national identity and unity as also dynamics of Indian polity, bringing Hindutva into the political centrestage from peripheries to which Nehruvians and Marxists had been able to push it for decades.

4. Dr Rajendra Singh alias Rajju Bhaiyya (1994–98)

He is said to be one of the leading nuclear scientists that India never had. A man of very high intellect, he joined the RSS during his days in BHU. He was very soft spoken and had a very pleasant, radiant personality. He had a calming effect on anybody who went to meet him. Maybe, this is why he was addressed as 'Rajju bhaiyya' by everybody. There was something spiritual about his inner core that reflected in his personality. He was a very good singer and had helped set music to many RSS songs. He would walk into his classes as a professor directly with his 'jhola' of the prachaarak, in his trade mark 'dhoti kurta' to give lectures on nuclear physics.

One of the most important beliefs of Rajju Bhaiya was: "All people are basically nice. One should deal with every person by believing in his goodness. Anger, jealousy, etc., are offshoots of his past experiences, which affect his behaviour. Primarily every person is nice and everyone is reliable."

His pleasant personality was the reason for his great rapport with social and political leaders across the spectrum from academicians to spiritual, social and political people. Many of the leaders of BJP accepted Rajju bhaiyya as their mentor. Incidentally, it was during his tenure that BJP ascended from being a bit player to become the leading player in national politics that ultimately led to BJP forming a government in the Centre.

Like other Sarsanghchaalaks he was a firm believer in the concept of Swadeshi and empowering rural economy. Initiating the rural developmental activities, he had declared in 1995 that the utmost priority should be of making the villages hunger-free, disease-free and literate (Kshudha mukta, roga mukta, tatha shikshayukt). Today, there are hundreds of villages where the rural development work done by swayamsevaks has inspired the people of surrounding villages and their experiments are being emulated by those people.

His passion for education encouraged the RSS associate organizations to reach out to the nook and corners of India and run thousands of schools during his tenure as Sarsanghchaalak. Interestingly, he was in the team of prachaaraks that included Nanaji Deshmukh and Bhaurao Deoras who initiated this education movement of Sangh way back in 1948-50s with encouraging support of Guruji.

5. Shri KS Sudarshan (1998 - 2009)

Sudarshan ji has a sharp intellect, great clarity of thought and is outspoken. An engineer by training, he is thoroughly read and marshals his thoughts crisply. He is a Kannadiga who studied and lived his earlier life in Madhya Pradesh and grew as a senior RSS prachaarak in this state. He is a polyglot with knowledge of six languages from South India to North India. He is impatient and blunt in his observations but nobody can challenge his analysis easily.

He is passionate about Swadeshi and still travels to remotest corners of Bharat whenever he hears about a successful or path-breaking experiment with innovative indigenous technologies. He is always there to encourage such people. His lectures used to be peppered with anecdotes about such experiments and successful models, illustrating forcefully that Swadeshi is not a dreamy philosophy but something that could make India self-sufficient and society more equitable. His stress on self sustaining rural economy, sustainable consumption - not just sustainable development, espousal about scientific Hindu way of personal, social and national life for national and global harmony has been his theme for many years.

To my mind, his signal contribution has been to bring back unapologetic reasoned aggression to Hindutva philosophy. He presented Hindutva in a scientific manner and explained how it alone could respond to challenges of environmental degradation, civilizational clashes etc.

Many analysts consider his inability to take along leaders of other allied movements of Hindutva a weakness in his leadership. But, I think, he was there in the historic period when the whole society and various Hindutva related organizations were in a big churn. Some organizational affiliates themselves are huge mass organizations with very senior ex-RSS people at their helm. Thus, it would not have been an easy task for anybody. His critics, specially in media, generally could not find anything objectionable in his analysis of a situation or his solutions, but were unable to come to terms with his blunt style and tried to present him in a negative light, rather than highlighting his scientific approach to Hindutva.

6. Shri Mohanrao Bhagwat (2009 –)

Mohanrao Bhagwat is a veterinary surgeon by training and second generation swayamsevak from Nagpur. His father was one of the first bands of prachaaraks and initiated Sangh work in Gujarat. He has radiance on his face and a twinkle in the eyes and a ready smile; a person with whom you can feel cheerful in any kind of situation. His meetings are generally lively with light hearted banter once in a while.

He is always open to new ideas and ready to listen. This openness is what attracts workers to him for any discussion. Behind this easy exterior is a firm mind that is focused on the heart of the RSS work i.e. the RSS shakhas. He is again, clearly an organization man giving top priority to organization above anything else. His lectures are precise, to the point, which show his clarity of thought.

The way he has conducted himself so far, it seems that he will bring in more vigour in the organization. He should be able to give new dimension to the Sangh work that will move with rapid societal changes and keep it relevant.

❑

Annexure II

1942, Quit India Agitation and RSS

Year 1942 was literally a year of comprehensive transformation in the history of the Sangh. Large number of swayamsevaks volunteered to become prachaaraks. Most of them were highly educated. From Lahore alone there were new 48 prachaaraks, 52 prachaaraks came from Amritsar while Nagpur saw 22 new prachaaraks that year. Other centres had similar experience.

But, there were already some of evil omens for the RSS. The Central government came out with a gazette on August 5, 1940. As per its sections 56-58, private organizations were prohibited from giving army training or wearing army uniforms. There is no mention of Sangh in it. But, the language of this gazette indicated for whom it was framed. Crafty British knew very well about the political background of Dr Hedgewar, so they were keeping a close watch on Rashtriya Swayamsevak Sangh founded by him. This is the reason Central government had issued a gazette eight years earlier on December 15, 1932 that termed participation of government servants in Sangh illegal. Sangh had come out of such trials successfully. Dr Hedgewar, who was well versed in public life, was gone and his successor Golwalkar seemed to be raw, relatively inexperienced. So, this seemed to be the right time to strangle it. This was the intention behind this government order.

Guruji took a step that would help swayamsevaks work undisturbed for their goal without being bothered with this order. Keeping this government gazette in mind, he wrote ten days later on August 16 to Professor Malkani in Sindh, "Our purpose is not to raise an army. We believe firmly in an organized society. Our goal is to generate a sense of unity in the Hindu society."[2] Similarly, he wrote a detailed letter with even more clarity to the chief prachaarak of Delhi, Vasantrao Oke. The intelligence bureau used to read all the correspondence of Sangh stealthily. In this letter Guruji wrote, "You know it well that we are not bound by any specific type of programme. We are not shackled by any situation and we modify our programmes and come up with plans for new programmes keeping in mind our core objective.

With this view, we had given up that part of our training syllabus in our programmes that was based on military terminology keeping in mind restrictions imposed by the notification issued in August, 1940. Earlier too, we used to impart only the training that would equip a person with qualities of discipline etc, so that they could have better capabilities to handle their daily lives."

Guruji had sent notifications with similar content from Nagpur central office to all the states. The report sent by the central police intelligence department on December 13, 1943 speaks about the impact of these communications. "It is not possible to build a case for banning the Sangh. But, it is equally clear that Golwalkar is creating a strong organization at a rapid pace that would obey orders, maintaining confidentiality and jump into any activity of sabotage or of any other type whenever required as per their leader's orders. The structure of this organization looks superficially like that of 'khaaksaars'. But, fundamental difference between the two is that the leader of Khaaksaar, Inaayatullah, is a loud mouthed imbalanced lunatic, while Golwalkar is a very cautious, crafty and much more capable leader." [3]

When Sangh was growing at such a pace, August Kranti (Quit India movement) of 1942 exploded onto the scene. This was the second freedom struggle in the lifetime of the Sangh. First one was the Salt satyagrah of 1930. Dr. Hedgewar had taken part in that movement in his personal capacity after handing over the responsibilities of Sarsanghchaalak to Dr LV Paranjape. Appaji Joshi of Vardha and Dadarao Paramaarth had also gone to prison with him. A circular was sent to all the shakhas that 'ordinary swayamsevak can take part in the satyagrah in his personal capacity after taking permission from the local Sanghchaalak'. After twelve years now, Guruji faced the question of taking part in 1942 movement.

During these intervening twelve years, strong hunger for independence had awakened the entire society across all sections of the populace. On the other hand condition of British was deteriorating rapidly in the fierce war. Feeling that their poor position implies our strong position, ordinary people of the country believed that independence was round the corner. Situation for the Sangh had also changed a lot for the better. Number of experienced workers had risen. Though, the growth was not very balanced, the Sangh had expanded geographically in large areas. But, it was also true that this expansion was limited to Mumbai Presidency and Central Province. In other places, its presence was more like a seedling. Still the tone of organization was that of growth. Guruji had to decide about the role of Sangh in this background.

Guruji convened a meeting of state level workers. It was decided to evaluate the state of the movement dispassionately. Famous revolutionary Dr. Pandurangrao Khaankhoje (who had earned his fame in Mexico) and Sangh strategist Balasaheb Deoras were sent to meet underground leader Jaiprakash Narayanji with this objective in mind. Guruji was keen to get satisfactory answers to seven questions. The questions were :

1. Part of 'Dying' is clear in the slogan 'Do or Die'. But what is to be 'Done'? Has the Congress working committee given any directions about it?
2. What is the immediate and long-term goal of the movement? That is, what do we want to achieve without fail?
3. What is the working methodology of the movement and how is it going to work?
4. How long will the movement run?
5. You must have estimated your strength, how big is this strength?
6. What is the next move after the movement is successful?
7. If it is unsuccessful, then what is to be done next?[4]

Dr. Khaankhoje and Deoras came back after meeting Jai Prakashji. Dr. Khaankhoje's opinion was that "none of the answers by Jai Prakashji was satisfactory. Not only this, there was no clear direction about what was to be done or not done by the people, next in line, after the front line leaders were arrested." In the light of this information, Guruji held discussions with his colleagues. He was aware of Sangh's strengths and limitations as an organization. He had also discovered the actual state of movement. In spite of all this, he had no two opinions about the lofty goals of this movement. Under the circumstances, Guruji decided that, "The agitation is being conducted for the freedom of the country. Therefore, swayamsevaks, as citizens, can take part in this agitation in whichever part of the country they are. But, as an organization, the Sangh will keep working for national cause, that is organizing the society; without getting involved in the agitation directly."

There is another direct source of information on this subject. That is a personal interaction of Dattopant Thendgi at that time. Here is his account: "Guruji had to go to Chennai after his programme in the port city of Mangalore in September 1942. Swayamsevaks and prachaaraks were deeply upset and they were in a state of dilemma due to impact of the movement that was shaking up the whole nation. Questions like, why is Sangh inactive in these times? What is the use of its strength? etc. hurt their souls hard. I was prachaarak in Calicut in Kerala those days. Brethren there insisted that we should meet Shri Guruji and inform him of these ground realities. With this objective, I met Shri Guruji in Mangalore. Summary of his detailed response is as follows:

1. The Sangh has its own code of conduct in such matters. According to these, when the Sangh founder Doctorji took part in satyagrah, he kept the Sangh out of the agitation and urged swayamsevaks to keep their Sangh work going without any disruption.
2. However, if we were to reach near the goal of independence by leaving aside this tradition, then we are not bound by it. Because our work and traditions have the same goal and independence is definitely our immediate goal.

3. It would have been desirable if the Congress had taken other parties and the Sangh into confidence before initiating the agitation. But, it did not do so. Still, there is no reason to be upset. Independence gained through this movement will be for all, not just for the Congress. So, it would not be right to show any ego in this matter.
4. It is a worrying prospect that the Congress leaders have not made any preparations before the launch of this agitation. People had to face and fight British rulers directly. There was no planned arrangement for this. Thought, it is true that in a period of revolution, things won't go as per plans; it is equally true that there should be some element of planning and leaders should be alert to take advantage of any situation that might arise. It is also true that policies and directions depend only on fervour of the people and leaders cannot do much about it. But, we must remember that it is fatal not to have any plans during a movement or revolution.
5. In spite of all this, if the country was to gain independence with the Sangh jumping into the agitation, we would have not been averse to it. But, when I took a comprehensive view, it was my firm belief that we would not be able to reach anywhere near the goal.
6. Many people have overestimated the Sangh's present strength. It is a situation where people who are in a place where Sangh is strong, believe that the Sangh is equally strong in other places too. But, this is not the reality. To be victorious in a struggle, many other things need to be favourable apart from your strength. Of these, first is support from common people and their cooperation. Second is dissatisfaction among police, armed forces etc. Attitude of these sections of government is crucial before one takes the path of struggle. Even if these factors were favourable, still chances of success of our struggle would be bleak, this is my assessment. I believe that our strength will be limited from Belgaum to Gondia. Will we be able to achieve our objective with these limitations?

   Truth is that our influence is limited to the central region of our country. Even if the struggle was to be successful in this limited area, it would be possible for our enemy to post its army from all the directions. People will get frustrated with such a development. But, if the zone of struggle were to be near the borders, it would be easy to put up a fight and would be more useful from strategy point of view.

   In such circumstances, I believe that it would be fruitless for the Sangh as an organization to get involved in this movement. It doesn't mean that we wish to save our skin. But the truth is that people will end up disappointed with this agitation."[5]

In short, the Sangh leadership comprehended the inherent inertia of this battle, practical view of Sangh's organizational status across India, society's mental state and permitted swayamsevaks as patriotic citizens to take part in this national struggle and extend wholehearted cooperation to it. As a result many swayamsevaks jumped into this battle and took part to the best of their abilities along with common people, as a part of the society. In Vidarbha, swayamsevaks of Chimur launched agitation under the leadership of Ramakant Deshpande. Breaking the bounds of non-violence it turned violent. A few British were also killed in an encounter. This encounter became famous in the history of this movement as 'Chimur Ashti episode'.

Similar was the heroic story of Hemu Kalani of Sakkhar town in Sindh. He was busy removing fishplates from the railway tracks with his brave colleagues. Their objective was to frustrate the plans to move forces to suppress the struggle in various areas. Unfortunately, Hemu was arrested. His friends escaped and were saved. Hemu was awarded death sentence by the Army Court in 1943. Sindhi brethren in Mumbai celebrate the memory of martyr Hemu Kalani in Mumbai to this day.[6] Unfortunately, his name is not celebrated as a freedom fighter in official records, probably because he was an RSS volunteer. He was disowned in Pakistan as he was a Hindu – from a community that was thrown out of Pakistan. And, he is not remembered in India because he belongs to an uprooted community that lost its entire land to Pakistan formation.

Apart from such activities, many swayamsevaks also helped the underground leaders of the movement. House of Sanghchaalak of North East Lala Hansraj was the secret place of stay for Aruna Asaf Ali. She herself speaks about it in an interview published in Hindi daily *Hindustan* in August 1967. She says, "I was underground in 1942 agitation, Delhi Sanghchaalak Lala Hansraj provided me refuge in his house for 10-15 days and arranged for my complete safety. He saw to it that nobody got information about my stay at his house. Since, underground workers should not stay at for long at the same place, I moved out of his house dancing 'Bhangra' in an embroidered ghagra and chunri in a baaraat (marriage procession). This dress was given to me by Lalaji's wife. When I went to return it in due course, she refused to take it back, saying, keep it with you as our gift with our best wishes."[7]

"When famous Vedic scholar Pandit Shripaad Damodar Saatavalekar was the Sanghchaalak of Aundh, he had given asylum for many days to the revolutionary underground leader Nana Patil who had experimented with the novel idea 'Patri Sarkaar'. Nana Patil's colleague Kisanveer had stayed at the house of Satara Sanghchaalak in Wai while working underground there. Famous Socialist leader Achyutrao Patwardhan had stayed at many Sangh swayamsevaks' homes when he used to work underground and change places according to circumstances. Not only these people, but even the life-long bitter opponent of Sangh, follower of Gandhiji, Sane Guruji used to stay at Pune Sanghchaalak Bhausaheb Deshmukh's house secretly."[8]

The Congress committee member of Solapur, Ganesh Bapuji Shinkar had taken part in the satyagrah to press for the removal of ban on Sangh in 1948. He had resigned from Congress on grounds of democratic ethics before joining the satyagrah. He issued a statement clarifying his stand and it was published on 12 December 1948. He says, "I had participated in Bharat Chhodo (Quit India) movement in 1942. Capitalist and agrarian community was scared of the government at that time, therefore we were not offered safe haven in their homes. We had to stay in the Sangh workers' homes to work underground. People from the Sangh used to help us happily with our underground work. They also took care of all our needs. Not only this, if someone from amongst us fell sick, the Sangh swayamsevak doctors used to treat us. The Sangh swayamsevaks who were advocates, used to fight our cases fearlessly. Their patriotism and value based living was indisputable." [9]

When anti-national Communists were acting like fifth columnists and getting agitating patriots arrested, the Sangh was doing its bit for the struggle. Eventually, the agitation cooled down after 75 days by the end of October. Scattered and weak leadership and disorganized agitation on one side and highly well entrenched ruling set-up of British on the other, led to death of a well intentioned movement in its infancy.

That British rulers were alert was well known. CID kept sending reports about the the RSS Chief regularly. The report of 30 December 1943 says, "Rashtriya Swayamsevak is moving ahead rapidly towards building a highly significant all India organization. Spokesmen of the Sangh keep saying that the basic goal of the Sangh is to achieve Hindu unity… In a programme in November 1943 in Lahore, MS Golwalkar declared that Sangh's objective is to remove the feeling of untouchability and weaving together all sections of Hindu society in a single unifying thread. … it is clear that the Sangh is bent upon expanding its area of influence and this year it has been able to bring on board, the famous religious saint Sant Tukadoji Maharaj from Central Province for spreading its message….."

"Membership of the Sangh is swelling continuously. In Central Province, membership has increased from thirty two thousand to thirty three thousand three hundred forty four. It has reached twenty thousand four hundred seventy six from eighteen thousand twenty nine in Mumbai and fourteen thousand from ten thousand in Punjab… A new dimension to their growth is their efforts to gain entry in the villages. MS Golwalkar laid a lot of stress on this aspect in the winter camp of Vardha that the Sangh should expand into villages….."

The "Sangh office bearers from its head office are touring the shakhas in remote areas continuously, so that they can heighten interest of swayamsevaks in the Sangh work, give them secret directions and strengthen the local organization. We can see the recent well spread out tour of the present Chief of Sangh, MS Golwalkar as an example of such efforts. In last month of April he was in Ahmedabad, in May he was in

Amravati and Pune. In June he was in Nashik and Benaras. He toured Chaandaa in August, Pune in September, Madras and Central Province in October, and Rawalpindi in November…."[10]

Thus, it is not true that the Sangh was not involved in Independence movement and particularly 1942 movement, a movement show cased as the cathartic period in independence struggle.

- Excerpts from Chapter 18 of Shri Guruji Golwalkar, Biography by Ranga Hari

Endnotes

1. Shri Guruji Punjab Mein, pp. 29-30
2. Shri Guruji Samagra, pp. 8-9
3. Sangh Beej se Vriksha, pp. 60-61
4. Raashtraay Namah, pp. 83-84
5. Pioneer of New Era, pp. 54-55
6. Rashtriya Swayamsevak Sangh – Sindh kaa Pravaas, p. 71
7. Rashtraay Namah, pp. 85-86
8. Ibid, p. 86
9. Pahli Agnipareekshaa, pp. 140-141
10. Sangh Beej se Vriksha, pp. 63-66

Annexure III

Background of Ban on RSS in 1948

In his book *Golwalkar and RSS* author Jagat S Bright writes, the "RSS had worked like Red Cross Society during period of independence and partition. The Sangh's contribution in saving innocent people from the explosion of Islamist blind faith before and after the independence was outstanding. Service that the RSS did for the society in those hours of grave danger was highly appreciated by the Deputy Prime Minister, Sardar Patel. Tireless efforts put in by the Sangh to resettle the refugees properly could not be overlooked by anyone even if one wished to. This very fact generated jealousy and dread in political circles. Responding to it pointedly, Guruji had noted in the Vijayaadashami festival of that year on 24 October 1947, "Reacting to the acknowledgement that Sangh has received for easing the pain of affected Hindu people of Punjab, an English daily has commented that it is 'Unfortunate, but true.' Various political parties also wish to confront the Sangh in a similar manner. They are worried that in case the Sangh enters the arena of electoral politics, what will be their fate. I wish to assure these parties trying to save their respective reputations with means fair or foul, that their fear is meaningless."[1]

It is true that Guruji did not accept the partition of the country till his last days. For example, in his lectures, he always used the term, "part of our country that is called Pakistan today." Still, he never spoke in a critical way like the Communists who used to say that, "this 'independence' is not independence", "independence day is a day of fraud". He accepted the unpalatable truth, even if with anguish.

Overcoming these feelings, he sought people's attention about their national duty, "First step upon attaining nation's independence is to take pride in our forefathers, and not in philosophies of other nations like Russia, America, England etc. When every individual owns up the goal of national welfare, forgetting about self, only then the nation can arise.... Independence will be founded only on selfless sacrifice."[2]

As the day independence drew near, he explained the meaning of this word to the RSS activists. To his mind, independence did not simply mean transfer of power. Getting rid of slavery and being independent – he looked at both conditions differently. For him, Bharat's 'independence' - not being dependent, and Bharat's freedom – being free - were not the same. Former word symbolizes lack of dependence while the latter symbolizes the power of 'self'. Addressing senior citizens in capital, Delhi, he said, "Liberating our intellect from the values (sanskaars) of other countries and evolving a system (tantra) of growth with our own feelings and will is 'swa-tantra' (system by self). But, a system that is born through ignoring our history, being slaves of intellect of others, inspired by other societies will not be 'swa-tantra' but 'para-tantra' (system of others, or slavery of others). A system based on Russia's directions will be a 'Russian-tantra', not 'swa-tantra'. A system inspired by the politicians of England, under their guardianship or their support, will be England's system. A federal system created with inspiration of free America would be an American system, never 'swa-tantra'. ..... We wish to envision the soul of our nation. We want to keep our sense of nationalism alive. We wish to make our nation powerful and prosperous. Philosophy of nationalism is not a philosophy about political rights... We do not wish to borrow talent from outsiders to build our lives. We have our own talent. We will create our own way of life from it. A system that will symbolize our sense of pride, that would be built around comprehensive 'Bharatiyata', that through which flows perennial Bharatiya tradition, that is the system of national way of life."[3]

Not even thirty days had passed since proclamation of independence when Muslim League hatched a conspiracy to blow up the top leaders of Bharat with a massive explosion. Alert swayamsevaks were doing their own investigation working day and night had done and passed on precise information to Sardar Patel. Based on this information, armed forces raided many places in Paharganj and surrounding areas and captured large cache of arms and explosives, and took action against the rebels. Dr. Bhagwandas, recipient of Bharat Ratna, lifted the lid off this conspiracy on page 19 in his book *Crises*, published from Allahabad. He notes, "I have confirmed information that some Sangh swayamsevaks of Delhi had gone to the extent of making a show of accepting Islam to gain trust of Muslim League members in order to get details of the conspiracy hatched by them. It is only because of this, that they could find and provide advance information to Sardar Patel about the conspiracy of 10th September to kill all the ministers and civil officers and thousands of Hindu citizens, unfurl Pakistan's flag on Red Fort and grab control of Indian government... If these young men, fired by ardour and patriotic feelings, had not provided information about this conspiracy in time, there would have no Indian government today."[4]

Just as Guruji was getting ready to leave for Kolkota on September 9, he received a message from Mahatma Gandhi, "Please meet me before leaving." "As you wish," saying so, he went with Lala Hansrajji to meet Mahatmaji in Birla Bhavan at 10.30 a.m. Situation was grave. Delhi was burning that week. Mahatmaji had reached Delhi only on September 9 after moving around in Kolkata. Situation in the capital had already turned for the worse before his arrival. Displaced commoner refugees moving into Ajmeri and Kashmiri gate of Delhi were livid with searing anger. Mahtama Gandhi and Guruji were meeting in the background of such an atmosphere. Probably, influenced by rumour mongers, truth seeker Bapuji asked him, "Even your hands are dirtied by blood, aren't they?" Guruji's answer was, "Not at all. They are not dirty, they are pure and clean." Grasping the meaning of what Mahtamaji was indicating, Guruji clarified, "I cannot claim to be aware about the conduct of each and every swayamsevak of the Sangh. However, the Sangh's objective is to serve Hindu society and Hindutva piously and the Sangh wishes to achieve this objective without inflicting injustice on anybody else. Though, the Sangh doesn't wish to attack anybody, still it doesn't believe in excessive non-violence. It teaches self defence. It has never taught about policy of revenge even by mistake. During the discussions, Gandhiji asked Guruji to give a written statement that would appeal people to be peaceful. Responding the suggestion, Guruji said, "Who will listen to me? Your words are respected everywhere, you are senior. So, it is ideal that you release the statement. If you wish so, you can mention my acceptance of your views." Finally, this is how the statement was released. In the evening prayer meeting, Gandhiji declared that 'Golwalkar had assured his full co-operation in establishing peace.' Newspapers also published this statement the next day.[5]

The Rashtriya Swayamsevak Sangh and Guruji were gaining popularity very rapidly in that atmosphere. Unfortunately, opposition to the Sangh was rising slowly in the Congress circles. Guruji had expressed his views on the reason behind this opposition in his Vijayaadashami lecture in Nagpur already.

Guruji had met Sardar Patel and Gandhiji in September. He had not been able to meet prime minister due to prime minister's busy schedule. When Guruji visited Delhi again during his tour in October, this meeting was possible. Talks lasted for nearly one hour. Guruji could gauge that Nehruji's attitude about the Sangh was different and not favourable. Clarifying the objectives of the Sangh, Guruji began by saying, "Lack of a fundamentally strong and capable organized power has resulted in our nation's inability to influence the world today." Diverting his target towards Sangh in an accusing tone, Nehruji said, "But such a power should not be evil." Guruji grasped the import of these words. Responding that his understanding of the Sangh power as evil was against the ground realities, he went on to present his analysis of disturbances in Northern states and added, "This sense of bitterness prevailing across the country is not because of the Sangh, it is because of tragic partition." After discussing about other related subjects, he took leave and requested him that atmosphere by the government should be created in such a way that feeling of cooperation would be encouraged."[6]

It was decided to hold a full fledged camp of young swayamsevaks of Western Maharashtra in Pune on November 1-2, 1947. One lac swayamsevaks were expected to attend this camp. Activists had taken leave from their jobs and businesses to make arrangements for the camp in sufficient numbers. Guruji's was to be present throughout the camp. Sardar Patel had agreed to come as the Chief Guest. Aakashwani (All India Radio) had also arranged for broadcasting the news about the camp. Support from all quarters for the camp was available as expected. There was an atmosphere of enthusiasm all around. But, there were evil souls in the Congress camp feeling uncomfortable and seething with jealousy. Ultimately, the state home minister gave an excuse of a grave situation and rescinded the permission for the camp. It was clear that the Sangh had become victim of internal pulls and pressures within the Congress.

Guruji sent out a notification immediately that there would be get-together rallies (saanghik) in full Sangh uniform in each district of Maharashtra and Guruji would be present in each of this get-together and he would be greeted with 'Sarsanghchaalak pranaam' - salutation to the Sarsanghchaalak. Anger of swayamsevaks was transformed into zeal, and they began working with a strong will to be victorious. Guruji toured all the thirteen districts from October 24 to November 5. When the final reports were prepared, it turned out that more than four lac swayamsevaks from 1300 villages and towns had attended these programmes.

This pre-emptive, meaningless abortion of the state level camp indicated the direction in which thinking of the Congress government's machinery was moving. Next month, in November, a meeting of chief ministers was called in Delhi. The topic of discussion was increasing popularity of the Sangh and challenge arising out of it. The problem facing them was how to bridle the Sangh. [7]

Around this time accusing swayamsevaks of fomenting riots in Kandaale in Uttar Pradesh, the Congress government there put up cases against them. (These accusations were proven incorrect later on). Such evil designs were witnessed in other places also.

According to daily *Dainik Kaal* dated October 13 1947, Satara Congress committee in Maharashtra passed a resolution and asked Chief Minister B G Kher to 'Uproot Rashtriya Swayamsevak Sangh'. In a threatening tone, the committee claimed that 'otherwise we would destroy the Sangh ourselves using 1942 type of terrorist methods.' Giving sagely advice to them, chief minister told them, "Don't take up an action in a mood of pessimism, or else you would be totally destroyed."[8]

Later on there was a meeting of All India Congress Committee on 17 January 1948 in Delhi that passed a strongly worded resolution against the Sangh. It demanded state governments also to take anti-Sangh steps. Lowest units of the Congress were also asked to follow this policy. During this time, the Central government also released a circular that said, "It was illegal for a government servant to be a member of the RSS". Leader of this anti-Sangh front was Rafi Ahmed Kidwai from Uttar Pradesh.

Even as newly independent nation was passing through a grave crisis, diverse pulls and pressures and tensions between Nehru-Patel came into open. Even Sangh had to suffer because of this. Speaking in a public meeting on 6 January 1948, Sardar Patel said, the "Congress people in power should behave in a different way with Sangh rather than laying stress on their own rights and powers. It is not possible to suppress an organization with the power of penal action. The Sangh people are not the type who will fight for selfish interests. They are patriots who love their motherland." Within a few days, Pandit Nehru, as if in response to this speech, spoke in Amritsar, the "Sangh and Hindu Mahasabha people have insulted our national flag. They are traitors. I will crush them."

One could talk of countless leaders who came to the Sangh offices begging for help in very difficult helpless situations when they were fleeing Pakistan or fighting Muslim League goondas. But, today all this had been forgotten. Why this sense of ingratitude? Historian of Kashmir, Kalhan, has already given answer to this 'yaksha prashna'- seemingly unsolvable riddle - in his book *Raajtarangini* written in eighth century. His conclusion is that just as a newborn baby completely forgets about the pain of living in the womb, similarly a ruler forgets about all that happened previously once he gets power.

On one side, there was a defeatist feeling about kneeling before the decision of partition, guilt complex that we are the cause of unexpected miseries and pains of countless people, the sense of failure that we couldn't lift a small finger to stop these excesses. On the other hand, there was this sense of brotherhood of swayamsevaks who jumped into defence of helpless displaced brethren and their rehabilitation without worrying about risks; pious emotions with which they brought leaders of various political parties to safety, without thinking about narrow party politics, to well appointed centres, live example of Guruji who jumped fearlessly into the terrible whirlpool of calamities and delivered life giving support for a hope filled future to the sufferers; and as a result, affectionate feelings of the populace towards Sangh. This was a factual, comparative scenario.

In the fag end of year 1947 on December 27, Guruji wrote to Rajabhau Deshpande of Pune, "...I am aware of the entire situation. This is a period of trial, not of loss. We shall come out of it stronger and in a bigger form. Do not fall into the evil trap of opposing or confronting and avoid bitterness in speech or action. Keep focused on duty, it will lead to success and a favourable environment."[9]

Madhya Pradesh's home minister Pandit Dwarika Prasaad Mishra's statement seemed like a statement given in favour of Sangh. Countering the allegations of the opposing camp, to *Nagpur Navbhaarat* (19 December 1947) he said in a statement, "The very idea that the Sangh can overthrow government on the strength of lathis is laughable. It is surprising that this allegation was not made against the local DSP I cannot believe at all that the Sangh is a political organization and that there is a possibility of it overthrowing Pandit Nehru's government."[10]

Vaartaa Vihaar of North Karnataka and South Maharashtra published the public speech of 'Karnataka Kesari' Gangadhar Rao Deshpande after another six days on 25 December 1947. In this speech he had said, the "Congress has passed a resolution recently very cleverly against the Sangh....strange are the games of fate that as soon as they got hold of power, they are parroting the idea of 'do not organize' whenever they think of the Sangh... But, looking back at my experience of past 50 years, I can state not once but again and again, that organizing Hindus is very crucial for maintaining peace in our country... I pray to the people in power not to shirk away from this organization. This organization will ultimately come to their rescue at a crucial time..."[11]

Most strident editorial appeared in the *Tribune* that was being published from Delhi itself. He wrote on November 26, "Pandit Nehru has instructed East Punjab government to ban the RSS and Akali Dal and destroy them. This news is so dreadful that it should not be true at all. And if it is true, then it can only be termed as a misfortune of this country... Because it is necessary for us to remind Pandit Nehru that if these nationalist organizations had not faced the cruel and inhuman Pakistanis with their bravery, then thousands of Hindu and Sikh sisters would have been raped, thousands of Sikh and Hindu children would have been butchered... we wish to say this with full force at our command that the Sangh and Akali Dal have made a place for themselves deep in the hearts of the people of this bordering state. Populace there looks at them as the sentinels of their state... It is nothing but ingratitude to brand these organizations communal or private armies. In fact, they are nationalist powers out to help us who have discipline like army, but have no arms. Indian government should be proud of them..."[12]

The Congress leadership never expected reactions of this order. They kept quiet for some time, but they were looking for the right opportunity. The real reason for this was pointed out by Shri Banahatti, the moving spirit of Sarvoday movement, in his weekly *Savdhaan*. He wrote openly that, "In this period, Rashtriya Swayamsevak Sangh is the only organization that can challenge the Congress. Talented, dedicated young class of high character is getting attracted to Sangh due to its organized strength. This is the reason the Sangh has become an eyesore for the Congress leaders. The Congress is taking the nationwide work of the Sangh, its impact on educated, intelligent youth and rare qualities like readiness of its swayamsevaks to work patiently in times of any disaster as a challenge to itself. The spiritual qualities due to which the Congress used to think of itself as a superior power; growth of same qualities in the Sangh is making the Congress uncomfortable."

The Congress government was bent upon not letting any competition nor any noble soul to grow. It was waiting with an evil intention for the right opportunity 'sooner or later' to disrupt the sustained hard work of the

Sangh. For them the incident that gave them this opportunity was unfortunate murder of Mahatma Gandhi. Thus, began the cycle of persecution of the RSS and its followers. This began with arrest of Guruji and ban on the RSS.

– Excerpts from Chapter 20 from Shri Guruji Golwalkar Biography by Ranga Hari

Endnotes

1. Shri Guruji Samagra 5, pp. 170-171
2. Shri Guruji Samagra 3, p. 176
3. Ibid, pp. 169-170
4. Maa. Sa. Golwalkar, p. 108
5. Ibid, p. 109
6. Ibid, pp. 109-110
7. Ibid, p. 119
8. Pehli Agnipariksha, p. 41
9. Shri Guruji Samagra 8, p. 44
10. Pehli Agnipariksha, p. 43
11. Ibid, pp. 43-44
12. Ibid, p. 32

Annexure IV

Exchanges between RSS, Patel and Nehru

Pre-Satyagrah efforts by RSS

MS Golwalkar, aka Guruji, was released on August 6 after nearly 6 months, but release was linked to many conditions. These conditions were – to stay within municipal limits of Nagpur, not to leave Nagpur municipal limits without written permission from district magistrate, not making any public speech, not writing for newspapers, writing letters in them without District Magistrate's permission, not acting or writing in a way that would create disaffection directly or indirectly against state governments, not keeping in touch with people who acted in such a way.

Conditions did not prohibit writing letters to people. He turned his attention to this condition and decided to move ahead on this narrow pathway. Without delay, he wrote to Home Minister and Deputy Prime Minister Sardar Patel on August 11, requesting him to rescind the ban on Sangh and give back its democratic rights to function. Case of Gandhiji's murder was being conducted in Red Fort in Delhi for two and half months. All the accused except two fugitives of Gwalior had been arrested. Even the charge sheet of the case did not even have a mention of either Sangh or Sangh swayamsevak. Therefore, people and rulers knew clearly that Sangh had no involvement in this incident. This was, but, a matter of common knowledge. But, there was another truth beyond this that was not known at that time but is well-known today. That is the report submitted by a high ranking police official Sanjeevi about Gandhi assassination within one month of the incident. He had completed his job in 17 days and handed over the complete report in writing to home minister. With same alacrity and sense of responsibility home minister had written a long letter to the prime minister on 27 February 1948, that is, on twenty ninth day of Gandhiji's death. Today this letter is available in the sixth volume Collection of Nehru Patel correspondence on page numbers 56 and 57. But, this was an unpublished government document at the time. Letter also exposes another truth of history. Parts of that document are as follows:

- All the materials received through known-unknown, true-untrue, named and unnamed sources have been sifted thoroughly. Ninety per cent of these are baseless speculative reports. Most of the allegations are about activities of the RSS - that they distributed sweets, held celebrations. All this was found to be false upon investigation.
- Strong opponents of Bapuji's policies and thoughts, many of whom were members of the Hindu Mahasabha and the RSS did welcome this murder. But, beyond this, there is no way one can drag the RSS and the Hindu Mahasabha members into this conspiracy on the basis of available evidence. The RSS may be responsible for some other disturbances but not for this one. (Page 57)
- Confessions of the conspirators prove that the RSS was not a party, in any way, to this conspiracy. (Page 56)

Thus, it is doubtlessly clear that when Sarsanghchaalak was writing letters to the prime minister and home minister, they already knew the truth about the Sangh for more than five months. Now, this entire correspondence between the two sides has been published in English and all other major Indian languages.

Bitter truth is that the political leaders of that time covered up the truth deliberately and did grave injustice to the Sangh. It was expected that the steps taken in the emergency that arose out of dark atmosphere because to Gandhi murder should have been corrected after true facts came to light later on. But, unfortunately, it did not happen. There was no acknowledgement from Prime Minister's office. Home minister's reply was sent after one month on September 11. Leaving aside the letter he had written to Prime Minister in the light of investigation of the police officer or pushing it under the carpet, he wrote, "Happiness that the Sangh people expressed and sweets they distributed on Gandhiji's death has resulted in more resistance from people."[1] There is another sentence in that letter with a tone of pious lecturing, "I have firm belief that the Sangh people can do justice to their patriotism only by working together with the Congress and not by opposing it or being separate from it"[2] As an honest, reputed and a person pledged to the Congress, Patel had all the right to sermonize anybody about party politics. But, here the letter was addressed to the home minister demanding undoing the injustice done to his organization, based on irrefutable facts. Home Minister's duty was to prove the allegations true or take them back in view of lack of proofs. But, one will have to say with all due respect for the home minister that party politics overrode his duty for rule of law.

Guruji did not express any reaction to Patel's sermon. He wrote to Pandit Jawaharlal Nehru again on September 24, "Eight months have passed since the Sangh was banned and every possible investigation in this regard has been conducted by now. I believe that you would have fully understood that the allegations leveled against Sangh are baseless and false. Therefore, it is only a question of administering justice in this matter now. We have a right to expect justice from our own government."[3] Much against the earlier bitter experience, a reply from Prime Minister's office was received on the fourth day. It was a repetition of the earlier government notification. Only one point was different - "Prime Minister had been informed about a note that United Province government had sent to you containing some evidence collected by the state government about the Sangh's above mentioned activities before the ban was imposed on the Rashtriya Swayamsevak Sangh. Other states also have such proofs."[4]

Within two weeks of Guruji's release from jail, there was Rakshaa Bandhan festival of the Sangh. Many swayamsevaks came to his house till late in the night, touched his feet and tied 'rakhee' on his arms. He heard the tragic stories of torture which they went through at the hands of so-called followers of Gandhiji.

The Sangh leadership decided that Sarsanghchaalak should go to Delhi to put forth his demand for justice and he should make Delhi his battlefield for these efforts. Guruji left for Delhi on 16th October. However, newspapers suppressed the news of 'departure of the head of an outlawed organization' under government's pressure. In spite of this, when the train arrived at 5.15 a.m. after a delay of 45 minutes, nearly ten thousand people had collected in the station campus. The Delhi government had already banned raising of slogans at station. As a counter to this policy, all the guests had arrived with rose and jasmine flowers. Arrival of Guruji was greeted with grand sweet fragrance of flowers. Writing about it, home minister informed prime minister, "Their discipline is still strong. I had made it clear that when he (Golwalkar) arrives in Delhi, there should be no display etc. There were three to four thousand people to welcome him at the station. They greeted him in full silence. Not a word came out of their lips. There was no display of any kind. Everybody listened to the orders of Guru Golwalkar. ...."[5] This welcome in the capital was a proof of the reality that the Sangh work had survived well despite a ban of nearly eight months. Guruji went to the house of Lala Hansraj Gupt from the station and stayed there till he was put under arrest again on November 12.

Topic of ban always used to come up during informal discussions. The RSS Chief took care that volunteers should not get agitated. "Ban on Sangh is totally unjustified. But, it is our government therefore efforts to get the ban lifted should be peaceful and within rule of law... ... We shall have to find an area of action .... We should strengthen the social life, taking recourse to just path. As far as the Sangh is concerned, victory is assured, because its foundation is based on truth."

The day Guruji reached Delhi, he met the home minister the same evening. Because the dialogue couldn't be completed that day, he met him again on October 23. But, discussions didn't move in the desired direction. Guruji's stand was, "Because the allegations against the Sangh have proven to be so patently untrue and baseless, government must lift the ban immediately. If the government still believes that these accusations have any basis then it is its bounden democratic duty to prove them in the courts." But, Sardar's pet theme was the sermon he had delivered in his earlier letter. "Only practical solution is to become part of the Congress." Sarsanghchaalak Guruji was totally against this suggestion. He was not ready to let die the freedom to organize. Thus, the dialogue failed.

Guruji had understood the mentality of the government in the very first meeting. Therefore, he invited journalists to the residence of Lalaji on October 19 at 9 in the morning. One of the question was, "Do you have any hope of the ban being lifted in near future?" Answer was, "I am always optimistic, but it is the job of the government to lift it." Second question was, "If the ban is not lifted, what would be your first step?" Response was, "Then, the government will have to prove that the Sangh is guilty. Current democratic government has a major responsibility in this regard. It is not possible to prove an innocent guilty. Therefore, I believe completely that government will lift the ban. Till this belief is firm why should have any other thought?"

The administration decided to take a more rigid stance about Sangh. Thus, Guruji received a message from Patelji that, "The job for which you had come to Delhi is over. Therefore, leave Delhi now." This order passed on October 28 was handed over by the government representative on November 2 at his place of residence. Guruji read it and expressed his disagreement with it, and wrote on the same page in English, "I believe that this order is unnecessary and it takes away the civil rights of a law abiding citizen. I also believe that I would be a party to this unjustified act and injustice if I accept it. By accepting this order, I would be failing to do my duty as a citizen of an independent state. Thus, I have to submit that I cannot accept this extraordinary order."[6]

Realizing that this government was following the footsteps of foreign rulers blindly and would use similar tactics, the Sangh team awaited the arrest of Guruji that same night. Guruji prepared two statements to present Sangh's side to the common people before this could happen, and got it distributed to newspaper world one after the other. First statement was refutation of government's action and second was clarification about the Sangh's position on various issues.

Main points of the first statement were –

1. We were aware even at the time when allegations were hurled against the Sangh that they were false and baseless. Still we had disbanded the Sangh, while not accepting those allegations.
2. During this period all the charges have proven to be untrue.
3. Nine months have passed, still this injustice waged against us has not been set right.
4. Orders were received that the Sangh should merge with a political party. This will mean that there is no freedom or right to anybody to organize non-political activity in this country.

Guruji appealed to the society further, "It is my appeal to the Hindu society not to fall prey to misleading false propaganda. We have already suffered a lot during last 1000 years due to our disunity. At least, now we should have unity and we should build a more healthy, strong and enlightened life based on mutual affection, dedication and trust; that would result in us, the ancient Hindu society making our sacred motherland, Bharatvarsh happy and prosperous in our own home."[7]

Second statement was about the Sangh's stand about symbols of national honour. Poisonous arrows of false propaganda were also being unleashed by various leaders about these issues. Clarifying about them, Guruji stated:

1. Flag - Confusion is being created deliberately about the Rashtriya Swayamsevak Sangh's views about flag.... the Rashtriya Swayamsevak Sangh has its own flag that symbolizes its urge to create cultural unity among Hindu race. ...Being a part of the nation, the Rashtriya Swayamsevak has complete faith and respect for the national flag. And I can say without hesitation that each member of the Rashtriya Swayamsevak Sangh will readily sacrifice his life to defend our national flag against any aggressor.
2. Faith in democratic system of governance - Time has proved that democratic state is the best and longest lasting and successful in comparison to all other systems of governance.
3. State is a secular institution - For a Hindu, state has always been a secular institution and so is it even now. .... Truly, it is unnecessary to give an adjective of 'secular' (asaampradaayik - non-communal) for a state that is already 'secular'.
4. Hindu state - the Rashtriya Swayamsevak Sangh does not propagate a Hindu state which has zero non-Hindu citizens.
5. We believe that no progressive organization can stay alive long and grow if it works in a secretive manner. Question of the Rashtriya Swayamsevak Sangh working in a secret manner also cannot arise as its work is cultural and it has no political ambitions.
6. It is state's duty to raise an army, not that of any non-government organization. Therefore, it is not right to compare the Rashtriya Swayamsevak Sangh's discipline with Army's discipline and its rules of work.
7. Idea of overthrowing the current government and capturing power taking recourse to violence is purely a figment of imagination. Keeping in view the Rashtriya Swayamsevak Sangh's cultural form of work and its efforts to keep itself aloof from political ambitions, this question too doesn't arise.
8. I feel that after this, my brethren of this nation will completely believe that allegations against the Rashtriya Swayamsevak Sangh are unjustified and propaganda against it is misleading, they will appreciate my efforts made to revive this organization with lawful means.[8]

Most of the newspapers published only a summary of these statements. But, the *Organizer* published it in full. The false and misleading propaganda against the Sangh and limited dissemination about it by the mainstream newspapers that was seen as a curse turned out to be a blessing in disguise. The Swayamsevaks took it up as a challenge. Both of Guruji's statements were translated in different languages and distributed in large numbers in different places all over Bharat. Many persistent college students made hundreds of hand written copies and distributed them.

The Government did not arrest Guruji on November 2 as expected by the Sangh team. Instead of this, Guruji received an intimation from the Delhi's magistrate that if he wished to meet prime minister then he can stay back in Delhi only for that work. But, this stay will be allowed only on the conditions that were imposed earlier on him by the Madhya Pradesh government. He also realized that government had not shut its doors completely. Therefore, he restarted his correspondence with the central leaders. He wrote a letter the same day to the prime minister on November 3.

He stated four major points in this letter:

1. I request to you that as our prime minister you should give us an opportunity in an impartial, justified and positive manner to negate the allegations and prove our innocence.
2. "Finding that the allegations are baseless, ban on the Rashtriya Swayamsevak should be lifted immediately."
3. "Adding new points to this issue should be avoided."
4. "I will be highly obliged if I am given an opportunity to meet you.
5. But, Prime Minister's response was not to the issues raised in the letter. Exposing his pre-conceived bias he wrote, "There is no relation between the declared objectives of the Sangh and the real objectives, and activities of its members. These real objectives are completely contrary to the resolutions of the Indian parliament and the rules and regulations of the proposed constitution. As per our information these activities are anti-national and generally destructive and violent. Therefore, you will agree that just an adamant stand will not be of much use."[9]

Guruji's suspicion proved correct. Now a new accusation had come up which was not there in the government notification. Maintaining his expression of respect Guruji wrote back with clarity, "It seems that on the basis of said information you have concluded that our activities are anti-national. This is a grave accusation and it is not proper to raise it against anybody lightly. One needs solid and factual evidence for such an allegation. It is meaningless to keep saying repeatedly that government has information without giving permission to the people against whom they have been raised to examine such allegations. Both of us should agree that 'just an adamant stand will not be of much use' .... As far as the talk about being contrary to the regulations of the proposed constitution is concerned, it would have been better if our prime minister had not written it. It is like punishing somebody for attempting to kill a person who is going to be born after a year or more than that."

Another point is that we do not know what actions of ours make you say that our declared objectives and activities are different from our real objectives and activities. ..... We are just simple servants of the society involved in creating character and unifying in the cultural field, keeping away from politics. There is no place in our work for the art that conceals real objectives from the declared objectives."[10]

Guruji had also written to home minister in the same period. Situation at that end was also not different. At the end, the Delhi mission proved to be a failure. He received the final directive from secretary of home ministry, H. BR Iyengar, to leave Delhi within 24 hours and return to Nagpur. Guruji and his colleagues realized where the future was heading. They decided to utilize every minute of these 24 hours well. First of all, he wrote to prime minister about this last directive in a forthright manner, "We claim to be a cultured state. Such unconstitutional uncivilized qualities can suit only a dictatorial government or to some extent a one party foreign rule. But in my opinion it does not behoove a modern cultured democratic government that claims to protect civil rights impartially.... Therefore I have decided to stay in the capital till this injustice to us is set right."[11]

For 11 days, from November 3 to 13, hand cuffs of the state were hanging in front of Guruji who was appealing for justice. He had worked on two fronts during these days. One - Meeting top people in power and demanding justice through letters. Two - Clarifying his stand in the newspaper world through dialogue with journalists and statements.

Now only one action was left - present his analysis of the situation and views in front of the swayamsevaks, for whom he had come to Delhi as their representative. He prepared a letter in Hindi and English containing 10 paragraphs. In this he described in complete details what had been done from his side so far and stated at the end, "thus, I am taking back the directive that I had given on 6 February 1948 to dissolve Sangh after giving it full thought and I request you to begin your activities regularly. Along with this, we should try our best that peace is maintained and feeling of enmity is kept under check. I have asked our Sarkaryavaah Shri Bhaiyyaji Dani to inform all swayamsevaks about this decision and decide on the day and date to restart our work as it was running earlier."[12]

Police officers arrested the RSS Chief on midnight of November 12, 1948 under the Bengal State criminal procedure act of 1818. This 130 year old act gave unbridled power to arrest anybody anywhere without any proof or reason. In the words of Nehru spoken just three days prior to this, was it not "against the rules and regulations of proposed constitution of Bharat?" Guruji was brought secretively to Nagpur on November 15. The tag put on his luggage by the police officers accompanying him in the flight was 'accompanying person." He was taken to Nagpur Central Jail from the airport. From there he was shifted to Sivni sub-jail after two-three days. Second imprisonment of Guruji commenced thus.

- Excerpts of Chapter 23 of Shri Guruji Golwalkar, Biography by Ranga Hari

Endnotes

1. Shri Guruji Samagra 10. p. 14
2. Shri Guruji Samagra 10. p. 14
3. Ibid. p. 15
4. Ibid. pp. 20-21
5. Sardar Patel Patraachaar. p. 261
6. Ibid. p. 24
7. Ibid. pp. 28-29
8. Ibid. pp. 30-32
9. Ibid. pp. 39-40
10. Ibid. pp. 41-42
11. Ibid. pp. 43-44
12. Ibid. p. 49

Annexure V

Satyagrah against 1948 Ban and its Successful Culmination

Plan of the Sangh was to fight the ban with a satyagrah by reopening the RSS shakhas. It was the beginning of the clash with government. It was a satyagrah that was different from the satyagrahas that had taken place so far. There was no disturbance like 'rastaa roko' nor did it involve sitting in 'dharna' in front of government offices. Common people were not to face any disorder in their daily lives. Form of this protest was very simple. A designated swayamsevak would send written information to the office of local administration that 'we are starting a daily Sangh shakha at xyz place at abc time.' A pre-decided team of swayamsevaks would reach that place at preplanned time and begin shakha activities shouting slogans like 'Bharatmata ki Jai', 'Sangh se pratibandh hatao'. This was the format of satyagrah. The Sangh satyagrah was not against anybody - neither the government nor the police; but it was definitely against injustice.

To strengthen this plan, all the prachaaraks who had been moved to different small and big places, came back to their areas. Satyagrahis were prepared with personal contacts by working overground, without going underground, without depending on motivating speeches and without support from newspapers. Whatever the reaction of police against conducting shakhas — whether lawful or unlawful — they bore it peacefully. There was not even a small counter- reaction anywhere. Leadership had taken common swayamsevak into confidence and informed them about the actual conditions on the field transparently. They were told bluntly that government can act in a devilish way, students' studies can be stopped, member's jobs can be at risk, government servants would, surely, be removed from jobs, farmers' properties may be confiscated, businesses may be shut down, some close brethren may lose lives due to unfortunate accidental attacks, families may force their members to seek pardon, imprisonment may be for longer period than expected etc. etc. Factual picture of the scenario was presented to the swayamsevaks. They were not given assurances like 'ban will be lifted in four weeks' as was done by leaders in earlier times who had assured that 'independence will be achieved in one year'. Members were reminded how they had suffered all the atrocities with bounden hands in the first week of February. After making all these preparations only, did Sarkaaryavaah Bhaiyyaji Dani declare that the Sangh shakhas would re-commence from December 9.

Guruji wrote another special letter for swayamsevaks who were to offer satyagrah. It was handed over to each satyagrahi. It was so inspiring that many swayamsevaks in jail learnt this letter by heart. Given below is a small extract of that letter:

".......There is no time for thoughts like 'me and mine' in this terrible time of calamity for Bhaaratmaataa. Whatever happens to us as individuals, we have to set Bhaaratmaataa free from the impact of un-Bharatiyataa (abhaaratiyataa). We have to rescue all the children of Mother from abduction of their natural rights by parties in power that are blinded by selfishness. We have seen that everybody benefits from free, happy and honourable life.

Our work is undoubtedly the finest, it is exalted, it is divine work of God, in its fulfilment is the highest achievement for mankind. It is like envisioning the Supreme Being. Therefore, arise and make up for the loss of ten months of inaction. Truth is with us. It is a sin to sleep at times of injustice, and live as its victim. Let us set right this injustice. This is a confrontation of dharma versus adharma, justice versus injustice, greatness versus pettiness, love versus evil. Victory is assured, because with Dharma is Supreme god and with him comes victory.

So, arise with victorious roar for Bhaaratmaataa's glory that would reverberate from the horizons of the heart to the horizons of the universe and rest not till work is accomplished."[1]

The Government side had begun its verbal assault from the beginning of December. Speaking in Gwalior on 5 December Sardar Patel cautioned in a threatening tone, "Hearts of the Sangh members are filled with venom of hatred, therefore they can never run a satyagrah agitation successfully. The Government is armed fully to accept their challenge."[2] While addressing the annual conference of the Congress in Jaipur, Pandit Nehru said, "This is not satyagrah, it is an ill conceived insistence of the Sangh urchins. We shall use all over power to suppress this agitation. We shall never allow these people to raise their heads."[3]

On the other side newspapers opposed this dictatorial and unjust steps of the government unhesitatingly. Editorial of 21 October in English daily, *Hitavaad,* from Nagpur noted, "Prove the allegations or remove the ban – this demand of Shri Golwalkar is logical and one cannot disregard it. People from the Congress should definitely not ignore it because they were in the same situation in 1942 that the Sangh is in today. The Congress had been declared outlawed and British government in its charge-sheet had claimed that the Congress is responsible for the disturbances of year 1942. So, Gandhiji had made a humble demand that allegations against the Congress should be presented to a court of law and they should be proven."[4]

Even in this short period of two weeks, the satyagrah left a strong impression on the people. The Government's idea that this kids' game would lose steam in 4–5 days proved to be totally wrong. The Satyagrah was running with same vigour even in third week of January. The truth was that all the major prisons of the country had not only been filled up by the second week of satyagrah, in fact they were packed to more than twice or thrice their capacity with satyagrahis. Most of the jailers had intimated the rulers of this situation through telegrams. But, how could satyagrah stop? So, government began another experiment. Police began picking up satyagrahis and pushing them into jungles that were 60-70 miles away from their homes. But, those people would come back again to take part in satyagrah as additional team after moving around from village to villages in small groups like the pilgrims of earlier times, partaking food in different homes and spreading the word about the Sangh too.

Within a month the threatening tone of rulers had mellowed down. The Government thought of opening the dialogue with Sangh again. For this satyagrah has to be stopped first. For this, Sardar Patel asked for cooperation of Moulichandra Sharma who was well known to both the sides. Moulichandra Sharma contacted the editor of *Kesari*, GV Ketkar in Pune to make Sardar Patel's idea successful.

Discussion went along expected line. Ketkar met Sardar Patel and reached Sivni again on 16th. Writing about it, journalist Ketkar says, "I went to Sivni again, met Guruji. Discussions went on for four hours. Guruji would read each and every word of the directive that I needed from Guruji to suspend the agitation very seriously and kept correcting it time and again. Four drafts were made one after another, but each was rejected due to incorrect construct of words. Fifth draft was made satisfactorily. Guruji would examined each word in depth so that prestige of the Sangh would not be compromised in anyway. Of the two copies of the fifth draft, Guruji kept one with him while I got ready to take the second copy to leave the jail."[5]

The coordinator of the entire satyagrah movement was Doctor Bhai Mahavir. After getting Guruji's directive through GV Ketkar, he gave a statement on January 21 about suspending the satyagrah. The statement said, the "Sangh had not begun the satyagrah to put government in difficulty. Its objective was to raise a strong voice against injustice being perpetrated against Sangh and seek attention of government and enlightened people. It seems that our voice has attained expected success. Therefore, experiencing a friendly atmosphere and to make next level of action a success, agitation is being suspended."[6]

Thus, satyagrah of the Rashtriya Swayamsevak Sangh ran for 45 days from December 9, 1948 to January 22, 1949. As per last count, number of satyagrahis was 77,090,13. This figure was bigger than number of prisoners held during 1942 agitation, that was recognized as the biggest movement for independence.

The *Statesman* of 22nd January carried both the editorial and statement about withdrawal of satyagrah together. It said, "For this, not only government, but Sangh leadership also deserves complements and thanks. Credit goes to them for the way they conducted satyagrah."[7]

Atmosphere of struggle mellowed down and environment for dialogue became positive. But one has to note with regret that yet again, the Congress government's stance was not straightforward. Leaving aside the points there were there in the notification about ban, they began throwing up unrelated issues like, the 'Sangh doesn't have a constitution so in its absence it is difficult to lift the ban.' Instead of sitting across and discussing issues in an atmosphere of friendly cooperation, their behaviour smacked of feudalism. TR Venkatraman and GV Ketkar had taken on the role of mediators between government and Guruji.

As he came out of Sivni jail after meeting Guruji, he told Eknath Ranade, "To make your Guruji agree to anything is like moving a mountain. Still, due to his respect for me, he agreed to my views with open heart. Now, provide me with the necessary material to help me prepare the constitution." Eknathji and Pandit Deendayal Upadhyay sat together to draw out the working methodology of Sangh. Finally, the constitution of Sangh took form. Shastriji reached Sivni again on March 10 with this draft. Explaining the whole story behind making of this document, he handed it over to Guruji who flipped each page and signed at the required place."

On advice from Shastriji, Guruji gave this authority to Shastriji through his signed power of attorney to him. The letter said, "I have read the constitution prepared by Shri TR Venkatram Shastri. I accept it. With a view of saving time and as a matter of convenience I am requesting Shri Shastriji to submit it to the Central government and accept him as my authorized representative." Shastriji came to Nagpur with these documents and met state home minister Dwarika Prasad Mishra and after handing over the entire material to him for the purpose of submission to the Central Home Minister, he proceeded for Chennai. This ex-advocate general had believed that next steps would take place without any hurdle. Howerver, home minister of free India managed to find one fault with the whole exercise. He sent all the documents back to Chennai with a letter stating, "Though you have prepared this constitution, it is the constitution of the Sangh. Therefore, following the right procedure, Golwalkar should himself send it to Central home department through Madhya Pradesh home ministry. The permission given to you for meeting Golwalkar was not given to you as a mediator." This behaviour of home minister was found distasteful by the elderly gentleman. But, he was sincere about making the job successful that he had taken up. But, in his age, that too at the height of summers, it was exhausting for him to travel to Nagpur again via Sivni. Therefore, he handed over all this material with another letter through Shivram Shankar Apte to deliver it to Guruji by hand, appraising Guruji about the unexpected hurdle put by the government and his suggestion about how to represent it. Apteji went to Sivni in April 1949 to overcome the hurdle.

Accepting various opinions and discussions, Guruji submitted the constitution of the Sangh to the Central government through Madhya Pradesh government from Sivni jail on April 11. Attached letter had following lines, "I am sending the written constitution of the Sangh alongwith. Now onwards, the organization will work as per its provisions. It contains mainly those provisions on which the Sangh was working for years."

"I hope that constitution prepared now will be acceptable and will fulfill a sharply felt weakness. With a hope that the administration will approve the constitution, I also hope that you show the courtesy of releasing a notification to lift the ban on the Sangh and let it work as per its constitution (which has been prepared and sent to you). When this possibility is created, I will get this constitution printed. The required notifications that are to be released, may be released fast so that the Sangh work can be conducted with ease."

"It pains me a lot that Bhaaratiya government looks at my words and general conduct with suspicion. But, time will prove my work, that weaves together a scattered and highly divided people into a cultural tie built with a common goal and common discipline and generates unity, will prove to be useful for overall good of the nation. Future alone will tell that my nature is of cooperation, maintaining a positive feeling for all, and not tuned to fighting with some group. I expect a positive response very soon."[8]

In fact, demand of government had been met fully. Now, all that was left was to lift the ban with a liberal and open heart. Expecting this, generous hearted Venkatram Shastri had written special letters to Madhya Pradesh home minister Mishraji on April 16 and Home Minister Patel on April 29 from Chennai. But the government had different ideas.

It had a different regrettable objective. There was a meeting of chief ministers on April 8-9 in which it was decided to continue the ban. Because of this, government decided to play some complex political games of its own. Instead of home minister, home secretary took over the correspondence in this matter. After that, the human contacts established so far, began to melt away. Dry bureaucratic processes took over. This group is known for its quality of always being more loyal than the king. Home secretary raised objections over sub-sections of the constitution. Guruji sent his reply to the letter sent by state home ministry in Sivni jail directly to Central Home Minister. This time he wrote in a more terse manner, "Even my demand for producing evidence against the allegations against us is more than six month old, but there no proof has come up during this period. In such a scenario, it doesn't behoove a supposedly cultured government to keep repeating the so-called allegations even after such a long lapse of time and showing disrespect to truth, justice and judicial system." And finally, drawing attention of the home minister, he clarified, "Before closing this letter, I would like to bring to your notice another fact that there is no constitution in which you cannot pick holes in some way. All constitutions can be amended suitably over time. Therefore I think that if somebody criticizes a constitution right upon its introduction and expects it to be perfectly complete like the final words of God, it is not right to have such a view. I have been told that government wants the Sangh's constitution in writing. I have submitted it. .... I feel that the right way is to implement the constitution in practice and change and improve it as situation arises. This is, in fact, constructive and useful way of doing it."[9] The response that Iyengar sent after a week exposed the true intent of the government. He had written in conclusion, The "Government's approach about the Rashtriya Swayamsevak Sangh is completely transparent and the without any confusion. It is the custodian of people's interest and this is how it should be. It is its duty to protect them from undesirable and foul elements. Till it is not fully assured that the Rashtriya Swayamsevak Sangh will not be in a position to repeat such incidents and it will be able to stop negative fallout of such actions that are a result of its activities in the past, it cannot take a lenient view about the organization."[10]

Guruji sent response to this letter, too, to home minister. Attacking the intoxication of power, he wrote in his last letter, "In a matter like this, a suggestion of an independent enquiry committee can come only from people who do not understand even the basics of governance' – I am obliged for being told about this. I accept my ignorance on this subject. Not just ordinary human being, but even Mahatma Gandhi, himself, had a right to this ignorance, so I consider this a matter of pride for me. If this is how your government basically thinks then it is dangerous... Letter dated 3 May 1949 gave me a sense of satisfaction. That is, that my assessment of the mentality about the people who have the right to rule, was not wrong."[11]

At this stage dialogue between the two sides stopped. In the meanwhile, many newspapers published the Sangh's constitution that had been submitted to the government. *Navbharat* of Delhi wrote in its editorial dated May 24, the "Sangh has submitted a written constitution due to adamant stand of the Congress government. Why is government silent now? After studying the constitution of Sangh, we have come to the conclusion that the Congress rulers should not object to any part of it." [12]

Having understood the thinking of government, Sangh began preparing a new strategy. Jail walls not only have ears but they also have lips. It doesn't matter whether Guruji is inside or Eknathji is outside. Leaders and organizers had kept message broadcasting systems very fast based on this truism. Because of this, morale of swayamsevaks was very high in spite of being in prison for four-five months. In fact, the Congress leadership's estimates about the scenario slipped off the tracks here. They had assumed that policy of procrastination will weaken the opposition. That is why they had dragged the matter for five months after suspension of satyagrah.

The Sangh leadership decided to get back onto the battle grounds again with support of a favourable society. Noticing the last sentence of home secretary's letter, the "Government cannot take a lenient view about the organization", Guruji decided to face the challenge head on. He handed over a letter head carrying his name containing his plan for struggle to the jail warden, to be handed over to Balasaheb Deoras who was to be released after a week. Jailer intercepted it and sent it directly to Dwarika Prasad Mishra, who sent it to Home Minister Patel.[13]

It seems that this could be a part of the RSS strategy. It gave an idea about the intentions of the Sangh leader. The Sangh leader had written to his closest colleague, "I had told Shri Venkatram Shastri from beginning that this is what government will do. He assured me that 'leave it to me'... I accepted his offer. But, my view is that it is not possible to resolve this issue without informing members all over and launching a powerful agitation again. Thus, without rushing into it, this agitation will run for many days with faultless preparations. With this understanding, there is no alternative but to re-launch this agitation in June end or at a suitable time. This is my opinion. It would be better to include and add other types of strikes etc. to this. A good resolution should be documented well. The copies of this statement should be distributed all over the country. The statement should also declare that as a result of government putting hurdles against the right of the people to assemble, we are launching this peaceful agitation because we have been left with no other alternative. This statement should be sent from an unmarked place by post to the central and state governments and agitation should be launched in a peaceful manner."

"This is, but, my opinion. However, you people, who are outside should sit together and take the right decision. My effort is only that this sense of indecisiveness must end. This situation of being 'neither here nor there' with washing away of mediator's efforts must come to an end. ...."[14]

As expected, Sarkaaryavaah Bhaiyyaji Dani and Balasaheb Deoras reached Nagpur after being released from jail on June 5. None of them received the above mentioned letter suppressed by the jailer, but they had received complete information from other 'information highways'. Eknath Ranade also joined them later. Opinion of all the three was similar to that of Guruji. Their assessment was that discussions about some agreement with government were like a cry in the wilderness and that government is playing a game of stretching and delaying the issue. They also assessed the situation on the ground. They could notice that atmosphere prevailing at the time of imposition of ban had changed radically. Now, people have understood the truth.

In the meanwhile, case of Gandhi's murder had also got over. In that, prosecuting lawyers had not even mentioned the name of any swayamsevak. In the judgment that Justice H. Atmacharan gave, the Sangh's name didn't appear anywhere. During the hearing, the accused had kept aloof of Sangh in the long statement that he read out in front of the judge. Thus, the case, the accused and the judge – all three had left out the Sangh. In short, the triumvirate came to conclusion that hearts of the swayamsevaks in jail were still ready for the struggle and ready to bear with more pain, but there was serious shortage of funds; when they looked towards their side. They decided not to bow down. All the underground volunteers were sent out this directive all over the country. Series of contacts, discussions and broadcasting of instructions were used to hone the souls of swayamsevaks to be ready for hard work.

The Government must have received information about the movement in Sangh camp through its intelligence department. Student organizations had started functioning in different states of country. Experienced and polished workers of the Sangh like Balraj Madhok, Dattopant Thengdi, Dattaaji Didolkar and Naagraaj Reddy were leading this activity. Large number of students from amongst displaced citizens had joined the organization in North.

Simultaneously, discussions and workshops began about desirability of new political party to make real democracy more effective in the new post-independence period. Professor Malkani wrote a series of articles in the weekly, *Organizer*, about the possible shape of a new political party. The Sangh had begun its moves. But, Sangh leadership was aware that government being run by Sardar Patel would not give way so easily. The Government was hatching conspiracy to create fissures among Guruji and his followers. After receiving the letter written from Sivni jail by Guruji, Sardar Patel wrote to Dwarika Prasad Mishra, "If this letter reaches the desired destination, it will have the authentic stamp of the Chief of the organization. In its absence there will be pulls within the organization about the problem. As a result, we shall face split up groups rather than a well united organization. Therefore, as a policy and strategy, it would be ideal to not let this letter reach the desired destination."[15] A manifestation of this move was shifting of Guruji under the orders of Dwarika Prasad on June 7 from Sivni jail to Baitul jail that was 200 km away. It was clearly a vengeful step of the government. Even the imperialist British used to put political prisoners in jails like Yerwada, Naini etc. with normal facilities. Dangerous prisoners used to be sent to cellular jail of Andaman or Mandalay jail in Burma. Baitul was a younger sibling of these two jails. Guruji was put in this oven in those hot days of summer. His physical condition was not good even in Sivni. It got worse in Baitul. But, there too, he stuck to his policy of 'no demands, no complaints.'

Dani-Deoras duo took an aggressive stance. When a government appointed anonymous person met Bhaiyyaji Dani to get Sangh's opinion, Bhaiyyaji showed him the typewritten copy of the document about formation of the proposed political party. Vasantrao Oke also followed the same strategy. When these details reached various ministries, many chief ministers started saying that, "we shall have to reconsider the proposal of April about ban on the Sangh." Many ministers expressed the opinion that if Sangh entered politics, it would be transformed from a 'brahmin' to 'brahmraakshas' (from a peaceful person to a demon). It seems Nehruji's thoughts were moving in the same direction. We can conclude so because the title of the chapter covering this issue in the words of Nehru is 'The less of these bans the better'.[16]

The Government seemed have made up its mind internally to somehow find a solution to this problem. To achieve this, dialogue that had broken down had to be reopened. There was an intractable hurdle here. Guruji had stopped his correspondence with the government and so had the government. Now, the dilemma was how to move ahead? Sardar Patel found a way out. Thus, Dwarika Prasadji reached Delhi and stayed with Food minister Babu Rajendra Prasad. He called Moulichandra Sharma who was known and acceptable to both the sides, and apprised him of the problem. And, he also told that this was a 'directive from Sardar Patel taking rest in Dehradun' Moulichandraji accepted the brief immediately. He reached Nagpur on July 7. Home minister made arrangement of a car for him. He met Dani and Deoras without delay. They informed him of their experience from the beginning to date and told him that their faith in government was finished; it was fruitless to talk with these people, and requested him bluntly to leave them alone on their path. Moulichandraji returned after meeting Mishraji and said, "Patelji really wants to lift the ban. If Golwalkar were to write a letter to Patel on the same issues that he had talked about in his statement last November on 2nd, that is, about national flag, system of governance, secular state etc. then it would be possible." Dani and Deoras did not soften their stance even this time. Both said very clearly, 'Whether they lift ban or not, there is no possibility of anybody from among us including Guruji of writing a word to the centre of power." Moulichandraji came back after meeting Mishraji and offered a new idea for a solution. According to it, Moulichandra Sharmaji would be the person who would ask for clarification, Guruji would give him clarification in writing. Ban would be lifted on the basis of that clarification. Sangh leadership was agreeable to this, only on one condition. They told Moulichandraji, "You will first give us the list of those questions, after expressing our opinion only will we pass it on to Guruji." According to this, Moulichandraji presented the list with eight issues given to him by Dwarika Prasad. They were about the Sangh's faith in Indian constitution and flag, the Sangh's view about working secretly, process of election in the Sangh, meaning of life long oath of the Sangh, admission of young boys in the Sangh, process of appointment of Sarsanghchaalak, balanced representation of members and system of income and expense.

Deoras-Dani duo didn't find anything unacceptable in this list. Actually, Guruji had given answer to most of these issues already. So, rather than getting stuck with it, they wrote together a detailed letter to Guruji, sealed it in an envelope and while handing it over to the mediator, they said, "Sharmaji, please do not read this, nor do allow anybody else to read it. Give it directly in Guruji's hands. Show Guruji's clarification directly to us, only then hand it over to Mishraji." He accepted the condition and while leaving said, "shubham bhavatu" (may good things happen). He kept his word. He did not hand over the sealed envelope to Mishraji taking refuge under his promise. Activities went ahead smoothly after this.

Moulichandraji reached Baitul by car on July 10. In words of Moulichandraji, "I kept the letters in front of him after this. He said, 'give these to me, I will sign them.' Opposing this, I told him, 'First read these letters properly, think over them. It is possible that some words in them may not be to your liking.'... He wrote that letter on a letter pad with his name, signed it and gave the letter to me."[17] Moulichandraji showed it to Dani-Deoras first and then gave them to Dwarika Prasad Mishra. He read it out to Sardar Patel in Dehradun on telephone, where he was taking rest after a heart attack. Sardar gave it his acceptance and directed that the letter be sent directly to Delhi office. The Dehradun-Nagpur-Delhi hotline did its work on the midnight of 11th and before sunrise on 12th July, Sangh ban was lifted.

There is an interesting sidelight. Guruji's authorized letter sent along with the Sangh documents sent by Venkatram Shastri was returned to the sender with the reason, "You are not official mediator." And now, Moulichandra Sharma sends a clarification given to him to the government, and that is accepted, though he has not been declared a mediator. Not only this, acceptance is done on telephone and with the brave spirit of a Napolean and the complex problem is resolved at a lightning speed. This is the mystical way of politics. Finally, ban was lifted on the midnight of July 11, news was broadcast on July 12 from Akashvani; and published in all newspapers on July 13. The RSS Chief was freed from Baitul prison on the morning of July 13.

- Excerpts of Chapter 24 of Shri Guruji Golwalkar, Biography by Ranga Hari

Endnotes

1. Shri Guruji Samagra 10, pp. 50-51
2. Pehli Agnipariksha, p. 101
3. Maa. Sa. Golwalkar, p. 148
4. Pahli Agnipariksha, p. 97
5. Jeevan Prasang -1, pp. 215-216
6. Pehli Agnipariksha, p. 215
7. Ibid, p. 215
8. Shri Guruji Samagra 10, pp. 56-57
9. Ibid, pp. 61-64
10. Ibid, p. 66
11. Ibid, p. 67
12. Ibid, p. 222
13. Living an Era-2, p. 78
14. Ibid, p. 78
15. Ibid, p. 80
16. Ibid, p. 56
17. Jeevan Prasang-1, p. 218

References

RSS, Vision and Mission – H. V. Sheshadri

Ayodhya the Finale – Science vs. Secularism, the excavation debate – Koenraad Elst

Tao of Physics – Fritjof Capra

A Survey of Hinduism - Klaus K Klostermaier

Indian Express (09-09-09) – From Indus to India – Prof. Dilip K. Chakrabarty

Indian Express (01-06-2008) – Story about Kolkota runway realignment

Biography of Dr. Hedgewar (Hindi) - Prof. Rakesh Sinha

The Beautiful Tree – Dharampal

Indian Science and Technology in 18th Century - Dharampal

Ayodhya and After: Issues before Hindu Society – Koenrad Elst

Koenrad Elst's Indology site - http://koenraadelst.bharatvani.org/

How I became a Hindu – an autobiography – Sitaram Goel - http://www.bharatvani.org/books/hibh/

Hindu Temples, What Happened to Them – Sitaram Goel

Negationism in Hinduism – Koenrad Elst

The Saffron Swastika: The Notion of Hindu 'Fascism' – Koenrad Elst

RSS: Enthu? Engott? (Malayalam) – Father Kundukulam

Communism apnee hi kasauti par (Hindi) – D. B. Thengdi

Hinduism, Hindutva & Secularism – P.D. Mathew, S.J.

Integral Humanism – Deendayal Upadhyay

Bharatiya Itihas ki Paramparayen (Hindi) – Babasaheb Apte

Kashmir – Past & Present, Unraveling the Mystique - M. L. Kaul

Shri Guruji Samagra – Complete works of Guruji

Shri Guruji – His Vision and Mission – Summary of Shri Guruji Samagra

Business of Freedom - Sandeep Singh

Malaa Umagalele Doctor ji (Marathi)- Ramesh Patange

Understanding Human Response in Organizations - A study of Rashtriya Swayamsevak Sangh with a Management Perspective - Dr. Sadhana Satish Modh, December - 2003

Now It can be Told – A. N. Bali

Shri Golwalkar Guruji – Jeevan Charitra (Hindi) – Ranga Hari

www.gurujigolwalkar.com

Readings

Proceedings of first International Conference of Ancient Cultures and Traditions - 2003

Lost City of Dvaraka - S. R. Rao

Indian Muslims, who are they - K. S. Lal

Arise again O' India - Francois Gautier

Kashmir My Frozen Turbulence - Jagmohan

Jyoti Jalaa Nij Praan Ki (Hindi) - Manikchandra Vajpayee and Shridhar Paraadkar

Science & Technology in Ancient India - Vidnyan Bharati, Mumbai

Myths = Mithya: A Handbook of Hindu Mythology - Devdutt Pattanaik

Third Way - D. B. Thengdi

Integral Humanism - Dr. Mahesh Sharma (DRI)

Hindu Economics -K.G. Bokare

Dadra Nagar Haveli Liberation - Doc on Wikipedia

http://www.hindunet.org/hindu_history/sarasvati - Dr. S. Kalyanaraman

http://www.RSS.org,

www.sanghparivar.org,

www.haindavkeralam.org

http://www.drpvvartak.com

Index